Theory and Practice in EFL Teacher Education

NEW PERSPECTIVES ON LANGUAGE AND EDUCATION

Series Editor: Professor Viv Edwards, *University of Reading, Reading, Great Britain*
Series Advisor: Professor Allan Luke, *Queensland University of Technology, Brisbane, Australia*

Two decades of research and development in language and literacy education have yielded a broad, multidisciplinary focus. Yet education systems face constant economic and technological change, with attendant issues of identity and power, community and culture. This series will feature critical and interpretive, disciplinary and multidisciplinary perspectives on teaching and learning, language and literacy in new times.

Full details of all the books in this series and of all our other publications can be found on http://www.multilingual-matters.com, or by writing to Multilingual Matters, St Nicholas House, 31-34 High Street, Bristol BS1 2AW, UK.

Theory and Practice in EFL Teacher Education

Bridging the Gap

Edited by
Julia Hüttner, Barbara Mehlmauer-Larcher,
Susanne Reichl and Barbara Schiftner

MULTILINGUAL MATTERS
Bristol • Buffalo • Toronto

Library of Congress Cataloging in Publication Data
A catalog record for this book is available from the Library of Congress.
Theory and Practice in EFL Teacher Education: Bridging the Gap/Edited by
Julia Hüttner...[et al.].
New Perspectives on Language and Education: 22
Includes index.
1. English language–Study and teaching–Foreign speakers. 2. English teachers–Training of
I. Hüttner, Julia Isabel.
PE1128.A2T457 2011
428.0071–dc23 2011035423

British Library Cataloguing in Publication Data
A catalogue entry for this book is available from the British Library.

ISBN-13: 978-1-84769-525-3 (hbk)
ISBN-13: 978-1-84769-524-6 (pbk)

Multilingual Matters
UK: St Nicholas House, 31-34 High Street, Bristol BS1 2AW, UK.
USA: UTP, 2250 Military Road, Tonawanda, NY 14150, USA.
Canada: UTP, 5201 Dufferin Street, North York, Ontario M3H 5T8, Canada.

Copyright © 2012 Julia Hüttner, Barbara Mehlmauer-Larcher, Susanne Reichl, Barbara Schiftner and the authors of individual chapters.

All rights reserved. No part of this work may be reproduced in any form or by any means without permission in writing from the publisher.

The policy of Multilingual Matters/Channel View Publications is to use papers that are natural, renewable and recyclable products, made from wood grown in sustainable forests. In the manufacturing process of our books, and to further support our policy, preference is given to printers that have FSC and PEFC Chain of Custody certification. The FSC and/or PEFC logos will appear on those books where full certification has been granted to the printer concerned.

Typeset by Datapage International Limited.

Contents

Acknowledgements vii
Contributors ix

Introduction
*Julia Hüttner, Barbara Mehlmauer-Larcher, Susanne Reichl
and Barbara Schiftner* xiii

Part 1: Conceptualising the Issue of Theory and Practice

1 Closing the Gap, Changing the Subject
  Henry G. Widdowson 3
2 The Dialectics of Theory and Practice in Teacher Knowledge
  Development
  Amy B.M. Tsui 16
3 Moments of Practice: Teachers' Knowledge and Interaction
  in the Language Classroom
  Joachim Appel 38

Part 2: Developing Language Teachers' Knowledge Base

4 Creating Language-Assessment Literacy: A Model for
  Teacher Education
  Armin Berger 57
5 Grammar Teaching: Theory, Practice and English
  Teacher Education
  Penny Ur 83
6 Cognitive + Communicative Grammar in Teacher Education
  David Newby 101
7 Towards a Stronger Intervention: The Role of Literature in
  Teacher Education
  Susanne Reichl 124

Part 3: Assisting Language Teachers' Knowledge Construction

8 Supporting the Transfer of
  Innovation into Foreign-Language Classrooms: Applied
  Projects in In-Service Teacher Education
  Sandra Hutterli and Michael C. Prusse 145
9 Developing Student Teachers'
  'Pedagogical Content Knowledge' in English for Specific
  Purposes: The 'Vienna ESP Approach'
  Julia Hüttner and Ute Smit 164
10 The EPOSTL (European Portfolio for Student Teachers of
  Languages): A Tool to Promote Reflection and Learning in
  Pre-Service Teacher Education
  Barbara Mehlmauer-Larcher 186

Part 4: Addressing Established Paradigms

11 NESTs Versus Non-NESTs: Rethinking English-Language
  Teacher Identities
  Irena Vodopija-Krstanovic 207
12 Multilingualism Pedagogy:
  Building Bridges between Languages
  Eva Vetter 228

Subject Index 247
Name Index 251

Acknowledgements

In putting together this volume, we could rely on the advice and help of several individuals at diverse places. We would like to express our gratitude to our colleague Christiane Dalton-Puffer, research director of the Centre for English Language Teaching at the University of Vienna, for her guidance and words of encouragement throughout the project. Thanks are due to Viv Edwards, the series editor, for her enthusiasm about this project, and to Anna Roderick and the editorial team at Multilingual Matters for their support in producing this volume.

Very special thanks go to Monika Boniecki and to Christina Gefäll for their careful copy-editing, proofreading and compilation of the name index.

We are indebted to the contributing authors, whose scholarship and commitment to language teacher education made this volume possible.

Contributors

Joachim Appel has graduated from the University of Constance. He holds an MSc in applied linguistics (Edinburgh) and a PhD (Munich). After teaching German at Edinburgh University, he trained and worked as a secondary teacher. He went on to teach English-language teaching methodology and applied linguistics at Munich University and at the Pädagogische Hochschule Freiburg. He is currently professor of applied linguistics and language teaching in the Department of English at the Pädagogische Hochschule Ludwigsburg. His current research interests include teachers' experiential knowledge and verbal interaction in language teaching.

Armin Berger studied English and religious education at the University of Vienna and the Australian National University, Canberra. After having taught in a number of secondary-school settings, he turned to tertiary education. He currently works as a senior lecturer in the language and teacher education programmes at the English Department of the University of Vienna, with a keen interest in language test development and teaching language testing and assessment to future as well as practising teachers. His research activities focus on assessing second-language speaking.

Sandra Hutterli is head of the Department of 'Compulsory School' at the Swiss Conference of Cantonal Ministers of Education (EDK). As an expert of foreign-language learning, she has national and international experience in research and language policy development. She has been a lecturer of didactics and language acquisition at Zurich University of Teacher Education in Switzerland. Engaged in teacher training and further training as well as project management and implementation of innovation, she has, together with Michael Prusse, planned and taught the CAS Teaching Foreign Languages. Her research fields are evaluation and assessment of foreign-language competences as well as organisational development and change management in the educational system.

Julia Hüttner holds an MA and a PhD from the University of Vienna, as well as an MSc (applied linguistics) from the University of Edinburgh. She is a lecturer at the University of Southampton, where she teaches applied linguistics and teacher education courses. She has researched and published a monograph (*Academic Writing in a Foreign Language*, Peter Lang, 2007) and various articles and book chapters on the teaching applications of genre and discourse analysis and on the effects and the implementation of CLIL (content and language-integrated learning). Her current research project investigates oral language use and proficiency.

Barbara Mehlmauer-Larcher studied English and German at the University of Graz and applied linguistics and EFL teaching at the University of East Anglia, UK. After having taught languages in secondary and tertiary settings in Austria and the UK, she turned to EFL teacher education. She currently coordinates the ELT methodology programme at the English Department of the University of Vienna. Her research interests focus on ESP methodology, computer corpora in the language classroom and pre-service language teacher education.

David Newby is associate professor of linguistics and language-teaching methodology and research at Graz University in Austria. He is the author of school textbooks, reference grammars and school drama. His main academic interest is the theory and practice of pedagogical grammar. He has coordinated several projects for the European Centre for Modern Languages of the Council of Europe and has worked for the British Council in a wide variety of countries. He is the co-author of the *European Portfolio for Student Teachers of Languages*.

Michael C. Prusse is head of the faculty upper secondary level (vocational instruction) at the Zurich University of Teacher Education in Switzerland. As a professor of ELT methodology and literatures of the English-speaking world, he trains English teachers at the lower secondary level and, together with Sandra Hutterli, he has planned and taught the CAS Teaching Foreign Languages. Apart from ELT methodology and the transfer of innovative concepts into the classroom, his main research interests are in postcolonial literatures, the 20th-century short story, children's literature and in the teaching of reading inside and outside the EFL classroom.

Susanne Reichl is associate professor at the Department of English and American Studies of the University of Vienna, where she teaches literature, cultural studies and teaching methodology. She holds an MA, a PhD and a 'Habilitation' (teacher qualification in higher education) from Vienna University, and has also taught at the University of Munster, Germany. Her research interests are the teaching of literature and culture in secondary and higher education, postcolonial studies, contemporary British literature and culture and literature for children and young adults.

Barbara Schiftner obtained a teaching degree in English and German from the University of Vienna in 2008. She taught German and English as a foreign language at several institutions in Austria and spent two semesters teaching German at Wabash College, Indiana, as a Fulbright language teaching assistant. She currently works as a research assistant for the Centre for English Language Teaching at the University of Vienna. Her research interests focus on learner corpus research and the application of corpus findings to language teaching; her recent research activities are concerned with coherence and cohesion in learner writing.

Ute Smit is associate professor in English linguistics at the University of Vienna. Her recent research interests concern English in the bi- or multilingual classroom, in its roles as object of learning, especially as regards English for specific purposes (ESP), as well as medium of instruction in the shapes of content and language integrated learning (CLIL) and English as a lingua franca (ELF). Recent book publications include *English as a Lingua Franca in Higher Education: A Longitudinal Study of Classroom Discourse* (De Gruyter, 2010) and *Language Use and Language Learning in CLIL Classrooms* (Benjamins, 2010; co-edited with Christiane Dalton-Puffer and Tarja Nikula).

Amy B.M. Tsui is pro-vice-chancellor and vice president of the University of Hong Kong and concurrently holds the position of Chair Professor of Language and Education. She obtained her PhD in linguistics in 1986 at the University of Birmingham, UK. She has published widely and given numerous keynotes at international conferences in the areas of teacher knowledge and development, discourse, and language policy. She also serves on the editorial/advisory boards of many international refereed journals. Her book *Understanding Expertise in Teaching* (Cambridge University Press, 2003) has been widely cited. Her most recent publication is *Learning in School-University Partnership: Sociocultural Perspectives* (Routledge, 2009) as lead author.

Penny Ur has 30 years' experience as an English teacher in elementary, middle and high schools in Israel. Now retired, she has taught MA courses at Oranim Academic College of Education and Haifa University. She has presented papers at TESOL, IATEFL and various other English teachers' conferences worldwide. She has published a number of articles, and was for 10 years the editor of the *Cambridge Handbooks for Language Teachers* series. Her books include *Discussions that Work* (1981), *Five Minute Activities* (co-authored with Andrew Wright) (1992), *A Course in Language Teaching* (1996), *Grammar*

Practice Activities (2nd edn, 2009) and *Vocabulary Activities* (forthcoming), all published by Cambridge University Press.

Eva Vetter is an applied linguist at the University of Vienna. Her research interests focus upon multilingualism with respect to linguistic minorities, historical multilingualism, language policy and language teaching and learning. From 2006 – 2010 she elaborated on theories and methods of multilingualism within the European multilingualism network LINEE (Languages in a Network of European Excellence). Beyond the focus on multilingualism, her research concerns text and discourse analysis.

Irena Vodopija-Krstanovic teaches courses on English-language teaching methodology and the sociocultural aspect of ELT in the TESOL graduate program at Rijeka University, Croatia. She received a PhD in TESOL from Klagenfurt University, an MA in TESOL from the Graduate School for International Training in Vermont and a BA in English and French from Zagreb University. Her research interests and publications focus on cultural issues in ELT, the intersection of language-culture-identity, the pedagogical implications of English as an international language and the native/non-native divide. Irena is extensively involved in language teacher education and national teacher certification in Croatia.

Henry G. Widdowson was professor of education at the University of London, with particular responsibility for the teaching of English to speakers of other languages, and professor of applied linguistics at the University of Essex. He was a founding editor of the journal *Applied Linguistics* and for 30 years acted as applied linguistics adviser to Oxford University Press. He has lectured and written extensively on the teaching of English. His publications include *Teaching Language as Communication*, *Aspects of Language Teaching* and most recently *Defining Issues in English Language Teaching*. Now retired but still (relatively) active, he is honorary professor at the University of Vienna.

Introduction

Julia Hüttner, Barbara Mehlmauer-Larcher, Susanne Reichl and Barbara Schiftner

Language teaching is a profession that has been under considerable public pressure of identifying itself as such. The widely held belief that good teachers are 'naturals', requiring no specific training or education, is detrimental to creating an image of language teachers as 'true' professionals, on a par with, say, lawyers or doctors. Pressure also comes from stakeholders closely involved in education, who criticise that teacher education does not prepare teachers adequately for their future practice, and even within teacher education, frequent complaints are made about the lack of impact that it has on teacher learning and teacher behaviour. This situation has led David Nunan (2001) to address the question of what constitutes a profession in the first place and apply this to language teaching. He identifies four main characteristics of a profession, namely 'advanced education and training', 'standards of practice and certification', 'a disciplinary base' and 'advocacy' (Nunan, 2001: 4–5), and notes that in all of these areas, language teaching faces a number of challenges. On a practical level, these are due to very diverse situations in private language teaching institutions and state-run schools and to a general lack of legislation to prevent untrained teachers from working; on a more conceptual level, these challenges are often caused by problems to 'define, refine and articulate [the] disciplinary basis [of language teaching]' (Nunan, 2001: 5). In addition, we would argue that teacher education programmes need to provide the conditions for future language teachers to develop knowledge from such a disciplinary basis, as well as autonomy and responsibility, three dimensions identified as key elements of professionalism in teacher education by Furlong et al. (2000: 4).

In line with the considerable progress made in the understanding of effective learning and teaching and the learning of teachers in general education (Darling-Hammond & Bransford, 2005: vii), language teacher education (LTE) has rapidly developed in finding its position as 'advanced education' and its 'disciplinary base', following intensive work on theories of LTE towards the end of the last century (Crandall, 2000: 34). Of paramount importance in a theory of LTE has been the realisation that developing relevant teacher knowledge from subject matter knowledge is neither a simple nor a straightforward process. Indeed, with Shulman's (1987) introduction of the concept of 'pedagogical content knowledge (PCK)' as the focal point of teacher knowledge, research interest has moved towards the means and the contexts of transforming subject matter knowledge into such PCK. This also means that teachers are no longer considered to be merely applying theory to practice, but rather as professionals constructing theory and theorising their practice. Underlying such a view of teachers as active mediators of knowledge and as constructors of new knowledge is a social-constructivist perspective of teacher learning (Johnson, 2009: 98). This learning takes place at various points in a teacher's development and requires collaboration, on the part of teacher educators and mentors, but also of peers or students. By definition, teacher learning is situated and contextual, and part of the development of teacher expertise lies in making use of the diverse contexts and situations for learning. All this is conceived of as a possible response to continued demands for improving LTE in order to address the complaints of practitioners and stakeholders who perceive novice language teachers as ill-prepared for their professional practice by existing programmes.

From a social-constructivist viewpoint, questions of how such collaborations should be devised for these diverse contexts in order to foster the development of teacher knowledge are of prime importance. Operating both on a theoretical and a practical level, the role of teacher educators is conceived in this paradigm as that of mediators between both theory and practice of language teaching and the sometimes diverse worlds of academia and school. Sharing this view, we consider the role of teacher educators as primary facilitators and initiators of teacher learning, with a strong focus on coaching and supervision when assisting student teachers in their developmental process of becoming professional language teachers.

The way in which such situated teacher learning fosters the development of professionalism has been the focus of LTE research over the last decades and also underpins the contributions in this volume. Dominant among these is the increased interest in the knowledge base of teachers, both general and experiential, and the ways in which this is built up, addressing both the development of PCK and the disciplinary base from which knowledge can be transformed. This correlates with the rising concern for fostering the professional development of teachers by means of guided and focused reflection of their own learning process and their actions in the classroom, and thus their construction of knowledge and expertise. The important role of critical reflection, which recurs in the contributions to this volume, also touches on issues such as teacher beliefs, teacher cognition and teacher identities. In addition, topics from language learning and teaching that contribute fundamentally to teachers' knowledge base, cognition and expertise are important issues in teacher education as well. To name both long-established and fairly recent developments in language teaching, we mention grammar teaching, the role of literature in the classroom, assessment and testing or multilingualism. All these can be seen to contribute to the body of theory developing in language teacher education. On the 'practice' side, we are looking at the actual collaborative partners: at teacher educators and student teachers in university-based pre-service teacher education, at in-service teachers who manage projects and thereby disseminate the insights gained from theory and practice and at a whole range of teachers, novice and expert, with a focus on the multi-factorial development of their identities as teachers.

Using theory and practice as a binary opposition for the conceptualisation of this book may create the impression that these are clear-cut notions. As our contributions show, matters are much more complex than this. Practice, especially, has been interpreted and conceived of as a whole range of states or activities, including the actual teaching of language lessons in the classroom, critical reflection as part of pre- and in-service education, project work on a local or national level or the provision of effective practice opportunities in pre-service teacher education. Relevant theoretical knowledge informs these practices in a variety of ways, developing teacher cognition and raising the potential for reflective practice. Such a diverse perception of practice and theory is clearly contingent on the roles that individuals perform in a given teacher education context. What these conceptualisations do, very much in line with the outlook of this volume, is an advancement of theory formation through a contextualised rethinking of the relationship of theory and practice.

The key concern of this book is the more precise nature of this relationship, which, for demonstrative purposes, we conceived of as a gap to be bridged. The obvious assumption would be that such a divide can be overcome if the diverse research results feed into the daily work of language teaching, but our contributions point towards a more complex relationship: the bridge from theory to practice is not unidirectional, it is a two-way road, and, much in the same way that research results find their way into classrooms, the insights gained in practice do impact on the theory formation in LTE. It is not just academics who produce results for teachers or student teachers who then, in turn, translate them into practice; it is also teachers who produce theory while reflecting upon the circumstances and rationales of their practice. Some of the contributions in our volume reflect this dynamic relationship between theory and practice by giving voice to practicing and pre-service language teachers who are evidently in the process of theory building.

This is compatible with a more recent view, namely that the knowledge construction of (student) teachers can have two different starting points. A more established approach views the process of knowledge construction as starting in theory classes. This leads to the application of theoretical concepts in specific classroom settings and, in this way, student teachers develop their situated teacher knowledge. Another way of looking at this is from a situated social perspective; here, the starting point of teacher knowledge construction is a specific classroom setting with teachers or student teachers as members of a 'community of practice' (Lave & Wenger, 1991). Within this concept of teacher knowledge construction the focus is on peer-supported and collaborative teacher learning, leading to joint reflections with the aim of relating gained teaching experiences to the relevant theoretical concepts (Korthagen, 2010: 104). These two options of teacher knowledge construction with their different starting points represent two alternative ways of teacher learning as well as two possible solutions to overcome the divide between theory and practice, and are both represented in our collection.

This volume consists of 12 chapters by experts in the thriving field of English language teacher education from a variety of geographical and institutional contexts. It is our conviction that theory and practice can only ever cohere in a particular context and that teacher learning is situated, and the contributors have therefore taken great care to alert their readers to the specificities of the respective contexts while, at the same time, addressing issues that apply to different places and types of institutions. The focus is clearly on English as a foreign language (EFL) rather than any other foreign language. This reflects the geopolitical landscape in language teaching, but we hope that many of the issues raised in connection with teaching EFL can be viewed as examples of possible teacher learning or teacher development, transferable or inspirational for other contexts and situations as well. Our last chapter confronts this issue head-on and questions the monolingual mainstream of language teaching, challenging the hegemonic position of English by suggesting a plurilingual approach to learning languages.

The first part of our volume, **'Conceptualising the Issue of Theory and Practice'**, brings together the work of three scholars working in the field of teacher education in diverse international contexts. Their contributions suggest a variety of ways of establishing the link between theory and practice for teachers and student teachers. **Henry G. Widdowson**, in his programmatic essay **'Closing the Gap, Changing the Subject'**, argues for a clear rationale of English as a subject that would indicate the aspects of language that such a subject should focus on, as well as the relevant classroom activities. By establishing such a rationale, Widdowson suggests, teachers close the gap between theory and practice by consciously activating their theoretical knowledge to conceptualise their everyday teaching practice. **Amy B.M. Tsui** bases her deliberations on **'The Dialectics of Theory and Practice in Teacher Knowledge Development'** on recent expertise and knowledge studies and argues for a dialectical relationship between explicit and tacit knowledge, and, ultimately, between theory and practice. **Joachim Appel**'s essay focuses on what he calls **'Moments of Practice: Teachers' Knowledge and Interaction in the Language Classroom'** as a unit for analysis of EFL teaching practice. These moments throw light on the students' task performance, on the teacher's development and on the values and beliefs underlying such a moment. Appel argues that such an analysis will help bridge the gaps between beliefs and values held by theoreticians and scholars of language education and those held by practitioners.

The second part, **'Developing Teachers' Knowledge Base'**, is devoted to the question of how EFL teachers' knowledge base can be expanded between the poles of theory and practice. It addresses the disciplinary base that informs teacher knowledge and offers suggestions for transformative processes between different kinds of knowledge. **Armin Berger**'s contribution **'Creating Language Assessment Literacy: A Model for Teacher Education'** argues that language testing, a budding research area for some years now, has not yet made an impact on much classroom practice, despite an increasing interest in standardisation in many European countries. Berger discusses three areas that seem crucial for an implementation of research results from language testing: an awareness of teachers, heads of departments and other stakeholders of the relevance of professional testing, a development of teachers' expertise in language testing and finally the structural and legislative basis necessary for such an implementation. In her article on **'Grammar Teaching: Theory, Practice and English Teacher Education'**, **Penny Ur** proposes an integrated model of grammar teaching that is based on a variety of teaching approaches, ranging from a focus on form to communicative tasks, and argues convincingly for such a practical integration on the basis of a discussion of the theoretical rationale behind each of these approaches. **David Newby** in his article on **'Cognitive+ Communicative Grammar in Teacher Education'** discusses the significance of cognitive grammar for language learning, and his contribution suggests a rationale for a pedagogical grammar as well as ways of introducing student teachers to Cognitive+Communicative Grammar so as to facilitate their teaching practice. **Susanne Reichl** in her contribution **'Towards a Stronger Intervention: The Role of Literature in Teacher Education'** argues for a new approach of literature teaching within university-based education programmes for future EFL teachers. This approach leads away from a mere accumulation of knowledge about periods and text types to a stronger focus on processes of meaning-making in connection with literary texts. It is these processes that should help student teachers to make the necessary connections between literary content knowledge and the PCK required for their teaching practice.

The third part of the volume, **'Assisting Language Teachers' Knowledge Construction'**, comprises contributions dealing with the challenge of supporting pre-service and in-service teachers in their process of constructing experiential knowledge as well as professional competences. The authors of this section focus on approaches and instruments that are meant to support both novice and experienced teachers through collaboration with others (such as peers, teacher educators or mentors) to reflect critically on their own understanding and beliefs of a language teacher's expertise as well as their learning process as (student) teachers and (future) professionals. **Sandra Hutterli** and **Michael C. Prusse**, in their contribution on **'Supporting the Transfer of Innovation into Foreign Language Classrooms: Applied Projects in In-service Teacher Education'**, propose a way of implementing change in educational contexts, despite the resistance that is often found against it. Their three-step model has been successfully put into practice at Zurich University of Teacher Education, and combines theoretical input, biographical learning and project work. From an in-service training course, participants go back to their communities of practice to implement innovations as part of a team. In their article on **'Developing Student Teachers' "Pedagogical Content Knowledge" in English for Specific Purposes: The "Vienna ESP Approach"'**, **Julia Hüttner** and **Ute Smit** discuss an innovative LTE module preparing student teachers for the teaching of written ESP genres. The aim of this module is to help novice teachers develop PCK in the area of ESP teaching by focusing on material development. Three student projects, which provide examples of genre-specific ESP teaching materials, demonstrate the successful implementation of this approach to teacher education in the field of ESP. **Barbara Mehlmauer-Larcher**, in her article on **'The EPOSTL (European Portfolio for Student Teachers of Languages): A Tool to Promote Reflection and Learning in Pre-service Teacher Education'**, reports on a new tool for self-assessment and reflection developed for the Council of Europe with the aim of helping student teachers to reflect critically on their methodological skills and knowledge. The article also comprises the description of a possible implementation of the EPOSTL as well as a report on first results of a qualitative study on student teachers' attitudes towards this new type of portfolio.

In the fourth part of the book, **'Addressing Established Paradigms'**, we offer two articles that address and challenge established paradigms in teacher education. **Irena Vodopija-Krstanovic**, in her essay on **'NESTs Versus Non-NESTs: Rethinking English Language Teacher Identities'**, investigates the idealised notion of the native speaker as an EFL teacher and analyses, through ethnographic data, how such a conceptualisation impinges on the teaching practice in a Croatian context. **Eva Vetter** addresses the issue of stepping outside the widespread English-only framework by considering the potential of drawing on the multilingual resources of learners and teachers in her contribution **'Multilingualism Pedagogy: Building Bridges between Languages'**.

At a time when, in many institutions, teacher education is faced with pressing demands from a whole range of stakeholders, we feel the need to develop the debate further and contribute our share in the formation of theory (and practice!). The putting together of this collection has certainly challenged us all to review our own conceptualisations of language teacher education and has given us countless opportunities to both learn from others and rethink our own theory-practice interface. With this volume, we hope to be able to continue the bridge building and promote the professionalisation of language teacher education by contributing an impetus for more theory development and more reflective practice.

References

Crandall, J.A. (2000) Language teacher education. *Annual Review of Applied Linguistics* 20, 34–55.

Darling-Hammond, L. and Bransford, J. (eds) (2005) *Preparing Teachers for a Changing World: What Teachers Should Learn and Be Able to Do*. San Francisco: Jossey-Bass.

Furlong, J., Barton, L., Miles, S., Whiting, C. and Whitty, G. (2000) *Teacher Education in Transition: Re-forming Professionalism?* Buckingham: Open University Press.

Johnson, K.E. (2009) *Second Language Teacher Education*: A Sociocultural Perspective. New York: Routledge.

Korthagen, F.A.J. (2010) Situated learning theory and the pedagogy of teacher education: Towards an integrative view of teacher behaviour and teacher learning. *Teaching and Teacher Education* 26, 98–106.

Lave, J. and Wenger, E. (1991) *Situated Learning*. Cambridge: Cambridge University Press.

Nunan, D. (2001) Is language teaching a profession? *TESOL in Context* 11 (1), 4–8.

Shulman, L.S. (1987) Knowledge and teaching: Foundations of the new reform. *Harvard Educational Review* 57, 1–21.

Part 1
Conceptualising the Issue of Theory and Practice

1 Closing the Gap, Changing the Subject

Henry G. Widdowson

Teachers teach subjects. English is a subject, like history or physics. So how is this subject to be defined? What aspects of the language should be focused on, and what kind of classroom activity is most appropriate for the activation of learning? Over the years, different answers to these questions have been proposed and promoted, and the subject thereby redefined. The rationale behind these different proposals for changing the subject is not always clear, and when clear it is not always convincing. There is therefore a need for teachers to resist being too readily persuaded by these proposals, and instead to submit them to critical appraisal so as to establish their validity in principle and their relevance in practice. In this way, they would not so much be bridging the gap between theory and practice as closing it by taking their own theoretical perspective on the subject they teach.

Theory and practice are often perceived as quite different, indeed opposing kinds of activity: this as opposed to that, them and us, East and West – and as Rudyard Kipling has it: 'East is East and West is West and never the twain shall meet'. As far as the difference between linguistic theory and language teaching is concerned, however, there are people who feel that some meeting of the twain can be managed by building bridges. But bridges do not, of course, diminish gaps. They are a way of crossing from one side to another. The gap is still there and the difference remains – on this side linguistic theory and on that side the practice of language teaching.

I would want to suggest another way of perceiving the twain, not as distinct domains in need of connection in this way, but rather as inseparably fused together – not so much two different sides of a river as two sides of the same coin. As I have argued before (Widdowson, 1990, 2003), all pedagogic practice presupposes theory of one kind or another. Whatever activity English language teachers introduce in their classrooms is based on ideas and assumptions about language and learning. They may be second- or thirdhand ideas and assumptions, established by custom, received wisdom, taken on trust, dogma disguised as common sense, so their theoretical nature may not be at all apparent. Language teaching practice then is bound to be informed by theory of one kind or another, and in this respect it can be understood as a kind of *implied* linguistics. If this intrinsic relationship is not recognised, then inevitably the gap between theory and practice will always remain to be bridged. If it is recognised and made explicit, however, the two are integrated and the gap closes.

Of course, some teachers may not want to know about any theory that might be implied by their practice, complacently content with what they do in the classroom, without feeling the need to enquire into the reason why. Why make practice problematic? If there is an underlying dogma or two, never mind, leave them undisturbed. Let sleeping dogmas lie. Some teachers may think in this way, but not, I assume, those who will be reading this chapter.

One obvious advantage in closing the gap and making explicit the theoretical implications of practice is that teachers are less prey to persuasion, less ready to accept approaches to teaching on somebody else's authority, whether this be supposedly based on linguistic expertise or pedagogic experience. If teachers can raise critical questions about theoretical assumptions that underlie the approaches that are proposed, they are in a position to establish their relevance to their own local circumstances and *adapt* rather than just *adopt* them. It is a common complaint in the English teaching field that fashions come and go, as if teachers had no choice but to conform. But they can resist too, of course. Fashions come and go, alas, and the pendulum swings to and fro. But where do the fashions come from and why should they be followed? Why does the pendulum swing? These are questions that teachers need to ask, and they are essentially theoretical questions.

In 1886, the German scholar Wilhelm Viëtor published a celebrated pamphlet, *Der Sprachunterricht muss umkehren!* (Viëtor, 1886[D1]). This is generally rendered in English as *Language teaching must start afresh!* (see Howatt, 2004) and as such it has been used in our field often enough since then as a rallying cry for change. Fresh starts, or better perhaps fresh fits and starts, have been much in evidence: the way we teach now is old-fashioned, is the cry; we must change the subject, start afresh. But 'to start afresh' is not an entirely satisfactory translation of *umkehren*. A more literal translation of *umkehren* would be 'to turn back', 'to retrace one's steps'. This suggests going back in the direction you came from, but looking out for where you went astray. This kind of critical pathfinding is rather different from the idea of just giving up and starting afresh by returning to square one. But changes in English language teaching over the past half century are better characterised as fresh starts rather than a retracing of steps. Ideas and proposals have generally been heralded as entirely new departures, new approaches, new directions, new ways, without going back to see how they might link up with paths that have already been taken. No development of critical enquiry, but just a change of subject.

What I want to do in this chapter is to carry out an *umkehren* exercise and do a little critical pathfinding, a little theorising about various changes in the subject that have been proposed over the years. It will be convenient to have a framework of reference to give some overall coherence to the exercise. The one thing about the subject English on which we can all agree is that, however we go about teaching it, its ultimate objective is to develop in learners a proficiency or competence that enables them to put the language to communicative use. If we can agree that this is the objective, it would seem to make sense to use a model of communicative competence as our frame of reference for investigating different ways that have been proposed for achieving it.

The best-known model is, of course, that of Dell Hymes and it is the one that is always cited as giving warrant to communicative language teaching (see, for example, Brumfit & Johnson, 1979). So it would seem particularly appropriate for our purposes. In a frequently (if not always accurately) cited paper, Hymes (1972) proposed that communicative competence involved the ability to make four kinds of judgement about something – some bit of the English language in our case.

(1) Whether (and to what degree) something is formally *possible*.
(2) Whether (and to what degree) something is *feasible* in virtue of the means of implementation available.
(3) Whether (and to what degree) something is *appropriate* (adequate, happy, successful) in relation to the context in which it is used and evaluated.
(4) Whether (and to what degree) something is in fact done, actually *performed*, and what its doing entails (Hymes, 1972: 281).

We can take these then as the essential elements of communicative competence and we can take them as bearings as we retrace our steps.

By formally possible, Hymes means what is well formed according to the encoding rules of a language. So, one part of communicative competence is knowing the degree to which a sentence is grammatical or not. And it was this factor, of course, that was the focus of attention in the so-called structuralist approach. Now because this approach has so often been dismissed, uncritically, as obviously misconceived, it is important to consider the rationale on which this approach was based. In the first place, there was the recognition that what was essential about English as a foreign language was that it was indeed *foreign*.

A language is a way of conceptualising different aspects of reality, and different languages encode reality in different ways: English encodes reality in a different way from Spanish, German, Turkish, Chinese and so on. In other words, what is formally possible in one language is not in another: the sound systems are different, the words are different and the grammars are different. That is what makes a different language difficult to learn, and the greater the difference between ways of encoding, the greater the difficulty.

Now if this is so, then it would seem to make good sense to focus on this difficulty in teaching the language, to focus on the formally possible, the encoded features of English, the words and grammatical structures that make it different as a conceptualisation of reality and so difficult for learners who are accustomed to another kind of encoding.

So the structuralist approach, in focusing on the formally possible, can be seen as taking account of the crucial conceptual aspect of communicative competence. This is not, however, much acknowledged. On the contrary, the approach has usually been dismissed as conceptually vacuous, an arid exercise that focuses on form *rather than* meaning. But, as I have often pointed out before (most recently in Widdowson, 2003), even a cursory glance at structuralist procedures would make it clear that the focus is very definitely on meaning:

Book. This is a book.

I match the structure with the situation so that it becomes clear that the word '*book*' means this object. **This is** *a book, the book is* **here**, as opposed to **that is** *a book, the book is* **there**. *This* and *here* are words that mean 'close to me', 'proximal'. *That* and *there* are words that mean 'away from me', 'distal'.

The door is there.

The word *the* means 'something we all know about'.

I am walking to the door/She is walking to the door.

The action is matched with the linguistic forms to demonstrate their meaning. This form of the verb means continuous and concurrent action. And so on.

Now notice that this procedure brings two other of Hymes' factors into play. The situation that the teacher contrives serves as a context *appropriate* to the demonstration of meaning, and in such a way that it is *feasible* in that it can be readily processed by the learners. But of course the meaning that is thus demonstrated is semantic meaning, meaning encoded in the language form, *informed* meaning, and for this demonstration to be effective, that is to say feasible for learning, the context has to be designed to match up with the form and *duplicate* its meaning. If the context does not correspond exactly with the language, it ceases to be appropriate to the purpose and the demonstration fails. So in this procedure, you start with a bit of language and then invent a context appropriate to it.

But of course, this goes against the natural communicative process of language use. We do not in the ordinary way have bits of language in our head and then cast about for contexts in which they might be appropriately used. On the contrary, it is contexts that regulate the language we use and not the other way round. And the language does not duplicate the context but *extends* or *complements* it. We do not normally go around stating the obvious. We use language to say things that are not apparent from the context (for further discussion of this, see Widdowson, 1990). So although we might accept that it is of crucial importance to make learners aware of how semantic concepts are encoded in the foreign language, the very feasibility of this procedure for doing so requires a reversal of the usual relationship between the possible and the appropriate in the normal pragmatic use of language.

And there is another problem. Learners do not only have to be made *aware* of these semantic concepts, to *notice* them, but they also have to *internalise* them, to *know* them. And here we come to a second feature of the structuralist approach: after presentation, practice.

So in the structuralist approach, the language had to be made feasible in two ways: it had to be presented so that it was readily processed for understanding, and it had to make provision for practice in the language so that it could be processed for learning.

But this makes the language even more remote from what normally makes it appropriate for communication. We do not normally fixate on encoded forms and go around with them in our heads hoping that some context will turn up to use them in, nor do we go around repeating them for no apparent purpose. So, the kind of pattern practice that the structuralist approach went in for seems to be self-defeating.

> Nothing could be more enslaving and therefore less worthy of the human mind than to have it chained to the mechanics of the patterns of the language rather than free to dwell on the message conveyed through the language. (Lado & Fries, 1957)

This we might readily endorse: out, then, with pattern practice. But this quotation continues to come to a quite different conclusion:

> It is precisely because of this view that we discover the highest purpose of pattern practice: to reduce to habit what rightfully belongs to habit in the new language, so that the mind and personality may be freed to dwell in their proper realm, that is on the meaning of the communication rather than the mechanics of grammar. (Lado & Fries, 1957)

This makes clear that as far as Lado and Fries are concerned, pattern practice is designed to meet a communicative objective by ensuring that knowledge of the formally possible, the semantic encoding in the language, is acquired as the essential resource for communication. The problem is that the focus on this particular aspect of communicative competence, the possible, results in language that is not appropriate in normal contexts of use.

This is a book. I am standing up. You are sitting down.

Nobody uses language in this way. So it is all very well to say that learners need to know what is possible in a language before they put it to use, but how do they internalise this *as a communicative resource* if it is presented and practised in *un*communicative ways – and therefore in ways, of course, that conflict with the learners' own naturally communicative experience of their first language. The very procedures in structuralist teaching that are designed to make the second language less *conceptually* foreign have the effect of actually making it more *communicatively* foreign.

So we can say of the structuralist approach that it deals with one aspect of communicative competence in the Hymes scheme, the formally possible, but at the expense of another: the contextually appropriate. Thus, learners may acquire linguistic forms without knowing how to put them to use, may internalise what is formally possible without realising its communicative potential. So we need to consider how to bring the appropriate factor into our teaching: we need to change the subject.

We come to communicative language teaching. This focuses on how language functions in use and so seeks to restore the normal relationship between the possible and the appropriate. The procedure here is to first identify or invent contexts of one kind or another, social transactions and interactions or tasks, for example, which would naturally motivate the use of certain linguistic forms to achieve a communicative purpose. The assumption here is the very opposite of that of structuralist language teaching. In the structuralist approach, the idea is that if learners get to know the language code, they will subsequently be able to infer how it is put to appropriate communicative use. In the communicative approach, the idea is that if learners put the language to appropriate use, they will be able to infer a knowledge of the code that enables them to do it, and therefore, of course, acquire this code not as an abstract system but as a communicative resource, thus realising the potential of the possible.

There is no doubt that the communicative approach, in realigning these two factors of communicative competence in this way, *does* bring the language subject into closer correspondence with the reality of actual language use. There is, however, a problem. In normal communication, as I have already noted, context does not duplicate linguistic information but complements or extends it. In the social interactions and transactions we engage in, we only use as much language as is contextually required, and no more, and sometimes we need very little language to be communicatively effective.

You can often function effectively in a language without making much use of what is formally possible in the code. So the learning of what is formally possible in a language, its potential as a communicative resource, does not necessarily follow from the achieving of communicative purposes. One way around this problem is to design contexts so that they constrain learners to focus on the possible, as is done in task-based instruction, but of course to do this is to compromise with the naturalness condition by contriving to make the context appropriate to the language. As a consequence, the kind of language that results, though it may not be as unreal as that of the structuralist approach, nevertheless falls short of the kind of real language that actually and naturally occurs in normal contexts of use.

But if the objective of the subject is to teach the English that really is appropriate to the context, then surely you have to get learners engaged with the language as it actually and naturally occurs. We come to the fourth factor in the Hymes scheme and to another change of subject. The focus of attention now shifts to the actually performed, authentic English, the English that carries the real language guarantee of having been produced by its native speakers in naturally occurring contexts of use. Now that corpus linguists have collected large quantities of this actual performance, real English is available for classroom use. As McCarthy (2001: 128) puts it: 'The language of the corpus is, above all, real, and what is it that all language learners want, other than "real" contact with the target language.' The appeal of the real is difficult to resist. What teacher, after all, would want to confess to teaching unreal English? But leaving aside the question of how real the language of the corpus actually is, what we need to ask is how 'real' can the learners' contact with it really be?

Here, for example, is some real English, taken from a corpus that McCarthy himself has been involved in assembling: a transcript of an actually occurring conversation:

S1: Now I think you'd better start the rice.
S2: Yeah (...) what you got there?
(4 seconds pause)
S2: Will it all fit in the one?
S1: No you'll have to do two separate ones.
S3: Right (...) what next?
(17 seconds pause)
S3: Foreign body in there.
S2: It's the raisins.
(Carter & McCarthy, 1997: 65)

What kind of contact would learners of English make with this text? In the first place, there are some things that would make it difficult for any reader, let alone learners, to connect with the text at all. 'Will it all fit in the one?' Will all *what* fit in the one *what*? What are these people actually referring to? 'Foreign body in there'. In *where*? And what's all this about a foreign body? It is all very mysterious. But not, of course, for the participants in this interaction. For them, these bits and pieces of language serve an entirely satisfactory communicative function. And this is because they can make them real, or realise them, for their purposes as appropriate to this particular context – the formally possible bits and pieces are complemented, extended by the context in the normal communicative way. Although the insider participants in this conversation are in the know about the context and can connect with it, outsiders like us are not in the know and cannot make the connection. We may know *what the language means*, but not *what is meant by the language*.

Now of course you can say that samples of actually occurring bits of English are real language, as distinct from the kind of invented sentences that were used in the so-called structural approach. But they are only real as communication for learners if they can *realise* the appropriate relationship they have with context and what purpose the language is being used to achieve. They are only authentic as actual use to the extent that they can be *authenticated* as communication. If, as a learner, you are not in the know about what is going on, if you cannot realise what these people are referring to with these fragments of language and how they are using them to relate to each other and to achieve their communicative purposes, then the fragments simply become a collection of linguistic forms – an interrogative sentence here, a noun phrase there. For the participants in the conversation, they take on a communicative function, of course, because they are contextual insiders, but if as an outsider you cannot realise this function, you make no contact at all with what makes the language real. All you can do is focus on form. What is contextually appropriate language for these users then becomes only formally possible language for learners.

So how can language be made appropriate for learners? The problem with real English proposals is that it defines what is appropriate only in terms of what is actually performed – the only real language is that which has been produced as appropriate to the purposes and contexts of actual native speaker use. The trouble is that these purposes and contexts represent a reality that learners do not share. The only English that can be appropriate for them is that which relates to *their* reality, their purposes and their contexts.

So what is this learner reality and how can English relate to it? Perhaps the first point to be made is that whatever English learners are relating to, it is necessarily English as a *foreign or other language*, and it will be foreign or other in radically different ways for different groups of learners. Furthermore, this other language is not experienced, as it is with native users, as naturally occurring and an integral part of the continuum of their social lives. As a subject at school, it occurs discontinuously in short periods inserted in a timetable according to administrative convenience, wedged between other subjects like history or geography or physics: once on Monday afternoon, perhaps, once on Wednesday, twice on Thursday. It does not just occur, it is controlled, it does not just happen, it is designed: it takes the form of things called lessons, which consist of prescribed activities called exercises or tasks or projects, and what learners do with the language is then measured by tests. This is the reality that English represents for its learners. It is hard to imagine anything more remote from English as it naturally occurs. But it is this learner reality that English teachers have to come to terms with.

Since there is so little time for teaching, it is obvious that the subject of English as a foreign or other language has to be designed to provide the best *investment* for learning. And if the objective of learning is to acquire a communicative capability, then we need to look for some way of relating the possible and the appropriate that is practicable, workable – in a word *feasible* in classroom conditions. Not real English but *realistic* English. What kind of language then would that be?

It has to be language that is appropriate in two ways. First, it has to relate to the context of the learners, to the *local* context of what they know of the language, but also to their attitudes, values, how they see the world – in short, their reality. So the English of the subject has to be something they can *engage* with and make real for themselves. In this sense, appropriate English is English that they can *appropriate*. But it also has to be appropriate in another way as well. It has to be appropriate to the language-learning purpose. The learners are after all engaging with the language in order to learn it, to find out what is formally possible in the language as conceptual encoding and as communicative resource.

So a second condition that the English of the subject has to meet is that it should be appropriate to the learning purpose. It has to be not only English that learners can engage with, but it also has to be English they can learn *from*. So they have to realise how and why aspects of the formally possible can be used as a communicative resource. And this means that whatever *samples* of language are provided, they have to be converted into *examples* – for it is only when a piece of language, or anything else for that matter, is recognised and internalised as an example *of* something that any learning takes place at all (for further discussion, see Widdowson, 2003).

The English of the subject English, I am suggesting, has then to meet two conditions: it has to be language that learners can engage with, make real for themselves. And it has to be language that they can learn from, that will activate the learning process. It does not matter how closely this resembles English that is actually performed by its native-speaking users. This does not mean that teachers should strive to avoid this kind of 'real' English as a matter of principle. Obviously, as learning proceeds, the language of the subject will approximate in many ways to natural native-speaker usage. But features of such 'real' language will come into the classroom not because they are 'real' but because they meet these conditions, in other words, because they are pedagogically justified. The kind of English that meets these conditions does not naturally happen, it has to be specially designed to be made feasible for learning. It has to be contrived, custom made for pedagogy.

This, of course, is what the structuralist approach contrived to do. Having retraced our steps, we seem to be back where we started. But not quite. The structuralist approach, as we saw earlier, was certainly concerned with contriving language so that it provided examples for learners to learn from. But it seemed to provide little else. There was no attempt to make the language real for the learners. This was not language they could easily engage with. So although it was appropriate in one way, it was quite inappropriate in the other. Here is an example, slightly modified, from a typical textbook. A picture showing a man and woman in a sitting room appears after the following text:

> This is a man. He is John Brown. He is Mr Brown. He is sitting in a chair. This is a woman. She is Mrs Brown. She is standing by a table. Mr Brown has a book in his hand.

The focus here is clearly on demonstrating meaning in linguistic forms by replicating the information already in the picture, thereby depriving these forms of any communicative value. So how can the language be made more communicative and thereby engage the interest of learners? Here is one way:

> This is a man. He is John Brown. He is Mr Brown. He is sitting in a chair. This is a woman. She is *not* Mrs Brown. She is standing by a table. Mr Brown has a *look* in his *eye* ...

Just three small changes, a negative particle and two little lexical items replaced, and it makes all the difference. Who is this woman? What does Mr Brown have in mind? What happens next? Read on. A context is created, and the language has become communicative. It is just as 'unreal' as naturally occurring language use, just as remote from the corpus data of what is actually performed by native speakers, but it takes on a reality that learners can engage with.

I make no great claims for this as a work of fiction, but I think it serves to illustrate two essential points. First that even the most contrived language can be made real. Learners, when given the opportunity, can engage with language in all kinds of imaginative ways, appropriate it in play and give it communicative significance. Secondly, by making it real in this way, they are able to relate the formally possible with the contextually appropriate, and therefore realise the potential of the possible as a communicative resource.

What I have been suggesting then is that if we think about English as a subject in relation to the factors of the formally possible, the contextually appropriate, the feasible and the actually performed, what becomes clear is the crucial importance of taking into account how this foreign, this other, language relates to the reality of learners.

There is a further matter that arises from this. As I mentioned earlier, the most obvious thing about English for learners is that it is indeed foreign, not part of the learners' familiar world. Now the most obvious way of making it less foreign is to relate it to what *is* familiar – namely the learners' own language. And this is, of course, what learners do: they translate. If we accept that the subject English should relate to the reality of learners, then we need to recognise that the learners' own language is always present, even if teachers try to pretend that it is not, that English as a foreign language is always a bilingual subject, and that there is a case, therefore, for translation in teaching it. And here it would seem that we have retraced our steps even further back to the discredited grammar/translation method. This surely must be a retrograde step, a step too far. But as with the structuralist approach, it will not do to be dismissive and simply defer to the dictates of received wisdom. If we are to reject the pedagogic thinking of the past, we need to understand just what this thinking was and on what grounds it was misconceived. Instead of rejecting translation out of hand, as Guy Cook has recently argued (Cook, 2010), we need to critically assess the case for and against it. I am not proposing that we should just return to past practices, but that we should think about the theoretical assumptions that underlie these practices – and that underlie their rejection. If there is no place for translation in the subject of English, then why not?

That concludes this little exercise in theoretical backtracking. There may well be disagreements about the pathfindings I have presented in this chapter, but that does not matter. My purpose is not to persuade teachers of English into my way of thinking but to provoke them into following their own. I would simply suggest that whatever practice teachers favour, it is professionally incumbent on them as reflective practitioners to critically examine its theoretical implications. As I said at the beginning, fashions come and go, and English as a subject will always be subject to change like everything else. All I would say is that in accepting or rejecting the change, we should first take the necessary precaution of closing the gap.

References

Brumfit, C.J. and Johnson, K. (eds) (1979) *The Communicative Approach to Language Teaching*. Oxford: Oxford University Press.
Carter, R. and McCarthy, M. (1997) *Exploring Spoken English*. Cambridge: Cambridge University Press.
Cook, G. (2010) *Translation in Language Teaching*. Oxford: Oxford University Press.
Howatt, A.P.H. (2004) *A History of English Language Teaching*. Oxford: Oxford University Press.
Hymes, D.H. (1972) On communicative competence. In J. Pride and J. Holmes (eds) *Sociolinguistics: Selected Readings* (pp. 269–293). Harmondsworth: Penguin Books.
Lado, R. and Fries, C.C. (1957) *An Intensive Course in English*. Ann Arbor: University of Michigan Press.

McCarthy, M. (2001) *Issues in Applied Linguistics*. Cambridge: Cambridge University Press.
Viëtor, W. (1886) *Der Sprachunterricht muss umkehren!* Heilbron: Gebr. Henninger.
Widdowson, H.G. (1990) *Aspects of Language Teaching*. Oxford: Oxford University Press.
Widdowson, H.G. (2003) *Defining Issues in English Language Teaching*. Oxford: Oxford University Press.

2 The Dialectics of Theory and Practice in Teacher Knowledge Development
Amy B.M. Tsui

1 Introduction

> What knowledge is essential to their [teachers'] work? Is there a lot to learn or a little? Is it easy or difficult? How is such knowledge generated and confirmed? Indeed, dare we even call it knowledge in the strict sense of the term? Is not much of what guides the actions of teachers nothing more than opinion, not to say out-and-out guesswork? [...] If any of what teachers claim to know about something qualifies as knowledge (and who dares deny that some does?), what can be said of its adequacy? [...] Is there more to teaching than the skilled application of something called know-how? If so, what might that be? (Jackson, 1968: 1)

In his seminal work on teacher knowledge, Philip Jackson raised a number of questions that reflected the popular perception of the knowledge, or lack of knowledge, within the teaching profession. As Schön (1983) pointed out, professions such as medicine and law had always been regarded as being grounded in specialised, systematic, rigorous and scientific knowledge, and were therefore considered 'major' professions, whereas professions like social work, nursing and education, which were not seen as being grounded in a sound and solid knowledge base, were considered 'minor' professions. The teaching profession was seen as skills oriented, and learning how to teach was merely a process of acquiring some practical skills, or 'a bag of tricks', as some would call it. Such views represented a lack of understanding of the immensely complex task of teaching and the nature of the knowledge needed to accomplish that task.

Since the 1970s, there has been an increase in the number of studies conducted on teachers' work. Many of the earlier studies focused on teacher thinking and decision-making in the classroom. They were influenced by an information-processing model of cognitive development, in which knowledge was regarded as something 'held' within an individual's mind and that existed independently of context. In the 1980s, the adequacy of such a model was queried, and since then alternative conceptions of professional knowledge have been proposed and debated. For example, studies of expertise have argued that the knowledge of experts is intuitive and tacit and that it is characterised by 'knowing how' rather than 'knowing that' (Ryle, 1949: 32). Expert knowledge, these studies have pointed out, is embedded in an expert's action, and such knowledge defies explanation. Similarly, studies of teacher knowledge have argued that teachers *hold a special form of knowledge* that is embedded in their everyday practice. This form of knowledge is *highly personal* and *tacit*, and is often difficult for teachers to articulate. This view of teacher knowledge, however, was criticised by Shulman (1986), who argued that any portrait of teacher knowledge should also include the theoretical knowledge of the subject matter that informs and is informed by their teaching. As Munby *et al.* (2001) pointed out, the research literature on teacher knowledge is characterised by a tension between the different views of what counts as professional knowledge and how to conceptualise that knowledge.

In the context of the different conceptions outlined above, this chapter explores the nature of teacher knowledge. Drawing on the findings of case studies of English as a second language (ESL) teachers reported in Tsui (2003) and conceptions of knowledge in Chinese philosophy, it argues for a dialectical relationship between theory and practice.

2 Conceptions of Teacher Knowledge

Adopting Bruner's (1985) two modes of thought, 'paradigmatic' and 'narrative', Munby *et al.* (2001) proposed that teachers' knowledge can be seen as paradigmatic, that is, it can be expressed in propositions that say what they mean and mean what they say. However, they also observed that teachers' knowledge is inextricably linked to the specific contexts in which teachers operate, and that their knowledge is often expressed in the narrative mode of anecdotes and stories. Munby *et al.* (2001) considered paradigmatic thinking as corresponding to what Schön (1983) referred to as the 'high ground' associated with major professions, whereas narrative thinking corresponded to the 'swampy low ground' associated with minor professions. In the rest of this section, I shall examine the main conceptions of teacher knowledge that have been influential in the field.

2.1 Teacher Knowledge as Practical Knowledge

One of the earliest systematic studies of teacher knowledge was Elbaz's (1983) study of an experienced high school teacher, Sarah. The study was motivated by the assumption that practical knowledge exists and that the nature and defining characteristics of this knowledge can be understood by examining teachers' everyday practice and the thinking behind it. Elbaz observed that *teachers hold a special kind of knowledge in distinctive ways*. She referred to this kind of knowledge as 'practical knowledge' because the term 'focuses attention on the action and decision-oriented nature of the teacher's situation and construes her knowledge as a function, in part, of her response to that situation' (Elbaz, 1983: 5). This kind of knowledge is oriented to a particular practical and social context, and is *highly experiential and personal*. It is intuitive and tacit and less accessible in a formally articulated form. However, she considered the call for the conceptualisation of teachers' work in practical terms inadequate as a characterisation of teachers' practice because teachers' actions are *informed by theory* rather than divorced from it. The theoretical orientation of the teacher's knowledge, however, is an implicit theory of knowledge that informs his or her practical knowledge (Elbaz, 1983: 21).

Elbaz summarised her conception of teachers' practical knowledge as encompassing five domains: (a) knowledge of subject matter, which includes not only knowledge of the subject discipline that the teacher is teaching, but also theories related to learning; (b) knowledge of the curriculum, which refers to the structuring of learning experience and the curriculum content; (c) knowledge of instruction, which includes classroom routines, classroom management and student needs; (d) knowledge of self, which includes knowledge of the individual's own characteristics such as one's own personality, age, attitudes, values and beliefs, as well as personal goals and (e) knowledge of the milieu of schooling, which refers to the social structure of the school and its surrounding community. She argued that the relationship between these five knowledge domains with the world of practice is dynamic. They embody 'knowledge *of* practice' as well as 'knowledge *mediated by* practice' (Elbaz, 1983: 47, my emphasis).

What Elbaz tried to do was to bring together two opposing perspectives of knowledge, the empiric-analytical perspective, which sees knowledge as declarative and propositional, and the phenomenological perspective, which sees knowledge as procedural and experiential. She attempted to develop a way of studying teacher knowledge that 'acknowledges the importance of theory while firmly situated in practice' (Elbaz, 1983: 23). Elbaz's conception of teacher knowledge went beyond a unidirectional interaction between theory and practice, which is the application of the former to the latter. However, knowledge and practice were still seen as two separate entities and their relationship was one of reciprocity.

2.2 Teacher Knowledge as Personal Narratives

Another approach to teacher knowledge is represented by the work of Clandinin and Connelly, who adopted an experiential philosophical approach and saw teacher knowledge as embodied in the narratives of a teacher's life (see Clandinin & Connelly, 1987). In their view, teachers 'live stories, tell stories of those lives, retell stories with changed possibilities and relive the changed stories' (Connelly & Clandinin, 1995: 15). What they meant was not just that teachers tell stories of specific children and events, but that teachers' way of being in the classroom was storied: 'As teachers they are characters in their own stories of teaching, which they author' (Connelly & Clandinin, 1995: 15).

Different from Elbaz, they perceived teaching not as *informed by* theory but as the *unification of* theory and practice through what they referred to as the *narrative unities* of experience of the teacher. Teachers' personal practical knowledge is therefore

> a kind of knowledge carved out of, and shaped by, situations; knowledge that is constructed and reconstructed as we live out our stories and retell and relive them through processes of reflection. (Clandinin, 1992: 125)

2.3 Teacher Knowledge as Content Knowledge[1]

Different from the conceptions outlined above, which emphasise the situated and experiential nature of teacher knowledge, Shulman's theory of teacher knowledge is conceptual and analytical (see Shulman, 1986; Wilson et al., 1987). He maintained that conceptions of teacher knowledge as practical knowledge presented a truncated view of teacher knowledge: Teachers have theoretical as well as practical knowledge of the subject matter that informs and is informed by their teaching; descriptions of teacher knowledge should include both aspects (in this sense, Elbaz's conception of practice being informed by theory is close to Shulman's). Shulman (1986) further pointed out that subject matter knowledge, which is a central aspect of classroom life, had been very much neglected in the research on teacher knowledge. He observed that little attention had been paid to the ways in which subject matter was transformed from the knowledge of the teacher into the content of instruction, and how particular formulations of that content related to what students came to know or to misconstrue. He referred to the lack of study of subject matter knowledge among the various research paradigms for the study of teaching as the 'missing paradigm' (Shulman, 1986: 6; see also Shulman, 1999).

Shulman proposed for investigation a theoretical framework that distinguished between three categories of content knowledge: subject matter content knowledge, pedagogical content knowledge and curricular knowledge. Subject matter knowledge includes the knowledge of the content of a subject discipline, that is, the major facts and concepts in that discipline and their relationships (see Grossman, 1990). According to Shulman, teachers' knowledge of the explanatory or interpretive frameworks used in a discipline and the methods of inquiry within that discipline have an important influence on their curricular decisions and their representations of the content and nature of the discipline to the students.

Pedagogical content knowledge refers to the representation of content knowledge by the use of analogies, examples, illustrations, explanations and demonstrations in order to make it comprehensible to students. In order for a representation to be effective, teachers need to understand what makes a particular topic easy or difficult for students to understand, what the students' preconceptions and misconceptions are and what strategies are effective in dealing with these misconceptions. Curricular knowledge refers to knowledge of the programmes and available materials designed for the teaching of particular topics at a given level. Subsequently, Shulman and his colleagues added four more categories of teacher knowledge: (a) general pedagogical knowledge, which is knowledge of the principles and skills of teaching and learning that are generally applicable across subjects; (b) knowledge of educational aims, goals and purposes; (c) knowledge of learners, including knowledge of learners' characteristics and cognition and their learning development and motivation and (d) knowledge of other content, that is, content outside the scope of the subject being taught. They pointed out that teachers drew upon all of these seven categories of teacher knowledge when they made decisions about their content teaching (see Wilson *et al.*, 1987).

Subsequent to Shulman's call to search for the 'missing paradigm', there have been a number of studies on how subject matter knowledge, or the lack of it, affects the process and quality of teaching, including mathematics teaching (see, for example, Ball, 1991; Ball & Bass, 2000; Ma, 1999), science teaching (see, for example, Carlsen, 1991; Cochran & Jones, 1998; Hashweh, 1987; Heywood, 2007; Rollnick *et al.*, 2008; Smith & Neale, 1989), English teaching (see, for example Grossman, 1990; Grossman *et al.*, 1989) and history teaching (see, for example, Wineburg & Wilson, 1991). These studies have shown that teachers' disciplinary knowledge often has decisive influence on the process, content and quality of their instruction. However, some studies have shown that although subject matter knowledge is necessary for successful teaching, it is not sufficient (see, for example, Munby & Russell's [1992] case study of a secondary chemistry teacher and Smith [2008] about subject matter knowledge and professional identities). These studies suggest that central to successful teaching is pedagogical content knowledge, namely the transformation of subject matter knowledge into forms of representation that are accessible to learners. The transformation process requires an adequate understanding of the subject matter, knowledge of learners, curriculum, context and pedagogy.

Among the studies of teachers' knowledge reviewed in the previous section, there seems to be a consensus that teachers' subject matter knowledge is something that can be identified as such, and that it can be set apart from other domains of teacher knowledge. However, as a number of researchers have pointed out, the distinctions made between the knowledge domains are analytical rather than real. Calderhead and Miller (1986) have pointed out that categories of teacher knowledge provide a useful analytical framework for thinking about teaching, but in the complex task of teaching, the boundaries between these knowledge bases may be less easily distinguishable, and less meaningful, *because they constantly intermesh in practice* (see also Bennett, 1993).

Let us take, for example, the distinction that is often made between general pedagogical knowledge and pedagogical content knowledge. Certain pedagogical principles and skills are generic to the teaching of all subject disciplines, for example, conducting pair work, group work and so on. In practice, however, the application of these general principles is situated in the specific subject content being taught, at a specific grade level and even for a specific class of students. For example, in ESL speaking skills lessons, pair and group work can be appropriately applied to the teaching of conversational skills in order to maximise the opportunities for speaking. However, in a pronunciation lesson that introduces phonetic symbols for the first time, pair and group work is often preceded by a fair amount of lockstep teacher-fronted instruction to demonstrate how sounds are produced. In other words, one cannot talk about general pedagogical principles without regard to what is being learnt and who the learners are.

The notion of domains or categories of teacher knowledge, as Lave (1988) has pointed out, connotes a body of knowledge structured as a bounded 'conceptual space' (97). This conception gives the impression that everyday practices are poorly realised or are simplified versions of a putative knowledge structure. In other words, practice is seen as an imperfect realisation of codified knowledge or theory.

2.4 Teacher Knowledge as Situated Knowledge

The conception of teacher knowledge as *situated knowledge* is influenced by an anthropological approach to knowledge, notably the work led by Jean Lave and her collaborators, who see knowledge as contextually developed when practitioners respond to the specific context in which they operate.

Lave's (1988) conception of knowledge as situated knowledge emanated from her study of everyday social practices. For example, in studying and comparing the practice of mathematics in a variety of common settings, such as in grocery shopping in the supermarket and in test situations, she found that the same people responded differently in different settings: The problem was defined differently and the answers so developed were different. For example, she found that while grocery shoppers were capable of doing mathematical calculations and coming up with correct answers very quickly in supermarkets, they failed miserably when the same mathematical problems were put to them in decontextualised test situations. In other words, when mathematical problems were presented to them in context, they were able to draw on routines they had developed and to quickly come up with answers. For example, in figuring out which was the best buy among different brands of the same product, instead of dividing the price by weight, the shoppers simply took packages with the same weight and compared the price. Or if they needed to compare the prices of packages of different sizes, they had developed ways of rounding off numbers to simplify the mathematical processes. However, once these problems were decontextualised and presented in a genre typical of educational knowledge (as opposed to everyday knowledge), they were at a loss. This showed, Lave argued, that the relationship between the problem and the answer is dialectical in that 'the problem was defined by the answer at the same time an answer developed during the problem, and [...] both took form *in action* in a particular, culturally structured setting' (Lave, 1988: 2; see also Lave *et al.*, 1984; Scribner, 1984). In the case of grocery shopping, the mathematical problem was defined by the answer, namely, getting the best buy amongst brands of similar quality, and in such a process, the problem can be, and is often, redefined. Lave referred to the supermarket, a physical and social structure, as an *arena*, and the supermarket, *as experienced by the grocery shopper*, as a *setting*. She maintained that 'persons-acting, arenas and settings appear to be implicated together in the very constitution of activity' (Lave, 1988: 170). A more appropriate unit of analysis, she argued, should be 'the whole person in action, acting with the settings of that activity' (Lave, 1988: 17).

The notion of situated knowledge has been adopted by a number of researchers as a way of understanding teachers' work and their professional knowledge. For example, Leinhardt (1988) investigated expert teachers' situated knowledge in selecting and using examples to explain elementary mathematical concepts. She found that, just as other forms of situated knowledge that is contextually developed, the knowledge that is embedded in the teaching act embodies the features of the teaching situation, such as who the students are, what the classroom is like, the physical environment of the school, the time of year and even the time of day. In other words, this kind of knowledge is 'embedded in the artefacts of a context' (Leinhardt, 1988: 148) and it is more effective in helping learners learn than 'generative knowledge', which is context-free and can be generalised across situations. And yet this kind of knowledge is often considered low level, limited and inelegant.

3 Revisiting Teacher Knowledge

The tension between the different conceptions of teacher knowledge could probably be summarised as mainly between teacher knowledge as personal, experiential, tacit and intuitive, context oriented and often not codifiable and teacher knowledge as both practical and theoretical. To examine this tension, I would like to go back to the conception of knowledge proposed by Gilbert Ryle (1949) and echoed by Michael Polyani (1966).

3.1 Dialectical Relationship between Theory and Practice: Knowing-in-Action

Gilbert Ryle (1949) was the first scholar to point out that the distinction made between 'knowing how' and 'knowing that' is a misconstrual of the nature of knowledge (29), and that asserting that the former is an application of the latter is a misrepresentation of what happens in practice. Michael Polanyi (1966) echoed Ryle and pointed out that explicit and formalised knowledge and tacit knowledge do not exist independently of each other, and the former cannot replace the latter. He argued that tacit knowledge is an indispensable part of *all* knowledge, and that the declared aim of modern science to establish strictly detached, objective and formalised knowledge is *misguided*. Knowledge of theory, he maintained, cannot be established until it has been extensively used to interpret experience, and true knowledge lies in our ability to use it. He used the term 'knowing' to cover both theoretical and practical knowledge (Polanyi, 1966: 7).

Influenced by the work of Polanyi, Donald Schön (1983) asserted that the labelling of professions such as social work and teaching as 'minor' professions on the grounds that they lacked a rigorous and scientific knowledge base was a misconception of what professionals do. He observed that in the world of practice, it was often impossible for practitioners to simply apply research-based theory to problem solving because *problems do not present themselves as given*. Practitioners have to identify problems by making sense of situations that are often ill defined, complex and fraught with uncertainties and confusion. Even when a problem has been identified, practitioners may find that its unique nature means that it cannot be solved by the simple application of established theory or technique. Following Polanyi, Schön proposed that what professionals do in their everyday work life is 'knowing-in-action', that is, their skilful practice reveals a kind of *knowing* that does not stem from a prior intellectual operation (Schön, 1983: 51). Echoing Ryle's (1949) conception of 'knowing how', Schön pointed out that knowing and action are not two separate things but are two parts of one thing: Knowing is in the action itself. In other words, theory and practice are mutually constituted and dialectically related. As Lave (1988: 146) pointed out:

> [a] dialectical relation is more than a declaration of reciprocal effects by two terms upon one another. [...] A dialectical relation exists when its component elements are created, are brought into being, only in conjunction with one another.

3.2 Knowing-in-Action in Chinese Education Philosophy

The concept of knowing-in-action is also deeply rooted in Chinese education philosophy, which dates back to the 12th century. *Zhu Xi* [朱熹] (1130-1200), a well-known Confucian philosopher, pointed out:

> [w]hen you know something but don't act on it, your knowledge of it is still superficial. After you've personally experienced it, your knowledge of it will be much clearer and its significance will be different from what it used to be. (Chu Hsi, [Zhu Xi], Chapter 9, 9.1a:6/148:5, translated by Gardner, 1990: 116)

In other words, one cannot say that one has knowledge of something unless one has experienced it, and more importantly, one's 'knowing' will be *different* after the experience.

The importance of the dialectical relationship between 'knowing' and 'acting' can be seen from the exposition of what teaching means. The Chinese word for 'teach' is *jiao xue* [教學], which translates literally as 'teach-learn'. This concept was expounded in *Xueji* [學記], a collection of writings by Chinese philosophers, as follows:

> Learn and you know your own deficiencies,
> Teach and you know the difficulties (in teaching),
> You know your own deficiencies and you are able to improve yourself,
> You know the difficulties (in teaching) and you are able to strengthen yourself.
> Therefore it is said that teaching and learning are mutually strengthening.
> (Xueji, translated in Gao, 2005: 1)

The above quotation, which has been widely cited in Chinese writings on teaching and learning, illustrates the centrality given to practice in teaching and learning in the Chinese philosophy of education and the dialectical relationship between teaching and learning. First, it is only when one is engaged in the act of learning that one realises the gaps in one's own knowledge, and this in turn provides the impetus for further learning. Similarly, it is only when one is engaged in the act of teaching that one understands the difficulties of teaching, which in turn prompts one to learn more about teaching. Second, just as knowing and not knowing are mutually constitutive, knowing how to teach and knowing what is difficult to teach are mutually constitutive (see Tsui & Wong, 2009).

Philosophical and anthropological approaches to knowledge, as well as ethnographic case studies of teachers' work and teachers' lives, show that the knowledge that teachers develop is jointly constituted by the teachers' acting and the setting in which they operate, that is, the context that they experience. As Putnam and Borko (1997: 1254) remarked, '[h]ow a person learns a particular set of knowledge and skills, as well as the situation in which a person learns, become fundamental parts of what is learned'.

4 Theory and Practice in Teacher Knowledge Development

Understanding the relationship between theory and practice is particularly important to understanding teacher knowledge development. We are familiar with Schön's (1983) conception of *reflective practice*[2] in professional knowing. Practitioners engage in 'reflection-on-action' when they reflect on what they have done or what they have experienced, often in order to prepare themselves for future actions. They also engage in 'reflection-in-action', which takes place during the action, especially when they encounter situations that are unanticipated, problematic or unique, and they arrive at a new way of looking at a phenomenon or a problem, hence generating new understanding leading to immediate action. The process of generating new understanding is called 'reframing'. Schön argued that when a practitioner is engaged in this kind of reflective process, he becomes a researcher in the practice context, and the knowledge acquired in this process is a legitimate form of professional knowing that is rigorous in its own right (Schön, 1983: 69).[3]

In the ensuing discussion, I shall present two cases to illustrate the relationship between theory and practice. Both cases are drawn from the study of Marina, an expert ESL teacher in a secondary school in Hong Kong (for a detailed report on Marina, see Tsui, 2003). The following is a brief outline of the context of the study.

At the time of the study, Marina was an ESL teacher with eight years of teaching experience in a secondary school in a working-class housing estate and was also the head of the English panel (equivalent to the English department) in the school. Marina was highly commended by her principal and her colleagues as an excellent teacher, and well loved by her students. The study of Marina's pedagogical practices and the knowledge that underpinned these practices took place over a period of one and a half years during which intensive observation of her teaching was conducted daily over a period of three months. Numerous interviews were conducted with Marina after lesson observations, focusing on her classroom teaching, as well as during less busy periods when she was asked to elaborate on her conceptions of teaching and her own professional development as a teacher. Interviews were also conducted with her students at both junior and senior levels.

4.1 Case I: Conducting Group Work

Group work is a regular feature in Marina's classroom. She had used group work ever since she had started teaching. Her initial understanding of the practice was simply to provide opportunities for students to talk in English and she tried to design tasks that she thought would interest her students. However, she soon found that the tasks that did not require students to produce outputs often did not work well. She realised that merely putting students into groups did not mean that they would collaborate; some of them simply worked on their own while others were off-task. She also found that when students did not have the linguistic resources to complete the task, they got frustrated and lost interest. It was challenging for her to manage group work in a large class of 40. First, it was difficult to monitor 10 groups of four; second, providing feedback to all groups immediately after group work in a double lesson of 80 minutes was onerous. It was common practice for teachers to ask students to report back the outcomes of group work. However, as time allowed only a few groups to do so, those groups that did not get an opportunity to report back obtained no feedback on their work and felt that their efforts were wasted. Moreover, when one group was presenting their work, other groups were often busy preparing for their own presentations, and the opportunity for peer learning was lost. Furthermore, as many students were soft-spoken and nervous when they presented their work and the physical classroom environment was noisy due to the busy traffic outside the school, students were often unable to follow the presentations and soon lost interest. These and other similar problems led to group work being regarded by teachers as time-consuming and dispensable, especially if they were pressed for time.

The question of how group work could be effectively and efficiently conducted was something Marina had been trying to address, and in one interview she commented:

[There is] the need for a purpose in-group work. In the PCED [Postgraduate Certificate in Education] programme, I was made aware of this. Previously, when I asked students to do group work, the purpose was to get them to talk in English. This is still one of the purposes now, but I'd ask myself something more – what is the aim of this group work. I know that I should tell students what the aim is.

Marina was introduced to the theory of group work in the teacher education programme that she attended. However, it was in practice that she gained an understanding of what purposefulness meant in group work. According to Marina, group work should lead to an outcome that could be shared. When groups listened to the presentations of other groups, there had to be a purpose for listening. In the course of using group work over time, she also began to see that group work was a means for collaborative learning. The new understanding that she came to shaped the way the tasks were subsequently designed.

In the following, I will provide an example from my observational data on how group work was enacted in Marina's classroom.

4.1.1 Marina's group work in action

The following is a group activity that she used for teaching the use of the modal verbs *should* and *ought* to give advice. To make sure that students were linguistically prepared for the activity, Marina presented five sample letters from the 'problems page' of a magazine and went over each of them with the class. Then she asked each group to write a reply to one of the letters, using the modal verbs. Each group wrote their reply on a large poster and posted them on the board. Since Marina had gone over all five letters with the class, all students had the contexts for making sense of the group replies posted. She then introduced the activity 'Agony Aunt', a column in a newspaper for youngsters where they could seek advice from Aunt Debbie. She split the class into 10 groups and asked each group to ask Debbie for advice on a particular problem. She then asked the groups to exchange their questions and give advice as if they were Debbie. The following is an example of a note sent to Debbie by one group and a reply to the note sent by another group.

> Dear Debbie,
> I love a girl in Form 3 (Secondary 3). She is very beautiful. But I don't know. I want to spend some time with her.
>
> A handsome boy
>
> Dear handsome boy,
> You shouldn't love a girl when you are study[ing]. You ought to study well in this time. You ought to love a girl after you study secondary school.
>
> Debbie

All 10 pairs of notes were written on large posters and put on the board, and Marina went over them one by one, eliciting comments from students and providing feedback. This allowed Marina to go over the work produced by all groups within 10 or 15 minutes, and the whole class was able to benefit from peer and teacher feedback. Finally, Marina chose the best products and put them on the classroom bulletin board for positive reinforcement.

4.1.2 Marina's theorisation of group work

When I asked her to explain how she organised group work, the following principles emerged from her explanation:

- Task design: The task must be designed in such a way that students need to collaborate in order to complete it.
- Purposeful collaboration: The collaboration must result in an outcome that needs to be shared with the rest of the class.
- Peer learning: To enable students to learn from each other, the teacher must provide a purpose for students to listen or read group

presentations and to provide feedback. (For example, in the Agony Aunt activity described above, each group was keen to read the advice given to their own group by Debbie.)
- Opportunity for peer and teacher feedback on outcome: Peer and teacher feedback are important for student learning, and time must be allocated for this.
- Management of large class size for learning: All groups must have the opportunity to share their work and obtain feedback.
- Maximising time and resources for learning: Routines must be set up to organise learning and students must be familiarised with these routines. Available resources can be used creatively.
- Positive reinforcement: Good work produced by students should be recognised and should serve as models for other students.

These principles were developed over time as she tried out group work and encountered problems. For example, the use of large posters for students to present their group productions was her answer to the problem of allowing all 10 groups in the class to present their work and provide peer and teacher feedback within limited time. Marina's theorisation, realised by the principles she outlined, and practice of group work were thus unified in the enactment of group work in the setting as experienced by her, and as she acted within the setting. As she encountered problems, she modified her organisation of group work, and in this process, her knowledge and theory of group work developed: She came to a new understanding.

4.2 Case II: The Teaching of Writing

A common practice among teachers in Hong Kong is to give students a composition topic, provide them with vocabulary items related to the topic, mark the composition in great detail and ask students to do corrections. Marina was very much aware of the enormous amount of time that teachers spent on marking compositions (which she described as 'very painful'), and the lack of impact this practice had on students. She commented in one of the interviews, 'marking compositions is very painful. After all the marking, you find that the students' [writings] are still the same: the content is very limited and uninteresting'. She also observed that her colleagues had the same problem:

> I looked at my colleagues, they were all suffering from marking compos [compositions]; marking is no fun. The students produced the ideas. These ideas ought to be very interesting, especially when they are in

their teens, and they should be very creative. But why did they have to do it merely as a piece of homework? [...] students ought to be able to do it better, the question is whether we are giving them the opportunity to do so. Their concept of composition is that they have written a piece of composition, the teacher's responsibility is to correct the mistakes, and then their job is to do the corrections and hand it in. But this is not what writing is about.

The teacher's job, in Marina's words, is reduced to 'proofreading'. To address this problem, Marina read up on references on the teaching of writing, especially those on process writing and found the ideas useful because they corroborated her own experience in writing. She said, 'even in my own writing, I don't have just one draft. I think if you want to produce good writing, it is not possible to accomplish it at one go'. She liked the idea of process writing partly because it was congruent with her conception of student learning:

I always think that we need to give students a second chance to do things again. [...] Their initial idea may be odd, but when they think about it again, they'll sort out the problem and try again. [...] This is the merit of process writing.

The following implementation of process writing illustrates well the dialectical relationship between theory and practice.

Marina worked with teachers of junior levels in her department to try out process writing. Initially, she circulated an article by Tsui (1996) that reports on a study on the teaching of process writing in a secondary school in Hong Kong. She gave the teachers only rough guidelines for implementation instead of a specific format that they all had to follow. The general guidelines pertained to the following: First, students should be given opportunities to revise their initial drafts on the basis of the feedback they received from the teacher as well as from their peers; second, students should focus on content when providing feedback on the first draft, and on grammatical accuracy in the revised draft, so that they would not be handling both content and form at the same time. She gave the teachers freedom to try things out and suggested that they would review the effectiveness of the process at the end of the year.

The students' first writing task was to write a description of their first impression of one of their classmates or teachers. One of the teachers, Eva, being the coordinator of junior levels, drafted a lesson plan that contained what she perceived to be four main sequences of process writing, namely: (1) a pre-writing task which prepares students for the task in terms of content; (2) a first draft, peer feedback and production of a second draft; (3) teacher feedback on the second draft and further revision to produce a third draft and (4) teacher feedback on grammatical accuracy on the third draft and revision to produce the final draft for assessment.

To scaffold the provision of peer feedback, Marina suggested to Eva that guidance should be provided by giving students a reader's comments form to fill out. Eva took the suggestion seriously and designed a simple two-part form. The first part listed the main aspects that should be covered and asked students to indicate whether each aspect was well written, difficult to understand or simply missing. The second part asked students to suggest ways in which their peers' writing could be improved. Again a checklist on possible ways of improving their writing and an open-ended question were given. The students were also given the opportunity to discuss in groups and report back to the whole class. The reader's comments form proved to be helpful because many students incorporated the points on the checklist in their subsequent revisions.

While other teachers in the English Department, including Eva, simply gave out the reader's comment form and went over it verbally with the whole class, Marina selected one of the first drafts and worked with the whole class on providing feedback on the comment form. This kind of 'learner training' is very important, and is often neglected by teachers (see Allaei & Connor, 1990; Leki, 1990; Stanley, 1992; Tsui & Ng, 2000). In order to make sure that students would not feel that their work was being criticised by their peers, she prefaced her instructions to students as follows: 'The following composition is written by your classmate. He has got some good ideas and some ideas can be even better.'

On the basis of the experience gained in the first writing task, Marina modified the steps when she designed and prepared materials for the second writing task, which was to write a description of a mystery location for the reader to guess. Finding that students had problems with text organisation, she built in an additional sequence that required them to produce an outline after the pre-writing task and to give comments on each other's outline before they started the first draft. The process was again scaffolded by the provision of a simple checklist for provision of feedback on the outline. This additional sequence again proved to be very useful to the students.

In addition to providing 'learner training' for peer feedback, Marina built in 'learner training' at the revision stage, in order to help students to respond to teacher and peer comments and make corresponding revisions. She also designed a worksheet in which she gave students a fabricated text containing comments from the teacher, and provided guiding questions to help them to rewrite the sentences by putting in more descriptive details and by changing statements into dialogues. For all writing tasks, Marina included exercises on grammatical accuracy at the final stage (i.e. when students were asked to correct the grammatical errors identified by the teacher). She also provided model examples of good writing and built in motivation for reading each other's writing. For example, for the first and second writing tasks, students were respectively asked not to reveal the identity of the person and the location described in their texts, and a follow-up activity was built which required students to guess which person and which location were being described in their peers' writing.

The second writing task, with the additional scaffolding sequences, was more successful than the first one. Hence, the steps in what Marina subsequently called the 'writing cycle' became more or less the blueprint for junior writing tasks for the rest of the school year. Figure 2.1 is a diagrammatic summary of the sequences in the writing cycle described by Marina.

5 Implications for Teacher Education

The two cases cited above illustrate the dialectical relation between theory and practice in teacher knowledge development. As pointed out earlier in this chapter, a dialectical relation is more than a declaration of reciprocal effects by two terms upon one another. Lave (1988: 146) elaborates, 'A dialectical relation exists when its component elements are created, are brought into being, only in conjunction with one another'. Marina's practice would not have been brought into being without her knowledge of the concept of process writing and the studies conducted, and her own theorisation, that is, her formulation of the guiding principles, of process writing, as crystallised in the writing cycle, would not have been possible without practice. Bereiter and Scardamalia (1993: 44) point out that

> [k]nowledge is not just one more factor to be added in with personality, aptitude and social factors to account for expertise. [...] [K]nowledge is part of expertise – a large part of what must be explained – and not part of something that lies in the background as part of a pattern.

The knowledge held by teachers, as pointed out by many researchers, is largely tacit and unarticulated. It is important such knowledge be explicitly articulated so that it can further inform practice. Shulman (1988: 33) argues that

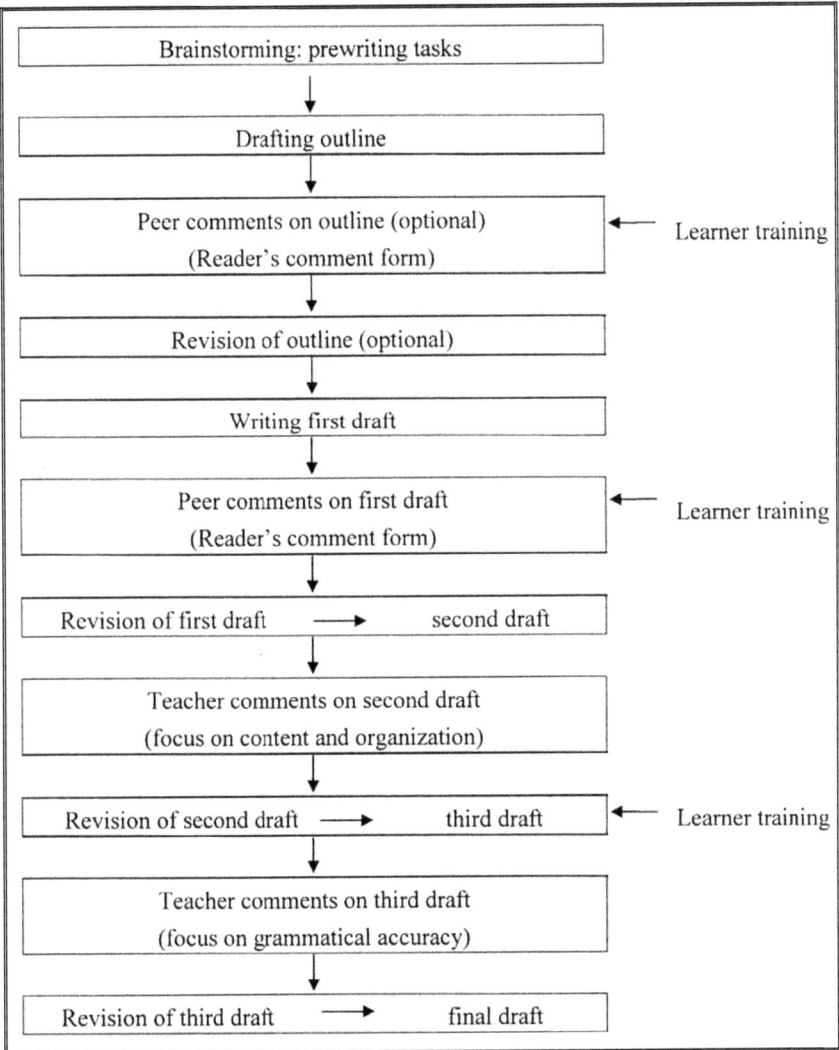

Figure 2.1 The writing cycle (Tsui, 2003: 230)

[t]eachers will become better educators when they can begin to have explicit answers for questions, 'How do I know what I know? How do I know the reasons for what I do? Why do I ask my students to perform or think in particular ways?' The capacity to answer such questions not only lies at the heart of what we mean by becoming skilled as a teacher;

it also requires a combining of reflections on practical experience and reflection on theoretical understanding.

And as Fenstermacher (1994: 51), echoing Shulman, points out, the challenge for teacher knowledge research is to show not 'that teachers think, believe or have opinions but that they know. And even more important, that they know that they know'.

The understanding of the dialectical relation between theory and practice is important for teacher education. It puts into question the predominant mode of organisation of initial teacher education programmes according to a theoretical component and a practical component (commonly referred to as the 'practicum' or 'school placement'), with the former typically preceding the latter. It helps us to understand why teacher trainees often complain that teacher education courses are too theoretical and that the practicum comes too late. It calls for a model of teacher education which is not predicated on such bifurcation, and which emphasises the centrality of reflection on practical experience and theoretical understanding as teachers engage in the act of teaching in specific settings.

Notes

(1) The term 'content knowledge' is used in the sense of Shulman (1986) and includes subject matter knowledge and pedagogical content knowledge, as opposed to pedagogical knowledge. In the teacher knowledge literature, the term 'subject matter knowledge' sometimes encompasses 'pedagogical content knowledge', and sometimes refers strictly to knowledge of the discipline. In this chapter, the term 'subject matter knowledge' is used in the latter sense. Subject matter knowledge for teaching will be referred to as 'pedagogical content knowledge'. For further discussion of Shulman's categorisation of knowledge, see the contributions by Hüttner and Smit, Mehlmauer-Larcher, Reichl and Vodopija-Krstanovic in this volume.
(2) For more discussions on the role of reflection, see the contributions by Mehlmauer-Larcher and Reichl in this volume.
(3) The distinction that Schön makes between reflection-in-action and reflection-on-action, as Eraut (1994) points out, is more theoretical than real. When real examples are examined, it is difficult to draw the line between the two and the distinction disappears. For further discussion of Schön's concepts, see also the contribution by Mehlmauer-Larcher in this volume.

References

Allaei, S.K. and Connor, U.M. (1990) Exploring the dynamics of cross-cultural collaboration in writing classrooms. *The Writing Instructor* 10, 19–28.
Ball, D.L. (1991) Teaching mathematics for understanding: What do teachers need to know about subject matter? In M. Kennedy (ed.) *Teaching Academic Subjects to Diverse Learners* (pp. 63–83). New York: Teachers College Press.

Ball, D.L. and Bass, H. (2000) Interweaving content and pedagogy in teaching and learning to teach: Knowing and using mathematics. In J. Boaler (ed.) *Multiple Perspectives on Teaching and Learning* (pp. 83–104). Westport, CT: Ablex Publishing.

Bennett, N. (1993) Knowledge bases for learning to teach. In N. Bennett and C. Carre (eds) *Learning to Teach* (pp. 1–17). London: Routledge.

Bereiter, C. and Scardamalia, M. (1993) *Surpassing Ourselves: An Inquiry into the Nature and Implications of Expertise*. Chicago, IL: Open Court.

Bruner, J. (1985) Narrative and paradigmatic modes of thought. In E. Eisner (ed.) *Learning and Teaching the Ways of Knowing* (pp. 97–115). Chicago, IL: University of Chicago Press.

Calderhead, J. and Miller, E. (1986) *The Integration of Subject Matter Knowledge in Student Teachers' Classroom Practice*. San Francisco, CA: Reed's Limited.

Carlsen, W. S. (1991) Subject-matter knowledge and science teaching: A pragmatic perspective. In J. Brophy (ed.) *Advances in Research on Teaching, Vol. 2: Teachers' Knowledge of Subject Matter as it Relates to their Teaching Practice* (pp. 115–143). Greenwich, CT: JAI Press.

Chu, H. (1990) *Learning to Be a Sage: Selections from the Conversations of Master Chu, Arranged Topically* (translated by D.K. Gardner). Berkeley/Los Angeles: University of California Press.

Clandinin, D.J. (1992) Narrative and story in teacher education. In T. Russell and H. Munby (eds) *Teachers and Teaching: From Classroom to Reflection* (pp. 124–137). London: The Falmer Press.

Clandinin, D.J. and Connelly, F.M. (1987) Teachers' personal knowledge: What counts as personal in studies of the personal. *Journal of Curriculum Studies* 19, 487–500.

Cochran, K.F. and Jones, L.L. (1998) The subject matter knowledge of preservice science teachers. In B. Fraser and K. Tobin (eds) *International Handbook of Science Education* (pp. 707–718). Dordrecht, the Netherlands: Kluwer.

Connelly, D.J. and Clandinin, F.M. (1995) Teachers' professional knowledge landscapes: Secret, sacred, and cover stories. In F.M. Clandinin and D.J. Connelly (eds) *Teachers' Professional Knowledge Landscapes* (pp. 3–15). New York: Teachers' College Press.

Elbaz, F. (1983) *Teacher Thinking: A Study of Practical Knowledge*. London: Croom Helm.

Eraut, M. (1994) *Developing Professional Knowledge and Competence*. London: Falmer Press.

Fenstermacher, G.D. (1994) The knower and the known: The nature of knowledge in the research on teaching. In L. Darling-Hammond (ed.) *Review of Research in Education* (pp. 3–56). Washington, DC: AERA.

Gao, S.L. (2005) *Xueji Yanjiu (Research on Xueji)*. Beijing: People's Education Press.

Grossman, P. (1990) *The Making of a Teacher: Teacher Knowledge and Teacher Education*. New York: Teacher's College Press.

Grossman, P., Wilson, S.M. and Shulman, L.S. (1989) Teachers of substance: Subject matter knowledge for teaching. In M. Reynolds (ed.) *Knowledge Base for the Beginning Teacher* (pp. 23–36). New York: Pergamon.

Hashweh, M. (1987) Effects of subject matter knowledge in the teaching of biology and physics. *Teaching and Teacher Education* 3, 109–120.

Heywood, D. (2007) Problematising science subject matter knowledge as a legitimate enterprise in primary teacher education. *Cambridge Journal of Education* 37 (4), 519–542.

Jackson, P.W. (1968) *Life in Classrooms*. New York: Holt, Rinehart & Winston.

Lave, J. (1988) *Cognition in Practice: Mind, Mathematics, and Culture in Everyday Life*. Cambridge: Cambridge University Press.

Lave, J., Murtaugh, M. and de la Rocha, O. (1984) The dialectic of arithmetic in grocery shopping. In B. Rogoff and J. Lave (eds) *Everyday Cognition: Its Development in Social Context* (pp. 67–94). Cambridge, MA: Harvard University Press.

Leinhardt, G. (1988) Situated knowledge and expertise in teaching. In J. Calderhead (ed.) *Teachers' Professional Learning* (pp. 146–168). London: Falmer Press.

Leki, I. (1990) Coaching from the margins: Issues in written response. In B. Kroll (ed.) *Second Language Writing: Research Insights for the Classroom* (pp. 57–68). Cambridge: Cambridge University Press.

Ma, L. (1999) *Knowing and Teaching Elementary Mathematics: Teachers' Understanding of Fundamental Mathematics in China and the United States*. Mahwah, NJ: Lawrence Erlbaum Associates.

Munby, H. and Russell, T. (1992) Transforming chemistry research into chemistry teaching: The complexities of adopting new frames for experience. In T. Russell and H. Munby (eds) *Teachers and Teaching: From Classroom to Reflection* (pp. 90–108). London: The Falmer Press.

Munby, H., Russell, T. and Martin, A. (2001) Teachers' knowledge and how it develops. In V. Richardson (ed.) *Handbook of Research on Teaching* (pp. 877–904). Washington, DC: AERA.

Polanyi, M. (1966) *The Tacit Dimension*. London: Routledge.

Putnam, R.T. and Borko, H. (1997) Teacher learning: Implications of new views of cognition. In B.J. Biddle, T.L. Good and I. Goodson (eds) *International Handbook of Teachers and Teaching*, Vol. II (pp. 1223–1296). Dordrecht: Kluwer Academic Publishers.

Rollnick, M., Bennett, J., Rhemtula, M., Dharsey, N. and Ndlovu, T. (2008) The place of subject matter knowledge in pedagogical content knowledge: A case study of South African teachers teaching the amount of substance and chemical equilibrium. *International Journal of Science Education* 30 (10), 1365–1387.

Ryle, G. (1949) *The Concept of Mind*. London: Hutchinson.

Schön, D.A. (1983) *The Reflective Practitioner: How Professionals Think in Action*. New York: Basic Books.

Scribner, S. (1984) Study working intelligence. In B. Rogoff and J. Lave (eds) *Everyday Cognition: Its Development in Social Context* (pp. 9–40). Cambridge, MA: Harvard University Press.

Shulman, L.S. (1986) Those who understand: Knowledge growth in teaching. *Educational Researcher* 15 (2), 4–14.

Shulman, L.S. (1988). The dangers of dichotomous thinking in education. In P. Grimmet and G. Erickson (eds) *Reflections on Teacher Education* (pp. 31–39). New York: Teachers College Press.

Shulman, L.S. (1999) Knowledge and teaching: Foundations of the new reform. In J. Leach and B. Moon (eds) *Learners and Pedagogy* (pp. 61–77). London: Sage.

Smith, D.C. and Neale, D.C. (1989). The construction of subject matter knowledge in primary science teaching. *Teaching and Teacher Education* 5 (1), 1–20.

Smith, R.G. (2008) Developing professional identities and knowledge: Becoming primary teachers. *Teachers and Teaching: Theory and Practice* 13 (4), 377–397.

Stanley, J. (1992) Coaching student writers to be effective peer evaluators. *Journal of Second Language Writing* 1 (3), 217–233.

Tsui, A.B.M. (1996) Learning how to teach writing. In J. Richards and D. Freeman (eds) *Teacher Learning in Language Teaching* (pp. 97–124). New York: Cambridge University Press.

Tsui, A.B.M. (2003) *Understanding Expertise in Teaching*. New York: Cambridge University Press.

Tsui, A.B.M. and Ng, M. (2000) Do secondary L2 writers benefit from peer comments? *Journal of Second Language Writing* 9 (2), 147–170.

Tsui, A.B.M. and Wong, J.L.N. (2009) In search of a third space: Teacher development in Mainland China. In C.K.K. Chan and N. Rao (eds) *Revisiting the Chinese Learner: Changing Contexts, Changing Education* (pp. 281–311). Hong Kong: Comparative Education Research Centre/Springer Academic Publishers.

Wilson, S.M., Shulman, L.S. and Richert, A.E. (1987) 150 different ways of knowing: Representations of knowledge in teaching. In J. Calderhead (ed.) *Exploring Teacher Thinking* (pp. 104–124). London: Cassell.

Wineburg, S. and Wilson, S.M. (1991) Subject-matter knowledge in the teaching of history. In J.E. Brophy (ed.) *Advances in Research on Teaching, Vol. 2: Teachers' Knowledge of Subject Matter as it Relates to Their Teaching Practice* (pp. 305–347). Greenwich, CT: JAI Press.

3 Moments of Practice: Teachers' Knowledge and Interaction in the Language Classroom

Joachim Appel

1 Introduction

The relationship between theory and practice has been conceptualised differently at various stages in the development of language teaching. One position sees practice as an area of application for preconceived academic knowledge. A second position assumes a need for mediation between academic knowledge and practice (Roulet, 1975; cf. the discussion on pedagogic grammar in Stern, 1983: 175). A third position, and the one that this chapter proposes, takes an ethnographic stance. It sees practice as a domain in its own right and tries to provide a platform for the practitioner's voice (Bailey & Nunan, 1996). Research on practice in this sense has been done in two areas: one is research into teachers' knowledge, beliefs and cognitions, the other is research on classroom interaction.

Research on teachers' knowledge started out from teachers' cognitions and decision-making (Calderhead, 1984, 1987; Clark & Peterson, 1986; Shavelson & Stern, 1981). It then moved on to personal and individual aspects of teaching knowledge (Clandinin, 1986; Freeman, 1996) and subject-specific ones (cf. Shulman's 1987 notion of pedagogical content knowledge).[1] The study of language teachers' subject-specific knowledge has come into its own since the 1990s (e.g. Appel, 2000; Bailey & Nunan, 1996; Tsui, 2003; Woods, 1996). It focuses on constructs like 'beliefs, assumptions and knowledge' (Woods, 1996), experiential knowledge (Appel, 2000) and expertise (Tsui, 2003).[2]

Whereas research into teachers' knowledge is primarily concerned with what teachers say in verbal reports, research into language-teaching interaction analyzes classroom events documented in recordings and transcripts. Research in this field can build on a long tradition encompassing work on discourse analysis (Sinclair & Coulthard, 1975; Wagner, 1983), classroom observation (Allwright, 1988) and current work done within a conversation-analysis framework (Seedhouse, 2004).

The following argument tries to bring together findings and methods from research on teachers' knowledge and from research on classroom interaction. It does so by using a model suggested by Hutchins (1995). The model was originally conceived for a domain of practice different from language teaching. It was developed to summarise the results of a study of navigation. The study argues that cognition does not exclusively reside in the individual's mind. Rather, it is situated and cultural. Similar arguments have been put forth in second-language acquisition research. Studies on teachers' knowledge have, with few exceptions (Appel, 2000; Breen, 1985; Feiman-Nemser & Floden, 1986), focused on individual aspects of such knowledge. In the following discussion, a case for the social and cultural nature of teaching knowledge will be made. The argument will use Hutchins' concept of a 'moment of practice' as a metaphor for looking at language-teaching practice.

Put very briefly, in any moment of practice, three developments come together. A first development is the *conduct of the activity*. This is the performance of a task over a limited stretch of time, usually involving a high density of interaction. In language teaching, this is a stretch of classroom interaction, be it an exchange, a transaction or a lesson. A second development is that *of the practitioners*. At any moment of practice, the practitioners involved will have reached a certain stage in the development of their knowledge, abilities and values. With regard to practitioners in the language classroom, this knowledge can be situational, i.e. knowledge about current states of the learning group, individual learners, the mechanics and agenda of a lesson, etc., or biographical, i.e. past language learning and teaching experience. A third strand is the *development of the practice*. The development of the practice includes the values and beliefs of teachers as members of a classroom and teaching culture and the collectively developed answers to the conditions and constraints of the teaching situation. It also comprises the 'official' history of language teaching, i.e. academic knowledge.

The argument will be illustrated with data from a secondary-school context in Germany.[3] These comprise an audio recording documenting a brief stretch of teacher–pupil interaction in a beginners' class of English. The students, aged 13 to 14, had just started with English as their second foreign language in secondary school, having had two years of French before. The episode was chosen because it exemplifies some basic concerns and dilemmas in classroom teaching (Lampert, 1985).

The second set of data is two interviews with the teacher; one was recorded the day before he taught the lesson and the other one immediately after the lesson. The teacher had 15 years teaching experience both in Germany and abroad. Let us now look at the three strands of the model in more detail.

2 Conduct of the Activity

The moment of practice to be considered here is a stretch of interaction documented below. It is a series of exchanges between a teacher and an individual student beginning in line (79) and lasting until line (98).

Extract 1
(79) Teacher: So right. So she has breakfast at seven o'clock. What about you, John?
(80) John: Ahm (2.0) I have (1.3) breakfast (1.9).
(81) T: At.
(82) J: At (2.1) *(laughter)* (2.5).
(83) T: John, come on *(softly)*.
(84) J: I have breakfast on.
(85) T: Not *on*.
(86) J: At six (1.3) at.
(87) (laughter).
(88) T: *(to class)*: Sssh.
(89) J: Ahm at six.
(90) T: At six o'clock?
(91) J: No, at six (1.5) ahm half past, half past.
(92) T: You have breakfast at half past six? Is that right? *(writes on blackboard: 'half past six')*. Is that it? Right. So, John has breakfast at half past six. John, say the sentence again please.
(93) J: I have breakfast (1.1) breakfast on half past.
(94) T: *(writes on blackboard 'I have breakfast')* Say it again, please.
(95) J: At half past six.
(96) T: The full sentence, please, John, sorry.
(97) J: I have breakfast at half past six.
(98) T: Okay. Marc.
(99) Mc: I have breakfast at seven o'clock.
(100) T: What about you, Isabel?
(101) I: I have breakfast at seven o'clock.
(102) T: What about you, Manuel?
(103) Ma: I have breakfast at. [...]
(104) T: OK. What about Nathalie?

Earlier on, the teacher had introduced the word 'breakfast'. He now wants his students to practice that word. He asks individual students when they have breakfast. In line (80), a student, John, has difficulties in answering the teacher's question and breaks off in mid-sentence. In (81), the teacher supplies the preposition 'at'. All the student is able to do, however, is to repeat this preposition in (82). The teacher softly tells him to try harder in (83). In (84), the student tries again, this time with the wrong preposition, 'on'. In (85), the teacher gives negative feedback on this in a meta-linguistic comment. In (86), the student corrects to the right preposition plus numeral. In (90), however, the teacher questions the truth of this statement, i.e. he momentarily focuses on the content of what is being said. In (91), the student corrects to a statement that is probably factually correct but incomplete. The teacher recasts the target sentence, writing the expression 'half past six' on the board (92). He then asks John to say the complete sentence. In (93), John comes up with a complete sentence but still with the wrong preposition. In (94), the teacher writes the first half of the target sentence on the blackboard. The student now produces a correct temporal expression (95). The teacher yet again insists on a full sentence (96), which John finally provides in (97). What follows in the next stretch of interaction (98)–(104) is a quick succession of exchanges in which no help by the teacher is needed.

In Hutchins' model, the conduct of the activity is characterised by limited duration and high density of interaction. 'Changes in this dimension happen quickly, and the elements of the task performance are in relatively intense interaction with each other' (Hutchins, 1995: 373).

This density of interaction can easily be seen in (79)–(97). Contributions are highly dependent on each other. Each student contribution triggers a new intervention by the teacher, taking into consideration the current stage of knowledge displayed by this student. The time available for interaction with an individual student is limited. The teacher is therefore under pressure to bring the exchange to an acceptable conclusion. It is indeed a highly significant feature of this moment of practice that a one-to-one exchange between teacher and student is maintained in front of an audience for a considerable length of time. This is made particularly salient by the contrast between (79)–(97) and the quick succession of exchanges that follows after (97).

'Elements of the task performance' are both the interactants and the media they use. In language teaching, verbal interaction between participants is at the core of the activity, although media like the book, worksheets, and visuals of all sorts also come into play. The teacher in our data uses the blackboard to support the student in (92) and (94). Language teaching interaction is, as the above episode shows, multimodal, a characteristic that deserves greater research attention.

A number of concepts exist to analyse the development of verbal interaction in language teaching. A first one, going back to conversation analysis, is the 'sequentiality' of interaction (Auer, 1999), a second one is the concept of 'footing' (Goffman, 1981) and a third one is the concept of 'pedagogical focus' (Seedhouse, 2004).

Sequentiality means that one utterance builds on the previous one. Work in conversation analysis has shown this dynamic character of interaction. Utterances can be understood only with reference to the place where they occur in interaction, i.e. in terms of their sequential position. In Extract 1, line (81) can be understood only with reference to (80), line (82) with reference to (81). Participants retrospectively display their understanding through what they say in their next turn. In (89), John may well be struggling with the composition of a time adverbial. In (90), however, the teacher displays an understanding of (89) as a statement about the time when John has breakfast, which John then subscribes to in (91).

A second concept is that of *footing*. Although (79)–(97) appears to be a dialogue between the teacher and an individual student, the class is still present as an audience, as (82) and (88) show. Classroom interaction is multiparty interaction, which produces the interactional density of the conduct of the activity and fundamentally shapes teachers' work (cf. Section 3). The multiparty character of teaching interaction is captured by Goffman's concept of *footing*. Footing describes speaker and listener roles and their dynamics. In terms of listener roles, it distinguishes between different ways in which participants are addressed and allowed access to the interaction. They may be 'addressed participants' or 'ratified participants', i.e. participants who are not directly addressed at a particular moment, but who are still intended partners in the communicative event (Duranti, 1997: 298). In lines (79)–(97), an individual student is addressed for a longer stretch of time with the class as ratified participants. In (98)–(104), the quick succession of individual exchanges is an implicit signal that everybody in the group is a ratified participant who may be called on by the teacher (cf. Appel, 2007; 2010). In terms of speaker roles, Goffman (1981) makes a distinction between a 'principal', i.e. someone who is responsible for the content of what is said, an 'author', i.e. someone who is responsible for the wording of what is said, and an 'animator' who lends his or her voice to the words and content decided on by the author and principal. We can identify such roles in (81)–(82) when John hesitantly picks up the teacher's correction 'at'. Here John acts as an animator, whereas in (90)–(91) he appears to act as a principal (or is at least cast in that role by the teacher), who wants to express the time when he has breakfast, and as an author, who struggles to find the appropriate expression in the L2.

A third concept is that of *pedagogical focus*. Seedhouse (2004) distinguishes between a focus on form and accuracy and a focus on meaning and fluency. A form and accuracy focus generates the type of interaction we find in (81)–(82), when John hesitantly picks up the teacher's correction 'at'. This type of interaction is governed by an insistence on exact wording and the correction of formal mistakes. In (90)–(91) there is, however minimal, a focus on meaning and fluency, because here the teacher no longer insists on a complete sentence but focuses on meaning; cf. (92: 'You have breakfast at half past six¿ Is that right¿'), where he checks whether he has understood the contents of what John has said correctly.

Which focus is chosen by the teacher at a given moment of practice and how much of a priority it is made not only depends on the exigencies of the teaching situation, but also on the teacher's agenda and his or her priorities, aims, principles and values in teaching. These come into a moment of practice through the development of the practitioners.

3   Development of the Practitioners

Insights into the development of the practitioners can be gained from research into teachers' knowledge and beliefs. Unlike the analysis of verbal interaction, which takes as its starting point actual classroom events, teachers' knowledge and beliefs are reconstructed from verbalisations, i.e. they are secondary data. Interviews may have different focuses that lead to different aspects of teachers' knowledge being articulated. The interviewer may, for instance, present the interviewee with the recording of a classroom event and ask him or her to comment on it. This was done with the episode presented in Section 1.

Extract 2
Q: How about John. You rather put him at the centre. You insisted a lot. Why did you do that¿
A: I can't remember.
Q: The boy at the back of the classroom. [...]
A: That was a language thing. [...] He is the one who has most difficulties. You can tell from the way he behaves in class, very insecure, and that's pronunciation, vocab, grammar, the lot. He is, in a way, the weakest. And that was the reason why I insisted. Whether that does him any good or whether he is just pushed back into his shell, that's of course an open question. [...] He does actually try. But he might not have the capacity.

In his first reaction, the teacher hardly seems to be aware of the episode. His retrospective comments on the event are general. This shows how difficult it is to access the so-called 'cognitions' that have been the focus of research into language teachers' knowledge. In fact, it is debatable whether we should take interviews like the above as a verbalisation of cognitions. Interviews are, just like the verbal interaction in the language classroom described in Extract 1, highly sequential. Statements by interviewees are made in the context of arguments unfolding and in the context of a process of negotiation between the partners in the interview. In our case, it clearly was the interviewer who put the 'John episode' documented in Extract 2 on the agenda. He thus set the theme for this part of the interview. In terms of a content analysis of what the teacher says, it is therefore hard to argue that he was conscious of this episode. What can be shown, however, is the way in which the teacher documents the reasons behind his practice. He does so using two categorisations. He first categorises the event as 'a language thing'. This ties in with the analysis of the interaction as being governed by a focus on form (Seedhouse, 2004).

In a second categorisation, the student is characterised as 'weak'. From a cognitive point of view, expert–novice studies have shown that 'labels' for students can be found in both inexperienced and experienced teachers' perceptions. For experts, however,

> categories appeared to be embedded in rich episodic memories about particular students of the particular type under discussion. The labels serve as broad sense-making categories for thinking about groups of students *and* [his italics] planned actions in the classrooms. (Berliner, 1987: 66)

This is borne out to some extent by what our teacher says. He formulates a number of observations (areas of weakness, the student's will to cooperate). He also has a general developmental scenario in mind (has the student the ability to cope with the course?) and, most importantly, his perceptions are linked to partly explorative, partly supportive action in the interaction documented in Extract 1.

A second area of knowledge is not so much related to a specific teaching situation, but rather to teachers' general values and principles. These are elicited in narrative interviews. Extract 3 comes from such an interview with the same teacher.

Extract 3

I don't know how achievement minded I am. That's the way it is at the moment. Let's say I have got expectations. And one expectation is simple. It is that when they have an English lesson that they somehow benefit from it, that they are able to do something after the lesson, that they know something. That's the primary aim. They should have something they can build on later. Of course this only works if the relationship is right. But just having a wonderful relationship with a class and never mind the subject, that's not for me.

When he says 'at the moment', the teacher positions himself on a developmental axis. The development that comes into this moment of practice is one towards more rigour and a kind of realism that does not gloss over students' difficulties but rather looks at what they are able or unable to do. This teacher's development[4] started 14 years ago with rather groping attempts to find a teaching identity as a beginning teacher. There followed a time when this identity was put to the test by a longer stay abroad during which the teacher worked in an environment that was ruled by rigorous and authoritarian values, which in turn triggered student resistance. The teacher stated that he could just about professionally survive in this environment. He returned to his old school having become a stricter teacher. At the same time, he had gained more experience. He now had a much firmer grasp of what he wanted to teach, including an image of what was to happen in the course of a whole school year. He tried to deliver the basics of the language, something his pupils could later build on. His ethos was a focus on the subject, i.e. the language. He could provide the security in the form of structured tasks and assignments assessed at regular intervals. This, he stated, enabled him to change his – still thoroughly designed – plans on the spot according to the needs of the situation. The episode above can easily be related to this type of knowledge. The interaction with John had not been planned. It was somewhat risky in terms of classroom management. Yet the teacher was able to 'neglect' the class during the first half of the interaction (79–97) and to regain their attention in the second half.

Research on personal aspects of teaching knowledge has provided a wealth of accounts of personal and professional developments like the one just mentioned (Bullough & Baughman, 1993; Tsui, 2003; Woods, 1996). Changes from one phase to another are typically triggered by so-called critical incidents, critical classes or critical persons (Measor, 1985). It is particularly classroom experience that makes teachers modify their instructional beliefs. These are 'mediated' by the realities of the classroom situation, such as student motivation, student ability and classroom management (Graden, 1996: 390-391). Teacher knowledge develops in response to the classroom context and its constraints (Golombek, 1998: 447; Numrich, 1996: 142). Both are important factors that make teachers' knowledge not just personal, but also social, situated and cultural.

4 Development of Practice

Teachers' knowledge tends to be portrayed as individual knowledge. Woods, for example, stresses the focus on the individual teacher in his study:

> This study is not ethnographic in that it does not attempt to describe that shared culture [i.e. the professional culture of language teaching, J.A.] and processes among groups; rather it focuses on processes within the individual. This gives the study a more cognitive focus. (Woods, 1996: 49, similarly 264)

Yet there is a strong case for looking at practice as something collective, social and cultural.

4.1 Cultural Nature of Teachers' Knowledge

It is not without reason that Hutchins talks of the development of practitioners in the plural and not of that of a single practitioner. The development of expertise described in studies of language teachers' knowledge does, as we have seen, not happen in a social vacuum. Rather it is a response to the teaching situation. 'Structural contexts provide frameworks which impinge on all teacher decisions and actions' (Hatch, 1999: 233). The study of language teachers' knowledge therefore needs to go beyond the individual.

The development of practice as a cultural enterprise takes place in two domains. The first one might be called the culture of the classroom, i.e. the teaching situation and the structural demands it makes on participants. The second one is the development of language teaching as a professional and academic field. The two domains can be related to each other in various ways. They may overlap, but there may also be tensions and contradictions between the two. It is here that the gap between theory and practice becomes most salient.

Research into teachers' knowledge as well as research into the specifics of the language-teaching situation have quite early on used the concept of classroom culture (Breen, 1985; Feiman-Nemser & Floden, 1986). The concept of culture here refers to the shared values, beliefs and practices in a particular setting. This setting can be characterised in terms of the social and situational constraints participants have to work with.

4.2 Constraints on the Teaching Situation

The constraints on the teaching situation have been described in studies on the sociology of the teaching profession (Connell, 1985; Lortie, 1975).

They are: a low degree of voluntarism, the grouped character of the teaching situation, the uncertainty of that situation and the importance of personal relationships. With regard to language teaching, the dominance of evaluation and the dominance of the coursebook have to be added. Each constraint produces tensions and dilemmas, which have to be addressed by the teacher.

4.2.1 A low degree of voluntarism

Student cooperation in a school classroom cannot be taken for granted. The teacher's insistence on John saying a 'whole sentence' gives an idea of how cumbersome the process of 'making students speak' can be in everyday life in the classroom. Although John is, as the teacher states in the interview, not an uncooperative student, it takes a lot of effort on both sides until John says what the teacher wants him to say. Teachers at the beginning of their careers have a tendency to attribute problematic student responses like the one documented here to a lack of willingness when in fact they are caused by deficient linguistic resources (Johnson, 1992) or communicative practices in the L1 where speakers' utterances are often elliptical. In our case, the teacher has had sufficient experience to see that John lacks the linguistic resources to solve the task put to him. This is the reason why he so rigorously establishes a form-and-accuracy context (cf. the analysis of Extract 2). The question might be asked how far the teachers' practice is in line with current mainstream pedagogical principles in EFL like learner autonomy, learner centeredness or a focus on meaning. Clearly, there is hardly any learner autonomy in the exchange. In terms of footing, the learner is hardly given any choices with regard to speaker roles. At the same time, the teacher does give a lot of attention to an individual student – something requiring professional skill and stamina within a whole-class framework. If the interaction between the teacher and John had not taken place within a whole-class context, it would probably have passed as a 'scaffolding sequence' (cf., for instance, Young & Miller, 2004) leading the student step by step to the mastery of an expression.

4.2.2 The grouped character of the classroom situation

Teaching is working with groups. And working with groups produces exactly the interactional density referred to in Section 2. The heterogeneity of students' abilities and resources in a class presents a constant challenge to the teacher because classes consist of individuals. Teachers therefore face a dilemma. In order to do justice to the individual's learning process, they have to attend to the needs of this individual. At the same time, they cannot afford to lose sight of the group as whole. This is visible in line (88), when the teacher asks the class to be quiet or in the quick succession of exchanges after (97), when he implicitly signals to the class that his questions are not a dialogue with individuals but addressed to the whole class.

Research on second-language acquisition (e.g. Pienemann, 1998) as well as suggestions in the field of teaching methodology (especially communicative and humanistic approaches, cf. Richards & Rodgers, 2001) have called for the individualisation of instruction. However, within classroom cultures, the knowledge collectively developed by professionals has at its core strategies to deal with groups as a whole. This means making sure that all pupils cover the syllabus and the units of the coursebook during a certain period of time. In order to solve this task, teachers have to 'synchronise' learning processes, i.e. they have to make sure the class proceeds through the course and particularly through the chosen coursebook and other materials at roughly the same pace. Again, the interaction between the teacher and John shows how difficult this can be. John needs more time and attention in order to solve the task than the students called on after him (who, of course, had more time to prepare themselves for this answer in the role of ratified participants, cf. Section 2). With regard to insights into second-language acquisition, the stage John has reached in his individual sequence of acquisition is hardly compatible with that envisaged by the syllabus and book. Attempts to guide John to the production of forms targeted there might therefore succeed only superficially.

4.2.3 Uncertainty

Central aspects of teachers' work are uncertain: student understanding, the overall effect of teaching, the teacher's status and authority, his or her mastery of instructional content as well as the assessment of students (Floden & Clark, 1988). Some uncertainties tend to be encountered at the beginning of a teaching career. The story told by the teacher above is an example of a gradual development from uncertainty towards more security. Other aspects of uncertainty are more permanent. Among these are, as Extract 2 shows, uncertainty about the teacher's effect on John. The teacher does not know whether his insistence on John forming a complete sentence will actually lead to learning. Uncertainty and doubts about the actual outcome of teaching remain an issue throughout teachers' careers, sometimes becoming even more fraught in later years.

> Certainty decreases even further when one shifts perspective from the instruction in a single class or on a single topic to the education of an individual over a period of ten to twenty years. Research has shown that the long-term effects of education are variable and unpredictable. This is driven home to teachers whenever a former student returns to

testify to the tremendous importance of a lesson or comment that seemed insignificant to the teacher at the time. (Floden & Clark, 1988: 510)

Teaching cannot guarantee learning outcomes. It can only provide opportunities for learning. Teachers may assume they have covered the syllabus, but ultimately there is no certainty as to how much and which aspects of the syllabus students have actually learned. Looking at the role of research, past discussions in language-acquisition research casting general doubts on the efficiency of instructed language learning have probably not made these uncertainties any easier. The same applies to current tests claiming to measure the efficiency of educational systems in general.

Teachers also seem inherently uncertain about the level of their performance. One key factor contributing to this type of uncertainty is the relative isolation in which they work. The sanctity of the classroom may be held up as a shared professional value (Denscombe, 1980, 1985). At the same time, working in isolation may constitute a potential barrier to professional feedback. Such feedback finds its way to teachers either through very informal channels like comments made by colleagues, students (cf. the quote above) and parents or through highly formal ones like inspections or centrally set exams. Predictably, such exams then have a backwash effect on teaching. A recent tendency towards standardisation and evaluation of learning in German-speaking countries has reinforced this trend. The kind of feedback that seems to be lacking for teachers is one that is not part of an assessment exercise but one that enables them to observe each other and exchange professional feedback on a peer level.

Uncertainty plays an important role in language teaching. Here the use of the foreign language increases the risk for comprehension difficulties and therefore is a potential threat to the stability of interaction (Breen, 1985). Reducing uncertainty therefore is an important task to be addressed by the language teacher. Reducing uncertainty is an interactive process between teacher and students during which expectations, regularities and patterns are established. Indeed, one of the tools of the trade considered most appropriate for reducing uncertainty is the establishment of and adherence to routines. Also, the use of the L1, in itself a matter of considerable debate within the profession, can be seen as a resource to stabilise interaction.

4.2.4 *Personal relationships and psychosocial climate*

A fourth constraint inherent in the language-teaching situation is the importance of personal relationships and the psychosocial climate in the classroom. The teacher observed explicitly says so in Extract 3. This concern affects the interaction in Extract 1, which is essentially a repair sequence containing negative feedback (Mitchell & Myles, 2004: 178). Seedhouse (2004: 175) has discussed questions of face work in language teaching interaction. He argues that too much mitigation of negative feedback might counteract both concern for the student's face and for the learning process, because making such feedback a taboo creates the impression that student errors do actually have negative connotations. In our case, the teacher quite clearly shows concern for the student's face. This can be observed in the interaction, when the teacher softly encourages John (83) when he tries to prevent the class from laughing (87-88), or when he apologises for having John repeat the sentence yet again in (96). On the other hand, the teacher does not avoid negative feedback. In fact, the feedback he gives is quite explicit, with some measure of mitigation in (83) and (96). Note that in Extract 3, he advocates a balance between a concern for relationship and a concern for learning.

Language-teaching methods have taken different stances towards the personal in language learning. Approaches like audiolingualism and early communicative methodology have tended to avoid personalisation of language and content. Stevick (1976) launched a major critique of language-teaching methodology on the grounds that it ignored whether the contents of what students said made any personal difference to them. Humanistic approaches subsequently provided a lot of suggestions as to how the personal and emotional could be harnessed for language teaching. Some of these suggestions have been criticised for merely utilising personal experience and emotions for language-teaching purposes (Appel, 1995; Legutke & Thomas, 1991).

4.2.5 The necessity to evaluate

Language classes have frequently been characterised as inherently evaluative (Breen, 1985). The interaction documented in Extract 1 took place in the immediate vicinity of a quiz where students were tested on vocabulary they had had to learn. It is inevitable that interaction that focuses on the evaluation of students will linger on as a frame for subsequent interaction. When the teacher co-constructs the sentence together with John in Extract 1, the interaction will, at least to some extent, be seen as an extension of the testing frame established earlier. Although the teacher does not actually examine John, the interaction is likely to be perceived by John as a test of his ability to produce the sentence.

4.2.6 The coursebook

In no other school subject do coursebooks exert a similar influence as in language teaching. The book is in fact often treated as the syllabus.

The teacher interviewed here states several times how much he is constrained by the book. This is visible rather through the language the teacher does *not* use. The book introduces the do-paraphrase relatively late and therefore does not provide the structures necessary for asking the appropriate questions in our exchange. Teacher and class cannot use the question 'When do you have breakfast?', a sentence that does indeed not appear in the data. Earlier on, the teacher says 'tell me when you have'. In a statement on his lesson planning, he said that it was taking him considerable self-discipline to avoid questions using the do-paraphrase. During the interaction recorded for our argument, he avoids such questions by using alternative formulations like 'What about you?'. Whether this actually helps students or whether it deprives them of input they could cope with at least receptively is an open question. Knowledge on how to work with a coursebook would well be worth more attention in teacher education, which has a tendency to focus on demonstration lessons that are designed as if no coursebook existed. Some basic techniques for work with the coursebook have been suggested by Stevick (1986).

5 Conclusion

The argument presented here has tried to contribute to an understanding of language-teaching practice. Using a model suggested by Hutchins (1995), it has looked at three dimensions of practice:

(a) the immediate teaching situation and the verbal interaction taking place there,
(b) the personal and biographical development of teachers' knowledge, values and beliefs,
(c) the structural constraints which shape teachers' work and the culture of the classroom.

What conclusions for the relationship between theory and practice can be drawn from this analysis?

First of all, the analysis has shown how complex practice is. In order to do justice to this complexity, a combination of data and methodologies seems appropriate. The study of verbal interaction in the language classroom and the analysis of teachers' knowledge are two research traditions available for the study of language-teaching practice. Both traditions do not automatically match. Especially the methodology used in conversation analysis, now increasingly applied in studies of verbal interaction in the language classroom, may not easily combine with methods of content analysis used for narrative data in teacher interviews (cf. the discussion in Schwab, 2009: 70-75). Yet it seems necessary to look for correspondences and resonances between findings from different avenues of research if the study of practice is to make any progress. The interpretation of the teaching episode documented above has tried to show some of these correspondences. If, for instance, the grouped character of teaching is a general constraint on teaching cultures, then a detailed analysis of the multiparty interaction in the classroom will contribute both to an understanding of teaching on a micro-level and to an understanding of general characteristics of classroom cultures.

Given its complexities and constraints, practice has to be seen as a domain that is reasonably independent from other domains like academic knowledge on language teaching. Both domains coexist. This should not prevent them from being useful to each other. Practical and experiential knowledge develops as a response to the realities of the teaching situation. Practitioners have little choice but to respond to the conditions they are confronted with. These conditions should be studied carefully. In a survey of research on teachers' cognitions, Borg (2003) has pointed out that much of this research 'has been conducted in language learning settings which are not necessarily, in a global sense, typical (e.g. small classes with adult learners in universities or private institutions)' (Borg, 2003: 94). Knowledge on language teaching will reach practitioners if it addresses the constraints of the teaching situation and if it offers inspirations for responding creatively to these constraints. It should be added that although practical knowledge is developed as a response to such constraints, practitioners have always found their own, often highly original answers to the demands of the teaching situation. One contribution the study of practice can make is discovering such solutions and making them available to a wider audience.

Notes

(1) For further discussion, see also Hüttner and Smit, and Reichl in this volume.
(2) For further discussion, see also Tsui in this volume.
(3) For a more detailed discussion, cf. Appel (2000).
(4) As he stated in a longer narrative interview, cf. Appel (2000: 144).

References

Allwright, D. (1988) *Observation in the Language Classroom*. London and New York: Longman.
Appel, J. (1995) *Diary of a Language Teacher*. Oxford: Heinemann.
Appel, J. (2000) *Erfahrungswissen und Fremdsprachendidaktik*. München: Langenscheidt-Longman.

Appel, J. (2007) Language teaching in performance. *International Journal of Applied Linguistics* 17 (3), 277–293.
Appel, J. (2010) Participation and instructed language learning. In P. Seedhouse, S. Walsh and C. Jenks (eds) *Conceptualising 'Learning' in Applied Linguistics* (pp. 206–224). Basingstoke: Palgrave Macmillan.
Auer, P. (1999) *Sprachliche Interaktion: Eine Einführung anhand von 22 Klassikern*. Tübingen: Niemeyer.
Bailey, K.M. and Nunan, D. (eds) (1996) *Voices from the Language Classroom*. Cambridge: Cambridge University Press.
Berliner, D.C. (1987) Ways of thinking about students and classrooms by more or less experienced teachers. In J. Calderhead (ed.) *Exploring Teachers' Thinking* (pp. 60–83). London: Holt, Rinehart and Winston.
Borg, S. (2003) Teacher cognition in language teaching: A review of research on what language teachers think, know, believe, and do. *Language Teaching* 36, 81–109.
Breen, M. (1985) The social context for language learning – A neglected situation? *Studies in Second Language Acquisition* 7, 135–158.
Bullough, R.V. and Baughman, K. (1993) Continuity and change in teacher development: First year teacher after five years. *Journal of Teacher Education* 44 (2), 86–95.
Calderhead, J. (1984) *Teacher's Classroom Decision Making*. London: Holt, Rinehart and Winston.
Calderhead, J. (ed.) (1987) *Exploring Teachers' Thinking*. London: Cassell.
Clandinin, D.J. (1986) *Classroom Practice*. London: The Falmer Press.
Clark, C.M. and Peterson, P.L.M. (1986) Teachers' thought processes. In M.C Wittrock (ed.) *Handbook of Research on Teaching* (pp. 255–296). New York: Macmillan.
Connell, R. (1985) *Teachers' Work*. Sydney and London: George Allen & Unwin.
Denscombe, M. (1980) The work context of teaching: An analytic framework for the study of teachers in classrooms. *British Journal of Sociology of Education* 1, 279–292.
Denscombe, M. (1985) *Classroom Control: A Sociological Perspective*. London: George Allen & Unwin.
Duranti, A. (1997) *Linguistic Anthropology*. Cambridge: Cambridge University Press.
Feiman-Nemser, S. and Floden, R.E. (1986) The cultures of teaching. In M.C. Wittrock (ed.) *Handbook of Research on Teaching* (pp. 505–526). New York: Macmillan.
Floden, R.E. and Clark, C.M. (1988) Preparing teachers for uncertainty. *Teachers College Record* 89 (4), 504–524.
Freeman, D. (1996) Redefining the relationship between research and what teachers know. In K.M. Bailey and D. Nunan (eds) *Voices from the Language Classroom* (pp. 88–115). Cambridge: Cambridge University Press.
Goffman, E. (1981) *Forms of Talk*. Philadelphia: University of Pennsylvania Press.
Golombek, P.R. (1998) A study of language teachers' personal practical knowledge. *TESOL Quarterly* 32 (3), 447–464.
Graden, E.C. (1996) How language teachers' beliefs about reading are mediated by their beliefs about students. *Foreign Language Annals* 29 (3), 387–395.
Hatch, A. (1999) What preservice teachers can learn from studies of teachers' work. *Teaching and Teacher Education*. 15, 229–242.
Hutchins, E. (1995) *Cognition in the Wild*. Cambridge, MA: MIT Press.
Johnson, K. (1992) Learning to teach: Instructional actions and decisions of preservice ESL teachers. *TESOL Quarterly* 26, 507–534.
Lampert, M. (1985) How do teachers manage to teach? *Harvard Educational Review* 55, 178–194.

Legutke, M. and Thomas, H. (1991) *Process and Experience in the Language Classroom*. London: Longman.
Lortie, D.C. (1975) *School-Teacher*. Chicago: University Press.
Measor, L. (1985) Critical incidents in the classroom: Identities, choices and careers. In S. Ball and Goodson, I. (eds) *Teachers' Lives and Careers* (pp. 61–77). London and Philadelphia: The Falmer Press.
Mitchell, R. and Myles, F. (2004) *Second Language Learning Theories*. London: Hodder Arnold.
Numrich, C. (1996) On becoming a language teacher: Insights from diary studies. *TESOL Quarterly* 30 (1), 131–153.
Pienemann, M. (1998) *Language Processing and Second Language Development: Processability Theory*. Amsterdam: Benjamins.
Richards, J.C. and Rodgers, T.S. (2001) *Approaches and Methods in Language Teaching* (2nd edn). Cambridge: Cambridge University Press.
Roulet, E. (1975) *Linguistic Theory, Linguistic Description and Language Teaching*. London: Longman.
Schwab, G. (2009) *Gesprächsanalyse und Fremdsprachenunterricht*. Landau: Verlag Empirische Pädagogik.
Seedhouse, P. (2004) *The Interactional Architecture of the Language Classroom: A Conversation Analysis Perspective*. Oxford: Blackwell.
Shavelson, R.J. and Stern, P. (1981) Research on teachers' pedagogical thoughts, judgements, decisions, and behavior. *Review of Educational Research* 51, 455–498.
Shulman, L.S. (1987) Knowledge and teaching: Foundations of the new reform. *Harvard Educational Review* 57, 1–21.
Sinclair, J.M. and Coulthard, M. (1975) *Towards an Analysis of Discourse*. Oxford: Oxford University Press.
Stern, H-H. (1983) *Fundamental Concepts of Language Teaching*. Oxford: Oxford University Press.
Stevick, E.S. (1976) *Memory, Meaning and Method*. Rowley, MA: Newbury House.
Stevick, E.S. (1986) *Images and Options in the Language Classroom*. Cambridge: Cambridge University Press.
Tsui, A.B.M. (2003) *Understanding Expertise in Teaching: Case Studies of ESL Teachers*. Cambridge: Cambridge University Press.
Wagner, J. (1983) *Kommunikation und Spracherwerb im Fremdsprachenunterricht*. Tübingen: Narr.
Woods, D. (1996) *Teacher Cognition in Language Teaching*. Cambridge: Cambridge University Press.
Young, R. and Miller, E. (2004) Learning as changing participation: Discourse roles in ESL writing conferences. *The Modern Language Journal* 88 (4), 519–535.

Part 2

Developing Language Teachers' Knowledge Base

4 Creating Language-Assessment Literacy: A Model for Teacher Education

Armin Berger

1 Introduction

Language testing and assessment has begun to feature more and more prominently on educational, social, political and business agendas in recent years. In many countries, politicians and educational boards are preparing the implementation of standardised language tests, educational institutions have noticed glaring discrepancies between what they promote as 'new learning culture' on the one hand and traditional testing and assessment procedures on the other, and businesses make high-stakes decisions for employment purposes based on test results. This growing centrality of language testing and assessment in many fields coincides with a serious lack of professional knowledge and training among those involved, including teachers and teacher educators. Given the importance of language testing and assessment in today's world, it is surprising if not alarming how little is known about it and how insignificant a role language testing and assessment plays in teacher education programmes. Teachers and other stakeholders are left struggling with their own tacit beliefs about assessment procedures that have evolved over time and resemble practices that look like their own experience as students rather than informed decisions based on theory. In short, teachers often lack even basic 'assessment literacy', a term coined by several writers to describe what teachers need to know about testing and assessment (Boyles, 2005; Malone, 2008; Stiggins, 1991; Stoynoff & Chapelle, 2005). One consequence of this gap between current demands of language assessment and the general lack of expertise is a growing need for teacher education programmes to equip teachers adequately for their roles as testers and assessors. Teachers need to be familiar with the theory and practice of language assessment in order to conduct their own assessments effectively, and teaching programmes need to offer systematic education in language assessment.

The fundamental question for teachers and teacher educators then is what assessment literacy entails, i.e. what teachers need to know and be able to do and how this expertise can be acquired. It is the main aim of this chapter with its theoretical rather than empirical, yet practically relevant, perspective to identify some fundamental issues involved in creating a broader assessment knowledge base and to propose a model for teacher education that can be used to operationalise the concept of language-assessment literacy for different (student) teacher populations and different purposes. It will be argued that any assessment-literacy programme can be positioned in a three-dimensional matrix featuring important facets of the WHAT, the WHY and the HOW of assessment literacy. Before describing this model in more detail, the chapter will briefly outline some fundamental issues in the current context of teacher education and compare different conceptualisations of assessment literacy over time. Section 4 will then describe the model, addressing the questions of what language teachers need to know to be 'assessment literate', what kind of provision can be made to equip teachers for their tasks and how assessment literacy can be developed. Section 5 will be illustrative of how existing assessment-literacy courses can be positioned in this model. Finally, some implications for second-language teacher education will be outlined.

Promoting the concept of assessment literacy, the chapter aims to provide language teachers willing to reflect their own practice critically and to acquire the relevant knowledge and skills with a starting point for their endeavour. At the same time, the chapter aims to outline a basic model for teacher educators to draw on when creating professional-development programmes targeted at future as well as experienced language teachers. It is hoped that the ideas and issues set out in this chapter will help to increase general awareness of the complexity of language assessment and the need to adjust current teacher education programmes to satisfy basic educational needs.

2 The Growing Need for Language-Assessment Literacy Programs

With a general movement towards more transparency in educational systems and an increasing demand for international comparability as to language proficiency, instructors and educational institutions are pressured to provide accurate information on students' progress and outcome. As a consequence, a number of countries, such as Austria or Hungary, have reformed or begun to reform their established educational systems to meet internationally accepted standards. In such contexts, new assessment procedures are created to align the local system with recognised standards or to replace traditional components completely. The ideas and resources set out in the Common European Framework of Reference for Languages (CEFR), which claims to be useful for the specification of test content, the definition of assessment criteria and the comparison of tests across different systems (Council of Europe, 2001: 178) have contributed to this kind of standardisation not only in Europe, but beyond.

Another sign of the growing importance of testing and assessment is increasing professionalisation in the field. Professional associations of language testers and language-testing organisations such as the European Association for Language Testing and Assessment (EALTA), the Association of Language Testers in Europe (ALTE), the Japan Language Testing Association (JLTA) and the International Language Testing Association (ILTA) have been established to promote the understanding of the basic theoretical concepts in language assessment and the implementation thereof in practice at a national and international level, for example, through a number of quality standards and guidelines for good practice, including most notably the EALTA Guidelines for Good Practice in Language Testing and Assessment (2006), the ALTE Code of Practice (1994) and the ILTA Code of Ethics (2000). Similarly, university institutions such as the Language Testing Centre (LTC) in Klagenfurt, Austria, aim at professionalising assessment infrastructures and practices on a national and local level. All these measures and initiatives have led to growing awareness of the need to provide adequate education and training in language assessment. At the same time, more and more people are directly involved in selecting and designing assessment instruments and/or using test scores for decision-making purposes. One might say with Spolsky (2008: 297) that 'testing has become big business', not only in a commercial sense.

Although professional organisations have sensitised teachers, language testers, educational authorities and other stakeholders to the problems of traditional assessment procedures and initiated a process of professionalisation, a major concern is that the standards for teacher education have not changed as rapidly as our understanding of language assessment. It seems that institutions offering teacher education have not yet reacted to the current trends and developments in the field of language assessment in a systematic way. In teacher education programmes at Austrian university English departments, for example, the subject matter of language assessment is covered to differing extents, ranging from virtually no coverage at all, to some coverage in more general teaching courses, optional one-semester courses on assessment and multiple compulsory components in the teaching programme. Not only do many institutions of teacher education lack adequate programmes, but there is not even consensus on what sort of knowledge and skills are required for language instructors to develop, select, administer, use and interpret tests. Therefore, the question remains as to what can be done to support teachers when they have to assess their students' language competence. One consequence of this void is a growing need for professional-development programmes in assessment targeted at pre-service and in-service language teachers.

3 The Concept of Assessment Literacy

It cannot be denied that language teachers need a strong knowledge of assessment practices if they want to make sound inferences about their students' language abilities and direct their teaching accordingly. Their efforts to improve teaching and learning based on assessment results will not be productive unless and until they understand the basic principles of classroom assessment. But what is the nature of this knowledge and what does it involve? The term 'assessment literacy' has been coined in recent years to denote what teachers need to know about assessment. Traditionally, it was regarded as the ability to select, design and evaluate tests and assessment procedures, as well as to score and grade them on the basis of theoretical knowledge. More recent approaches embrace a broader understanding of the concept when taking account of the implications of assessment for teaching. Stiggins (1991), for instance, defines assessment literacy as the ability to distinguish between sound and unsound assessment, evaluation and communication practices. Assessment literates ask two key questions: (a) What does an assessment tell students about the achievement outcomes we value? (b) What is likely to be the effect of this assessment on students? (Stiggins, 1991). Knowing and understanding the key principles of sound assessment and translating these into quality information about students' achievements and effective instruction are considered essential. Similarly, Boyles (2005) characterises assessment literacy as the understanding of the principles and practices of testing and assessment. Language teachers 'need the necessary tools for analysing and reflecting upon test data in order to make informed decisions about instructional practice and programme design' (Boyles, 2005: 18). Both extend the notion of assessment literacy to include not only technical knowledge about how to select and create appropriate assessment instruments for specific purposes, but also the ability to analyse empirical data to improve instruction. Thus, being literate in assessment involves a move away from a passive interpretation towards an active application of data that will impact on teaching.

Clearly, the notion of language-assessment literacy has changed over the years. Societal and educational developments in theory, policy and practice have brought about changes in the nature of language assessment and its underlying philosophies, which have, in turn, effected a change in what is considered prerequisite knowledge in the field of language assessment. Several writers have attempted to delineate the conceptual transformations in the past and present of language assessment (Barnwell, 1996; Malone, 2008; Shohamy, 1997). What has not yet been described in detail are the implications of recent trends and developments for the knowledge base of language assessment. Arbitrary as such periodisations may seem, Spolsky's (1978, 1995) renowned division of language testing into three eras – the pre-scientific or traditional, the psychometric-structuralist or modern and the psycholinguistic-sociolinguistic or postmodern – provides a useful point of reference for the description of these changes from a historical perspective. Each period features different definitions of second-language competence and procedures for measuring it; each period has its own values and beliefs regarding the knowledge and skills dominant in the educational assessment traditions of the time. The pre-scientific, traditional era, before the 1960s, was characterised by a strong reliance on the judgments of experts as and when they assessed student performances. The labeling of this period as 'pre-scientific' indicates that 'science' in terms of educational measurement was not yet applied to such assessments. While the lack of scientific enquiry initiated debates touching upon questions of reliability of written and oral exams administered to large groups of students and rated by different instructors, essential properties such as reliability and objectivity were largely underrepresented. As there was little systematic training for instructors on how to develop test questions or guidelines for raters, the required knowledge can be described as intuitive in the sense that the expert status of teachers and linguists was sufficient to legitimise their judgments in the testing or rating process.

The next period, from the 1960s onwards, in contrast, was dominated by the psychometric paradigm that prevailed in much of the measurement scene. The psychometric approach, which is concerned with measurement in psychology and education, is part of the positivistic paradigm and assumes an independently existing reality that can be discovered and measured using objective, scientific methods. In the wake of placing emphasis on scientific approaches, statistics were increasingly applied to language testing to achieve objective and accurate measurement. Concepts such as validity, reliability and attention to item characteristics became fundamental requirements for test instruments. As a consequence, open-ended test questions gave way to discrete-point items testing structural aspects of the language such as vocabulary, grammar, pronunciation and spelling, usually in a decontextualised form on the sentence level. It is in this context that multiple-choice, true/false and short-answer items gained increasing popularity. The pedagogical focus of this measurement paradigm is described as 'assessment *of* learning' (Gipps, 1994), in which learning outcomes are assessed summatively at the end of a learning period, and the set of beliefs underlying it constitute what has been called a 'testing culture', in which formal tests prevailed over other more informal and process-oriented forms of assessment (Wolf *et al.*, 1991). In this 'testing culture', teaching and testing are two distinct sets of activities. Whereas teachers provide instruction to students, testing organizations develop large-scale tests to measure the students' progress (Malone, 2008). The knowledge required to create such test instruments was composed of (statistical) knowledge in educational measurement residing in the realm of testing experts, not teachers. In the classroom context where teachers had to evaluate their students' language, testing was seen as an additional activity, as a mere appendage to teaching.

In the wake of communicative approaches to language teaching, at the end of the 1970s and early 1980s, a new shift occurred towards the sociolinguistic period, in which not so much the knowledge of structural aspects of the language but rather the appropriate use of language specific to the context and audience became the center of attention. It was believed that the complexity of language use necessitates testers to consider the sociolinguistic norms involved in actual communication and incorporate sociolinguistic and sociocultural rules in language tests (Jakobovits, 1970; Jones & Spolsky, 1975). In assessment, this shift manifested itself in the move from a psychometric focus towards communicative language assessment. In the mid-1980s, discrete-point items were replaced by communicative tests designed to measure meaningful communication in life-like situations.

The trend towards communicative forms of assessment is continuing today and new models of assessment are emerging in many countries. The literature seems to reflect a strong focus on situationally and interactionally authentic (Bachman, 1991) performance-based assessment to make inferences about what learners can do with the language in non-test situations. Furthermore, there is an increased emphasis on methods of collecting information from learners, such as portfolios presenting language samples from an extended period of time, student self- and peer-assessment and authentic assessment of real-life tasks. It seems that a broader notion of 'assessment' (as opposed to 'testing') has gained ground in research and practice. As Inbar-Lourie (2008: 385) points out, this development signals 'not merely a semantic change but a profound conceptual one' that goes beyond notions of alternative assessment, perceiving the language evaluation process as a socially constructed activity embedded in the local context with teachers, students and other community members recognized as meaningful assessment partners.

In this new understanding, assessment is perceived as a means to promote learning rather than merely observe and record it, hence 'assessment *for* learning' (Gipps, 1994; Stiggins, 2002). That is, information gained from broader forms of assessment is used in addition to testing, not so much to monitor student outcomes or to certify the end products of learning, but rather to improve instruction and help students learn. Parallel to a 'learning culture' (Shepard, 2000), an 'assessment culture' (Inbar-Lourie, 2008) has emerged, in which assessment *for* learning entails 'the process of seeking and interpreting evidence for use by teachers to decide where the learners are in their learning, where they need to go and how best to get there' (Assessment Reform Group, 2002). Yet another step in this development is 'assessment *as* learning', which directs the focus of attention away from the teacher and towards the learner. It concentrates on the role of the learner as the crucial connector between assessment and learning. Assessment is used as a process of developing and supporting metacognition for students so that they themselves can use information from assessments for new learning. In this understanding of assessment as learning, students are enabled and encouraged to monitor autonomously what they are learning and effectively use feedback from assessment to make adjustments in their learning. In other words, assessment is a vehicle for helping students acquire and practice the ability to reflect and analyze critically their own learning (Earl, 2003). As a result of these developments, the gap between assessment and teaching has narrowed; assessment is seen as an integral part of teaching and learning. These developments offer a new lens through which the nature of assessment literacy can be understood. It is expanded to include competencies needed to conduct assessment in an educational context and to utilise assessment information to promote learning, and thus it is particularly teachers who need expertise in language assessment.

Taylor (2009) addresses yet another aspect of assessment literacy, placing a stronger emphasis on the people involved. Though it is mainly teachers and instructors who need some measure of assessment training,

> the concept of assessment literacy could be expanded to describe the level of knowledge, skills, and understanding of assessment principles

and practice that is increasingly required by other test stakeholder groups. (Taylor, 2009: 24)

As language testing and assessment has grown exponentially over the last decades and with it the general awareness of its social dimension (McNamara & Roever, 2006), there is an urgent need to promote the concept of assessment literacy more broadly to include the wider community, that is, educational advisors or government officials, policy planners and decision makers, the media and the general public.

As can be seen, the notion of assessment literacy is a dynamic one that has been transformed in response to social, political and epistemological changes mirroring the current values, expectations and attitudes in language teaching and assessment. While in the early days, language-assessment literacy was not yet an epistemological category, in the psychometric period, it concurred with expertise in scientific measurement. The most recent understanding of assessment literacy draws a substantial connection between language assessment, learning and teaching. The shift from a 'testing culture' towards an 'assessment culture' is congruent with views that learning and assessment are intertwined. Past developments and current trends, notably the notion of 'assessment *for* and *as* learning', provide the backdrop against which the nature of language-assessment literacy programmes need to be discussed. Three questions guide this discussion: (a) What are essential components of assessment literacy?, (b) What qualifications need to be acquired? and (c) How can the development of assessment literacy be fostered? These questions provide a basic frame for assessment-literacy programmes in teacher education. The following section will elaborate on this and propose a conceptual model for assessment-literacy programmes. Considering the focus of this chapter, the discussion will remain within the confines of the language-teaching perspective.

4 A Conceptual Model for Assessment-Literacy Programmes

As we have seen, institutions of teacher education are increasingly confronted with the need to provide assessment-literacy programmes and explicate their main contents and objectives. The following model is intended to help describe and revise existing and plan new assessment programmes, individual courses or course components aimed at future and practicing teachers in terms of three dimensions: the content of the programme, the purpose and rationale of the provision made to educate teachers and the mode of learning in terms of the degree of collaboration in acquiring assessment literacy. Each dimension is to be understood as a continuum stretching between two endpoints along which any specific assessment-literacy programme can be arranged. Although categorisations of this kind bring about ineluctable simplifications, it is useful to distinguish some basic perspectives from which assessment-literacy programmes can be approached. These perspectives, which are essential but by no means exhaustive, can be placed along the three dimensions mentioned above: The first dimension is concerned with the content level, that is, the 'what' of the programme, which can range from the more specific topic of (large-scale) formal language *testing* to the broader and more general topic of (classroom-based) language *assessment* (cf. Section 4.1). The second dimension concerns the kind of qualifications needed to perform everyday assessment tasks; it stretches between what might be referred to as language-assessment *skills* and *principles* (cf. Section 4.2). Finally, the third dimension pertains to the degree of collaboration, unfolding between *self-directed* and *collaborative*, that is to say, it distinguishes whether the content is processed individually or in a process of collaboration and cooperation (cf. Section 4.3). It is worth mentioning that the endpoints of each dimension are not seen as diametrically opposite poles, but as two related points along the same continuum, which complement rather than mutually exclude each other.

4.1 The Content of Assessment-Literacy Programs: Large-Scale Testing and Classroom-Based Assessment

Teacher educators find themselves confronted with the fundamental question as to what assessment-literacy programmes should focus on. In other words, what do future and practicing teachers need to learn about language assessment to be adequately equipped for their day-to-day work as assessors? While Section 3 of this chapter has outlined the changing views on the content of assessment literacy in the wake of changing educational paradigms, this section will characterise the content base of assessment literacy with regard to its scope and perspective, stretching between language *testing* and language *assessment*.

On the one hand, teacher education courses have focused on technical aspects of language testing. The term 'language testing' is used here in a somewhat restricted way to denote issues surrounding the planning, designing, developing, administering and monitoring of language tests as 'a procedure to elicit certain behavior from which one can make inferences about certain characteristics of an individual' (Carroll, 1968: 46). Much of the content is focused on the construction of test instruments to elicit a specific sample of performance to make inferences about a person's language ability. Many textbooks used in professional-development programmes reflect this focus and indicate that language teachers need to be introduced to a diversity of testing techniques. Topics covered in such books typically include aspects of language testing that are central to large-scale testing, such as an analytic approach to language and its use, that is, the question of what is meant by the ability to use a second language, along with technical issues in language testing such as validity, reliability, practicality, test construction, administration and analysis of test results. This narrow sense of language testing is reflected in a study by Bailey and Brown (1996), in which the characteristics of basic language-testing courses in the context of language teacher education programmes were investigated. The overall purpose of their study was to identify the characteristics of the preparation language teachers received in language-testing courses at the time. The characteristics under investigation were, among other things, the topics covered in class. General topics included norm-referenced testing, criterion-referenced testing, achievement testing, aptitude testing, diagnostic testing, placement testing, proficiency testing, measuring attitudes, measuring the different skills, assessment at different levels and critiquing published tests. Some 10 years later, the study was replicated to find 'the presence of a stable knowledge base that is evolving and expanding, rather than shifting radically' (Bailey & Brown, 2008: 371). Again, test critiquing and test analysis received more extensive coverage in teacher education than other topics, even though new topics such as alternative assessment, washback, testing in relationship to curriculum and classroom-testing practice were introduced.

On the other hand, the shift towards an 'assessment culture' (as opposed to a 'testing culture') outlined in the previous section has led to an expansion of the content base of related courses, in which the subject matter is conceptualised in a broader sense. Thus, testing ceases to be isolated from language teaching. On the contrary, testing is seen as an integral part of a broader assessment approach interacting with knowledge about current language-teaching pedagogy. Black and Wiliam (1998) were among the first to emphasise the central role of formative assessment for improving student achievement. Information obtained from assessment during learning processes should be used to promote learning, which is in contrast to summative assessment at the end of an instructional period. Assessment is integrated into teaching and learning in the sense that the feedback is used to make adjustments and adaptations in instructional processes.

As Fulcher and Davidson (2007) point out, the difference between classroom assessment and large-scale testing is frequently not taken into account, leading to considerable confusion. Given the focus on large-scale testing in teacher education courses and textbooks, it is not surprising that the classroom context has long been considered an irrelevant variable. However, it is this very context that is the major difference between large-scale *testing* and classroom-based *assessment*. The learners are there as learners, and the teachers are there to interact with the learners in the learning process. The classroom is a social environment characterised by learners, teachers, relationships between them and tasks and activities, and learning is based on interaction between these components. One of the major objectives in the classroom, therefore, is to provide opportunities for learning experiences that lead to communication and the acquisition of language. In large-scale testing, however, this social environment is not given. In fact, context is dismissed as one form of construct-irrelevant variance to be minimised. Consequently, much of the theoretical and practical lessons learned from large-scale testing cannot be directly applied to the classroom. Teasdale and Leung (2000), for example, emphasise the inadequacy of applying traditional validity criteria to all classroom-assessment processes. What teachers need to know then is how to utilise the principles from large-scale testing in the classroom, that is, not only knowledge about how to select and develop test instruments effectively but also how to use them appropriately to impact student learning in a positive way. In other words, they need to understand how assessment can drive instruction.

Although language testing focusing on principles of (large-scale) test construction cannot be readily applied in the classroom situation, the former does not stand in direct opposition to the latter. Rather, the two concepts form two points of a continuum. For Stiggins (2002), assessment *for* learning must be balanced with the traditional assessment *of* learning in order to assist the students' learning process. Both of these assessments, those in everyday classroom interactions between teachers and students using an array of (alternative) assessment tools and those set at the end of a learning process, are important. Testing cultures have not been eradicated or rendered insignificant by the new focus on assessment cultures (Inbar-Lourie, 2008). The focus of teacher development programmes on one or the other point of the continuum will very much depend on the professional context and the target audience. Different teachers will require different knowledge depending on the nature and extent of their primary language-assessment activities. The standards for teacher competence in educational assessment of students put forward by the American Federation of Teachers, the National Council on Measurement in Education and the National Education Association (1990), which are intended for use as a guide for teacher educators in designing programmes for teacher preparation and development, reflect a balanced agenda somewhere between testing and assessment:

- Teachers should be skilled in choosing assessment methods appropriate for instructional decisions. [...]
- Teachers should be skilled in developing assessment methods appropriate for instructional decisions. [...]
- Teachers should be skilled in administering, scoring and interpreting the results of both externally produced and teacher-produced assessment methods. [...]
- Teachers should be skilled in using assessment results when making decisions about individual students, planning teaching, developing curriculum and institutional improvement. [...]
- Teachers should be skilled in developing, using and evaluating valid student grading procedures that use student assessments. [...]
- Teachers should be skilled in communicating assessment results to students, educational decision makers and other concerned stakeholders. [...]
- Teachers should be skilled in recognising unethical, illegal, and otherwise inappropriate assessment methods and uses of assessment information. (American Federation of Teachers, 1990)

4.2 Assessment Qualifications: Skills, Knowledge and Principles

The second dimension of the conceptual model proposed here is concerned with the qualifications gained in assessment-literacy programmes and the kind of the provision made to teachers to furnish them with these qualifications. The reference points of this dimension, which, parallel to models of general teacher education, can be referred to as *skills* practiced in teacher training, *knowledge* acquired in teacher education and *principles* established in teacher development, reflect different purposes and approaches to providing teachers with the required qualifications. Although it is conceptually difficult to demarcate clear boundaries between these approaches, it might be useful to highlight some basic differences and subtleties in emphasis in order to characterise more effectively assessment-literacy programmes.

The differences between assessment skills, knowledge and principles are outlined in a study by Davies (2008). In his review of a number of influential textbooks commonly used to teach language testing between 1960 and today, Davies observed a trend towards an expansion of the field's own view of the knowledge base required by its members. While until recently there was a strong focus on the skills and knowledge approach to teaching testing, there is now a move towards an attempt to take account also of principles. Skills concern practical training in essential and appropriate methodology such as item writing, statistics, test analysis and increasingly software programmes for test delivery, analysis and reportage, whereas knowledge provides the pertinent theoretical background in measurement, language description and context setting. Principles, however, refer to issues surrounding the adequate use of language tests, test fairness and washback, including questions of ethics and professionalism, responsibilities of language testers and the impact of their work on all stakeholders. According to Davies (2008), the movement over the last years seems to be from 'skills' to 'skills and knowledge' to 'skills and knowledge and principles'. He argues that skills are essential, but not sustainable without knowledge of the context in which skills operate. Eventually, the profession has internally begun to query its own professional and ethical foundations, which has led to the development of assessment principles and a new approach in which 'the new principles-informed knowledge is operationalised and incorporated into skills' (Davies, 2008: 335). Thus, for example, the technical skill of item writing requires the knowledge and understanding of the context and purpose for which the items are being written as well as the principled ethical and professional justification for their use in live tests. The teachers' ability to reflect, explain, justify and judge becomes important.

The degree of concern for the three aspects proposed by Davies is reflected in the different terms that are used to denote programmes for (student) teachers. The terms 'teacher training' and 'teacher education' can be seen as couched within a transmission paradigm, in which knowledge and skills are passed on to and received by teacher candidates. The function of teacher training is to introduce and practice the skills required in the practice of language teaching and the range of methodological choices at the practitioners' disposal. The role of teacher 'trainers' then is to acquaint (future) teachers with the techniques available, which in language assessment would typically include, for instance, the range of testing techniques and strategies for testing reading, listening, speaking and writing, test construction, item writing and statistical analyses. Similarly, the role of teacher education is to transmit the knowledge underlying the practical skills. Teacher 'educators' then familiarise candidates with the basic terms and concepts that constitute the common ground in language teaching. Although training and education differ in that the former is solution-oriented and implies 'that teachers are to be given specific instruction in practical techniques to cope with predictable events' whereas the latter 'seems to be problem-orientated, and to imply a broader intellectual awareness of theoretical principles underlying particular practices' (Widdowson, 1997: 121), they share the tendency that in both approaches the individual teacher passively acquires commonly accepted, externally imposed and authoritatively prescribed content. Teacher candidates or experienced teachers are regarded as passive recipients of central tenets of contemporary teaching philosophy. Arguably, this kind of knowledge and skills is more 'trainable' than awareness, attitude and critical reflection. What is neglected, however, is the role that individuals play in their own professional development.

By way of contrast, 'teacher development' reflects greater recognition of the belief that teachers themselves play a central role in their professional development. Rather than assimilating transmitted information, teachers are actively involved in a lifelong process of critical reflection and self-generated growth and development. This approach is mirrored in Wallace's (1991) reflective model of language teacher education, in which teachers reflect, evaluate and adjust their own practice, or Freeman's (1996) model of teaching as knowing what to do, in which teachers reflect upon and interpret why they do what they do in different contexts. In assessment, the teacher development orientation would include, for example, a critical reflection of the teachers' immediate assessment context, the integration of previous experience, the flexible adaptation of relevant testing concepts to suit the local needs and the confidence to continue to learn about language-assessment autonomously. A broader focus on teacher development can counterbalance top-down approaches of teacher training/education models outlined above.

4.3 The Degree of Collaboration: Self-Directed and Collaborative Learning

If the first dimension concentrated on the 'what' of assessment literacy (formal, large-scale testing and classroom-based assessment) and the second dimension offered a 'why' (skills training, teacher education and development), the third dimension, finally, refers to an aspect of the 'how' in creating assessment literacy. While one end of the continuum focuses on the individual acting as a *self-directed* agent in the process of constructing assessment literacy, the other end acknowledges more strongly the social context in which language testers operate, providing opportunities for *collaborative* learning.

In practice, language testing and assessment is carried out either individually or by a team. Bachman and Palmer (1996) point out that since low-stakes classroom tests are often developed individually and individual teachers may want to create their assessment procedures alone, there is a place for one-person efforts. In particular, experimental tests are often the product of one person's creative thinking. However, while individual efforts may be appropriate for low-stakes situations, interactive teamwork is required as soon as testing and assessment start to affect a number of people in a profound way. Then, collaboration among all involved becomes essential, as it will tend to produce more satisfactory assessment instruments and eventually lead to greater validity and reliability in the long run. Davidson and Lynch (2002), for example, emphasise the importance of teamwork when developing test specifications. Products of team efforts are usually of higher quality, because of both the range of viewpoints that can be incorporated in the test development or review process and the greater diversity of creative thought that can be utilised when writing the items (Bachman & Palmer, 1996).

Both approaches, individual and interactive, can be incorporated into assessment-literacy programmes. The former is echoed in the concept of self-directed learning, which is based on locally orientated approaches encouraging teachers to critically consider their own contexts and construct their own knowledge and understanding of what is appropriate in their classrooms. Teachers assume individual responsibility for setting aims and standards in terms of self-development and for managing and controlling their own learning. Assessment-literacy programmes at this end of the continuum may predominantly include individual activities such as self-monitoring, journal writing or portfolios. Arguably, an orientation towards this end reflects more realistically real-life environments, in which practical conditions and constraints often force teachers to act individually as sole agents in classroom assessment.

The other end of this dimension embraces teamwork and collaboration with others in a process of mutually supportive learning. As Johnson and Johnson (1999: 40) observe,

> that working together to achieve a common goal produces higher achievement and greater productivity than does working alone is so well confirmed by so much research that it stands as one of the strongest principles of social and organizational psychology.

Collegial forms of learning promote greater interaction between individuals, creating learning environments in which shared understanding can develop and individual meaning can be challenged. It is the negotiation of meaning within social interaction that often leads to learning and allows individuals to restructure their concepts. That is, collaborative forms of learning create a social context in which joint efforts will produce new knowledge and lead to a critique of accepted knowledge. This principle applies to general learning contexts as much as it does to teacher education. In fact, collaborative approaches to learning, in which student teachers are encouraged to study together and see each other as collaborators, have become central to current pedagogies of teacher education (Richards, 2008). Assessment-literacy courses at this end of the continuum will incorporate expressly the notion that language assessment is a concerted effort and heavily depends on people working together in teams. At the same time, these courses acknowledge the fact that special effort often has to be made to develop the ability to work in teams. Thus, opportunities need to be provided for participants to work and learn together through mutual and reciprocal action in one-to-one or group-based activities with shared goals, responsibilities and joint problem solving such as peer observation, peer coaching, critical friendships, team projects or support groups. It is the shared knowledge, experience and thinking of the participants together with the course content and classroom artefacts that provide the resources of learning (Richards, 2008).

5 Relating the Dimensions to Each Other

In order to describe or plan assessment-literacy programmes, it is useful to combine and relate to each other the three dimensions outlined in the previous section as I suggest in Figure 4.1 below.

This axonometric diagram with its horizontal, vertical and diagonal distances representing the constituent dimensions of assessment-literacy programmes helps to conceptualise the model proposed here. The *content* dimension is a key consideration in this model, stretching between what has been described as formal (large-scale) *testing* and classroom-based *assessment*. The focus upon one or the other end of the continuum will govern the balance between six content components, including selection, creation, implementation, interpretation, translation and evaluation. While the *selection* component is concerned with issues involved in critically choosing suitable methods to assess how well learners can communicate in a foreign language, *creation* refers to the issues surrounding the development of appropriate and accurate test and assessment instruments for a given purpose and context. *Implementation* pertains to the process of putting a testing or assessment system into operation, i.e. the appropriate use and administration of instruments and procedures. Another content component deals with the *interpretation* of test scores and assessment results, that is,

Creating Language-Assessment Literacy: A Model for Teacher Education

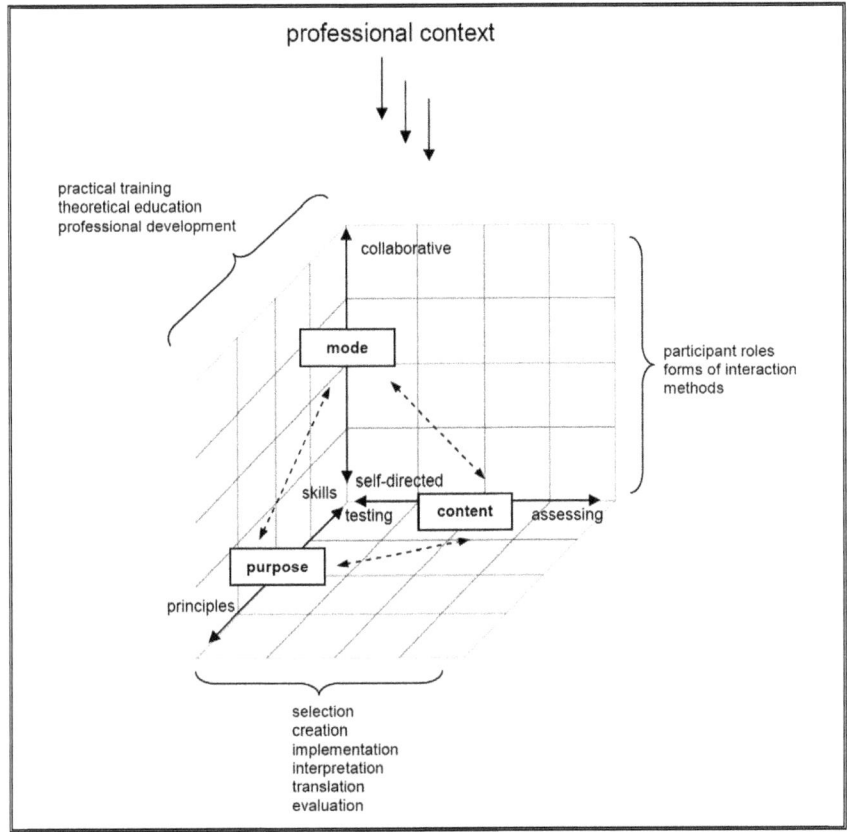

Figure 4.1 Three-dimensional model for assessment-literacy programs

making valid inferences about people's language ability. *Translation* is concerned with the decisions based on these inferences and the measures taken to direct or redirect teaching as a consequence of testing and assessment, that is, translating test and assessment results into pedagogical action. Finally, *evaluation* is the process of providing evidence to support the validity of test scores as well as the decisions and actions based on them. Ultimately, teachers and testers need to be able to ascertain that all the professional standards that govern the field are respected. It goes without saying that teachers need expertise in all these areas. Having said that, courses on testing may predominantly, though not exclusively, address aspects of creation, interpretation and evaluation, while programmes focusing on classroom-based assessment may concentrate more on issues of selection, implementation and translation.

The second dimension of the model, labelled *purpose*, is concerned with the kind of qualifications gained in assessment-literacy programmes. It stretches between practical *skills* required in language testing and assessment, the underlying theoretical *knowledge* and professional *principles*. The qualifications aimed at determine the kind of provision made to equip teachers with these qualifications: *practical training* will focus on skills, *theoretical education* will provide an understanding of the fundamental concepts in language testing and assessment and *professional development* will inform this understanding by professional and ethical principles accepted in the field.

Finally, the third dimension relates to the dominant *mode of learning*, ranging from *self-directed* to *collaborative* forms. The mode of learning will in turn influence the *roles* the participants assume in the programme as well as the *forms of interaction* between them and the *methods* employed to realise the learning objectives. It is the *professional context*, including, for example, professional considerations and needs (individual and social), the participants, the environment and practical constraints (e.g. financial resources, the availability of expertise) that will determine the precise nature of the programmes and their position along the three dimensions as well as the nature and extent of the interplay between these dimensions. If, for example, there is need for practical rating skills training as part of the implementation of a new rating scale, collaborative rating sessions might prove effective. Consolidating the knowledge of statistical concepts to evaluate the reliability of test instruments, however, might require self-directed efforts.

Although there are no watertight boundaries between the categories, existing language-assessment courses can be placed in this diagram. The position will depend on what aspects of content have been selected as focal points, what methods have been chosen to master the content and the purpose of the course. Traditionally, courses have been situated in the back bottom left section of the diagram, that is, they have been oriented towards the more traditional testing paradigm focusing on standardised tests and the practice of statistical procedures related to item analysis, internal consistency and validity of tests (Bailey & Brown, 1996). The major target group has been individuals with a professional interest in language testing.

Regrettably, the precise nature and orientation of most language testing and assessment courses offered in teaching programmes is rarely elaborated on in the literature. In fact, very little research has specifically addressed the content and objectives of such courses. While Bailey and Brown (1996, 2008) investigated a number of courses in terms of the instructors, course characteristics and students, more detailed descriptions of individual courses are rather scarce. One exception is Wharton (1998), who outlines the language-testing component of a pre-service training course at a British university. In terms of language-testing content, the objectives of the course are to become familiar with some of the testing procedures used in well-known public examinations, to think about question writing, options for marking and score reporting and test backwash. Although the latter is important in classroom-assessment contexts, the larger part of the course objectives reflect the skills and knowledge-focused testing paradigm. As the course sought to encourage an exploratory approach to learning in pairs, groups and whole-class discussions as well as individual activities and to develop self-confidence to carry on learning about assessment, the course seems to balance between self-directed and collaborative learning. In other words, the course described by Wharton (1998) will approximate the back center left area of the diagram.

More recently, there has been a change of focus in teacher education courses towards the front top right section of the diagram to embody the more comprehensive concept of principles-focused classroom assessment. O'Loughlin (2006), for example, describes a postgraduate elective in the TESOL and modern languages programmes at the University of Melbourne entitled *Assessment in the Language Classroom*. The course objectives were

> to enable students to develop (a) a sound understanding of key concepts in second language assessment, (b) their ability to critically evaluate existing assessment instruments, and (c) their capacity to design or adapt assessment instruments for their particular teaching contexts. (O'Loughlin, 2006: 73)

Both practical elements and discussion of theoretical concepts were part of the course. The topics covered included: introduction to second-language assessment, theoretical and practical aspects of designing assessment tools, assessing speaking, listening, reading and writing, evaluating assessment tools, self- and peer-assessment, integrating assessment and learning, policy and social issues in language assessment, current trends and future directions. An online forum was offered as an asynchronous adjunct to the face-to-face classroom sessions, in which students were required to contribute regularly. According to O'Loughlin, the forum fulfilled the intended functions of enabling students to reflect on the class sessions actively in an interactive environment, of helping to create and sustain collaborative learning and enabling the lecturer to evaluate student learning as well as the quality of teaching. Although full details of the course content and management are unknown, the course described above can arguably be situated in the top right front section of the conceptual model for assessment-literacy programmes.

Similarly, Kleinsasser (2005) describes a course with a focus on second-language educational assessment. He provides a narrative account of how a language testing and assessment course that had been offered to postgraduate students of applied linguistics and TESOL studies for some time was transformed from 'a content focus to a learner-centered teaching content focus' (Kleinsasser, 2005: 83). Following constructivist notions of active student participation at various levels, the teacher and the students collaboratively changed the course focus from content-focused learning about language testing and assessment to developing language teaching and assessment materials while reading and learning about them in a process of ongoing negotiation. As regards the course contents, a number of topics were covered, including item writing, test development, questions of construct validity, uses of language assessments, critical considerations, social impact and standards in language assessment. The strong emphasis on group discussions, interaction and joint negotiation of meaning even with respect to the final course grade helped create a professional community of collaboration. In conclusion, this course can be said to have a disposition towards classroom-based assessment and assessment principles in terms of content and purpose, respectively. Owing to an unequivocal emphasis on joint negotiation, the course ranges high up on the collaborative dimension.

Clearly, language-assessment literacy courses can come in all shapes and sizes, differing according to their overall purpose, core objectives and target audience. Although little is known about how course designers select and prioritise aspects of the syllabus, this section has attempted to exemplify how the model can help describe language-assessment literacy courses and to illustrate how the dimensions of the model interact. The following section will consider some major implications for teacher education and development.

6 Some Implications for Teacher Education

One central observation facilitated by the model for assessment-literacy courses is that programme designers need to adopt a broader view of language assessment. As the previous sections have shown, the testing paradigm focusing on formal large-scale testing needs to be expanded to include the notion of classroom-based assessment, which recognises the fact that the classroom context has its own rationale. Teachers need to understand how principles from large-scale testing can be adopted for the classroom rather than applied directly. Assessment-literacy programmes need to reflect this broader view of language assessment accordingly. Especially in countries that do not have a long history of professional language-assessment initiatives and that have introduced a process of professionalisation in language assessment only recently, a potentially narrow understanding of the training required by language teachers and other stakeholders might prevail. However, McNamara and Roever (2006, quoted in Taylor, 2009) caution against a limited view of academic training with a focus mainly on technical aspects of language testing. What is needed is a well-rounded teacher education that includes a broader view of language assessment as well as a critical view of assessment and the social consequences. In terms of the model, one could say that a more balanced approach is needed that conceptualises assessment-literacy programmes between the center and right section along the content dimension.

Similarly, it has become apparent that current trends suggest a shift towards the principles-based end along the skills-principles dimension. Taylor (2009: 27) echoes Brindley's (2001) views when she says that the

> current trend in thinking seems to be that training for assessment literacy entails an appropriate balance of technical know-how, practical skills, theoretical knowledge and understanding of principles, but all firmly contextualized within a sound understanding of the role and function of assessment within education and society.

Thirdly, assessment-literacy programmes need to highlight the importance of active collaboration in language assessment between teachers and other stakeholders. There seems to be a general consensus that extensive collaboration between all stakeholders is a key prerequisite for effective language assessment. The EALTA *Guidelines for Good Practice* (2006), for example, consider collaboration a cardinal principle equivalent to validity, reliability, respect for the students/examinees, responsibility and fairness. The fact that collaboration is listed in the same breath as validity and reliability is sufficient indication of its great significance. Collaboration in language assessment is essential not only between colleagues within the shared context of the same school, but also between different stakeholders at all levels, including schools, universities, testing organisations, teacher educators and policy makers. Assessment-literacy courses need to take into account the central role of collaboration at all levels by integrating it into the course objectives and preparing future teachers for the peculiarities of this form of work.

Finally, language-assessment literacy courses need to be modified or tailored according to the needs of the local professional context. As Freeman (2002: 12) points out, the 'notion of context moved from backdrop to interlocutor in the creation and use of teachers' knowledge'. A clear picture of the context in which teachers operate as well as their experience, thinking and beliefs about assessment will, therefore, be essential when creating assessment-literacy programmes. Different teachers will require different levels of qualifications depending on the nature and extent of their engagement in language assessment. While some teachers might need to be able to create and analyze in detail formal tests, others may be concerned with language assessment in their own classroom context only. Some courses will be directed towards future teachers in their pre-service programme, while others may address experienced teachers as part of their in-service development. Courses for future teachers might, for example, address the candidates' desire for 'hard information' (Mann, 2005: 107) and skills training to a greater extent than courses designed for experienced teachers, which can capitalise on the teachers' experiential knowledge. Just as the target audience will differ, so will the course purposes and objectives. As developments in the field of language testing and assessment do not take place synchronously in all parts of the world, the needs in terms of language-assessment literacy programmes will vary locally. In countries in which language-assessment issues have only recently begun to figure more prominently on the agenda of educational authorities, teachers will require different programmes than in countries with a long history in professional language assessment. Therefore, it is

> important that professional development programmes are flexible enough to allow teachers to acquire familiarity with those aspects of assessment that are most relevant to their needs. (Brindley, 2001: 129)

Courses will need to be designed to meet the specific local needs rather than adopt existing syllabi from other contexts.

The central challenge for teachers and teacher educators then is to select and set priorities. The previous sections have evidently shown that developing language-assessment literacy is a multidimensional process of acquiring a range of competencies in different areas. As a consequence, teacher educators as well as teachers are confronted with the difficulty of selecting and prioritising language-assessment issues. While educational authorities have to offer appropriate programmes, course designers have to make a choice as to the foci of their course syllabus; teachers have to select suitable programmes to acquire expertise according to their needs. The model depicted above may help to make these choices and set priorities in a more principled way. While it cannot and does not intend to suggest a normative taxonomy of components of assessment-literacy programmes and while it has not been empirically validated as yet, the model may be used to guide course instructors commissioned to develop new assessment programmes or to evaluate existing ones to make decisions and judgments in a more systematic way. It is a grid reference by means of which course programmes can be analyzed and, if necessary, adjusted to the specific local needs. The three-dimensional model can also provide a rationale for defining course objectives and research agendas. Course participants, on the other hand, might find the model useful to get an overall idea of how professional-development programmes might be organised, and to explore the range of courses in order to select the one most appropriate to their individual needs and interests should they be in a position to choose.

7 Conclusion

The present chapter has raised some issues involved in creating assessment literacy among language teachers. Just as the field of language testing and assessment has matured over the years, so has the notion of language-assessment literacy. While in the early stages of professional language testing, psychometric knowledge for external large-scale testing was the main focus of educational programmes, more recent developments stress the difference in nature between formal large-scale testing and classroom-based assessment, recognising at the same time the wider social, political and institutional dimensions of assessment. Recently, also a general consensus on the need for more extensive assessment-literacy programmes for teachers has begun to emerge. Not only do teachers need to have the basic knowledge and skills in test construction, but they also need to understand the basic principles of proper test use, fairness, washback and impact. Much as learning how to design tests and assessment instruments is part of the parcel of being assessment literate, it is not the only aspect. What seems most relevant for teachers is a critical understanding of the differences between large-scale formal testing and classroom assessment and how the principles of the former can be meaningfully adapted for use in the latter. In essence, language assessment in the classroom should aid learning. Traditional assessment *of* learning will, therefore, have to be balanced with assessment *for* and *as* learning so as to enable students to learn better. The fundamental issues that arose from the discussion concern the questions of what language teachers need to know in terms of assessment and how this knowledge can be developed. Based on available information about assessment-literacy courses, a three-dimensional model was suggested that could help to classify future or existing programmes along three key dimensions: the content, the qualifications and the degree of collaboration. This model might be useful for teachers who want to get a general overview of some possibilities in acquiring language-assessment literacy. For teacher educators who are confronted with the task of providing assessment-literacy programmes, the model might help to expose and specify possible shortcomings in the current system in terms of assessment literacy, make adjustments and define objectives according to the most immediate educational needs. One of the key insights that have emerged from this model is that current trends in the educational sector call for more principles-based collaborative assessment courses. What is needed on a large scale is the provision of teacher education programmes to educate pre- and in-service practitioners to use the principles and tools of language assessment effectively in their classrooms to promote learning. It is the responsibility of educational authorities to provide these programmes. Any proceedings along this line are hoped to prove beneficial for the professional development of both individual teachers as well as educational institutions.

References

ALTE (1994) *The ALTE Code of Practice.* Online at http://www.alte.org/cop/index.php

American Federation of Teachers (1990) Standards for teacher competence in educational assessment of students. Online document: http://www.unl.edu/buros/bimm/html/article3.html

Assessment Reform Group (2002) Assessment for learning: Ten principles. Online document: http://www.assessment-reform-group.org/CIE3.PDF

Bachman, L.F. (1991) What does language testing have to offer? *TESOL Quarterly* 25 (4), 671–704.

Bachman, L.F. and Palmer, A.S. (1996) *Language Testing in Practice.* Oxford: Oxford University Press.

Bailey, K.M. and Brown, J.D. (1996) Language testing courses: What are they? In A. Cumming and R. Berwick (eds) *Validation in Language Testing* (pp. 236–256). Clevedon: Multilingual Matters.

Bailey, K.M. and Brown, J.D. (2008) Language testing courses: What are they in 2007? *Language Testing* 25 (3), 349–383.

Barnwell, D. (1996) *A History of Foreign Language Testing in the United States from its Beginnings to the Present.* Tempe, AZ: Bilingual Press.

Black, P. and Wiliam, D. (1998) Inside the black box: Raising standards through classroom assessment. *Phi Delta Kappan* 80 (2), 139–148.

Boyles, P. (2005) Assessment literacy. In M. Rosenbusch (ed.) *New Visions in Action: National Assessment Summit Papers* (pp. 18–23). Ames: Iowa State University.

Brindley, G. (2001) Language assessment and professional development. In C. Elder, A. Brown and E. Grove (eds) *Experimenting with Uncertainty: Essays in Honour of Alan Davies* (pp. 126–136). Cambridge: Cambridge University Press.

Carroll, J.B. (1968) The psychology of language testing. In A. Davies (ed.) *Language Testing Symposium: A Psycholinguistic Perspective* (pp. 46–69). London: Oxford University Press.

Council of Europe (2001) The Common European framework of reference for languages. Online document: http://www.coe.int/T/DG4/Linguistic/Source/Framework_EN.pdf

Davidson, F. and Lynch, B.K. (2002) *Testcraft: A Teacher's Guide to Writing and Using Language Test Specifications*. London: Yale University Press.

Davies, A. (2008) Textbook trends in teaching language testing. *Language Testing* 25 (3), 327–347.

EALTA (2006) EALTA guidelines for good practice in language testing and assessment. Online document: http://www.ealta.eu.org/guidelines.htm

Earl, L. (2003) *Assessment as Learning: Using Classroom Assessment to Maximize Student Learning*. Thousand Oaks, CA: Corwin Press.

Freeman, D. (1996) Renaming experience/re-constructing practice: Developing new understandings of teaching. In D. Freeman and J.C. Richards (eds) *Teacher Learning in Language Teaching* (pp. 22–32). Cambridge: Cambridge University Press.

Freeman, D. (2002) The hidden side of the work: Teacher knowledge and learning to teach. A perspective from North American educational research on teacher education in English language teaching. *Language Teaching* 25, 1–13.

Fulcher, G. and Davidson, F. (2007) *Language Testing and Assessment: An Advanced Resource Book*. London: Routledge.

Gipps, C. (1994) *Beyond Testing: Towards a Theory of Educational Assessment*. London: Falmer Press.

ILTA (2000) ILTA code of ethics. Online document: http://www.iltaonline.com/index.php?option=com_content&view=article&id=57&Itemid=47

Inbar-Lourie, O. (2008) Constructing a language assessment knowledge base: A focus on language assessment courses. *Language Testing* 25 (3), 385–402.

Jakobovits, L.A. (1970) *Foreign Language Learning*. Rowley: Newbury House.

Johnson, D.W. and Johnson, R.T. (1999) *Learning Together and Alone: Cooperative, Competitive, and Individualistic Learning*. Boston: Allyn and Bacon.

Jones, R.L. and Spolsky, B. (eds) (1975) *Testing Language Proficiency*. Arlington: Center for Applied Linguistics.

Kleinsasser, R.C. (2005) Transforming a postgraduate level assessment course: A second language teacher educator's narrative. *Prospect* 20 (3), 77–102.

Malone, M. (2008) Training in language assessment. In E. Shohamy and N. Hornberger (eds) *Encyclopedia of Language and Education*, Vol. VII, (pp. 225–239). New York: Springer.

Mann, S. (2005) The language teacher's development. *Language Teaching* 38, 103–118.

McNamara, T. and Roever, C. (2006) *Language Testing: The Social Dimension*. Oxford: Blackwell.

O'Loughlin, K. (2006) Learning about second language assessment: Insights from a postgraduate student on-line subject forum. *University of Sydney Papers in TESOL* 1, 71–85.

Richards, J.C. (2008) Second language teacher education today. *RELC Journal* 39, 158–177.

Shepard, L.A. (2000) The role of assessment in a learning culture. *Educational Researcher* 29 (7), 4–14.

Shohamy, E. (1997) Language Assessment. In R. Tucker and D. Corson (eds) *Encyclopedia of Language and Education*, Vol. IV (pp. 141–152). London: Kluwer Academic Publishers.

Spolsky, B. (1978) Introduction: Linguists and language testers. In B. Spolsky (ed.) *Approaches to Language Testing: Advances in Language Testing Series: 2* (pp. V–X). Arlington, VA: Center for Applied Linguistics.

Spolsky, B. (1995) *Measured Words: The Development of Objective Language Testing*. Oxford: Oxford University Press.

Spolsky, B. (2008) Introduction – Language testing at 25: Maturity and responsibility? *Language Testing* 25 (3), 297–305.

Stiggins, R.J. (1991) Assessment literacy. *Phi Delta Kappan* 72, 534–539.

Stiggins, R.J. (2002) Assessment crisis: The absence of assessment for learning. *Phi Delta Kappan* 83 (10), 758–765.

Stoynoff, S. and Chapelle, C. (2005) *ESOL Tests and Testing: A Resource for Teachers and Program Administrators*. Alexandria, VA: TESOL Publications.

Taylor, L. (2009) Developing assessment literacy. *Annual Review of Applied Linguistics* 29, 21–36.

Teasdale, A. and Leung, C. (2000) Teacher assessment and psychometric theory: A case of paradigm crossing? *Language Testing* 17 (2), 163–184.

Wallace, M.J. (1991) *Training Foreign Language Teachers: A Reflective Approach*. Cambridge: Cambridge University Press.

Wharton, S. (1998) Teaching language testing on a pre-service TEFL course. *ELT Journal* 52 (2), 127–132.

Widdowson, H.G. (1997) Approaches to second language teacher education. In R.G. Tucker and D. Corson (eds) *Encyclopedia of Language and Education*, Vol. 4 (pp. 121–129). London: Kluwer Academic Publishers.

Wolf, D., Bixby, J., Glenn, J. and Gardner, H. (1991) To use their minds well: Investigating new forms of student assessment. *Review of Research in Education* 17, 31–125.

5 Grammar Teaching: Theory, Practice and English Teacher Education

Penny Ur

1 Introduction

The teaching of grammar has always occupied a central place in foreign-language teaching in general and in English teaching in particular. This is partly for historical reasons: the teaching of modern (spoken) languages was at first based on the teaching of dead languages such as Latin and Ancient Greek, which placed a strong emphasis on the learning of grammatical rules and the construing (translation) of texts. Hence arose the grammar-translation method of teaching modern languages.

But the historical background cannot fully account for the continuing focus on grammar in English teaching today. It does not explain why, even after the advent of the communicative approach, with its message of priority of meaning over (accurate) form, the explicit teaching of grammar continues to play a central role in most classrooms. Even if, as claimed by some writers, the fault is in the unthinking conservatism of the teaching profession (e.g. Skehan, 1997: 94), this cannot be true of all teachers; and many experienced and successful practitioners continue to teach grammar and believe in its worth. Nor does it explain why grammar teaching continues to be prominent on the research agenda (see the reference list of this chapter for a selection of recent research-based publications).

The above arguments would provide a strong a priori case for the inclusion of grammar teaching in principle in formal courses of study of English as an additional language. This chapter will therefore take as a basic premise that grammar instruction should take place in such contexts; it will not discuss any further *whether* grammar should be taught, but rather *how*. Selected research on this topic will be discussed, and some practical conclusions suggested. The main focus of such conclusions will be teacher education, and recommendations will relate to components of teacher preparation programmes: in particular, the need for a rethinking of a communicative-based methodology, for a critical approach to research and for substantial input in the area of practical grammar-teaching procedures.

2 What Is 'Acceptable' Grammar?

Grammar can be defined as the way a language manipulates and combines words (or bits of words) so as to convey meanings effectively and acceptably. The question arises, however, as to what is 'acceptable', and whether 'effectiveness' should not be the major, or even sole, criterion. Some scholars would suggest, based on data from the VOICE corpus (2009), that since many fluent and effective speakers of English as a lingua franca express themselves perfectly effectively using variant forms such as *she go* or *the people which*, such forms should be considered an acceptable part of the language variety used by such speakers (Jenkins, 2006a). The implication for teachers and test designers would be that such forms should not necessarily be 'corrected' if they occur in learner speech, or penalised in tests (Jenkins, 2006b).

However, others express more cautious conclusions. There is no evidence that the majority of fully competent speakers of English as a lingua franca (this term would include a substantial minority of native speakers of one of the varieties of English) in fact use such forms; nor is there evidence that it is true of the written language. A more moderate view would be that grammatical errors that *do* produce problems of communication (for example, the use of a present instead of a past tense) should be taught and corrected more carefully than 'unproblematical' variants like the examples above.

In practice, then, my opinion (and not only mine, see for example Maley, 2009) is that the conventional correct forms of standard grammar will, and should, continue to be related to and taught as acceptable, with some priority given to the forms that are crucial for effective communication.

3 Implicit or Explicit Teaching and Learning

Most (school) teachers whom I have observed, or with whom I have spoken, teach grammar *explicitly*, through a traditional 'presentation-practice-production' (PPP) model: they present a rule and then practise it through conventional exercises based on strategies such as gapfills or matching. As a result of these exercises, learners are expected to be able to produce the grammatical structures correctly in their own production.

The problem is, of course, that they often do not succeed in doing so. Even after extensive practice based on such exercises, many learners continue to produce unacceptable forms in their own spontaneous writing and speech.

As a result of this well-attested phenomenon, some writers have argued as follows: if we assume that the ultimate goal is for learners to be able to spontaneously produce acceptable grammatical forms – in other words, to have an *implicit* knowledge of the grammar – then would it not be more effective to teach them from the beginning through implicit strategies? Such arguments are indirectly supported by the *teachability hypothesis* (Pienemann, 1984), according to which learners absorb morphosyntactical features in a set order, impermeable to instruction (R. Ellis, 1989). In other words, it is no good trying to teach a grammatical feature for which the learner is not ready in terms of features he/she has previously mastered. This argument has led many to the conclusion that it is useless to teach explicitly at all, and it is better to allow learners to absorb new features gradually, as they are developmentally ready for them, through incidental encounter during communicative procedures.

Krashen (1999) therefore claims that the best way to learn language in general, and acceptable grammar in particular, is through naturalistic acquisition, made available through massive provision of *comprehensible input*. This would mean exposing learners extensively to acceptable forms within meaningful discourse, without explanations or practice, in the expectation that they will absorb the grammar intuitively and unconsciously.

But research indicates that this does not bring about any better mastery of grammar than the apparently discredited 'PPP' model does. In Canadian immersion programmes, anglophone students are exposed for several years of schooling to large amounts of comprehensible input in French from francophone teachers in school lessons. They emerge at the end of 12th grade with a fluent and confident, but far from accurate, command of French: they continue to produce basic errors in gender, for example, that would not appear in the speech of native speakers (Turnbull *et al.*, 1995). Swain (2000) drew the conclusion that learners should be 'pushed' to produce output, and that the provision of some explicit formal instruction is likely to lead to better results.

A later model of implicit teaching was *task-based instruction*. As originally proposed (Long & Crookes, 1992; Skehan, 1996), such a model implies the use of communication-based tasks only as a basis for language learning: learners tell each other about their families, fill in missing information on maps in information-gap activities, discuss the solution to a series of dilemmas, write letters to each other and so on. But studies of task-based classroom interaction in practice (e.g. Seedhouse, 1999) have cast doubt on the effectiveness of tasks as a vehicle for the learning of acceptable grammar, and task-based instruction in its 'strong' form has been criticised on these and other grounds by writers such as Richards (2002) and Swan (2005a).

Yet another, totally different, kind of implicit learning and teaching of grammar is that based on the repeated encounter with, or learning by heart of, short or long unanalyzed passages of text. There is a connection here with the mid-20th-century method of *audiolingualism* that had learners hearing, mimicking and memorising, drilling and reciting, while being discouraged from any conscious discussion of rules. Audiolingualism was largely abandoned by the 1970s, and learning by heart was rejected by many as 'unthinking' and 'mechanical'. However, the value of hearing, reading and repeating 'chunks' of language as a basis for acquiring grammatical knowledge through analogy has recently been recognised by various writers: N. Ellis (2002) talks about frequency of encounter with what he calls 'constructions' as a basis for learning grammar; Cook (2000) recommends the use of language play, including learning by heart; and Graham's popular jazz chants (e.g. Graham, 1993) are based on the same rationale. The literature on the teaching of formulaic language ('chunks') includes some discussion of its relevance to grammar learning (Wray, 2000). There has also been some interesting research on the learning by heart of extensive texts by Chinese learners and its positive results in both fluency and accuracy (Ding, 2007).

Growing criticism of purely implicit language-teaching models was reinforced by Schmidt's work on the concept of *noticing* in language learning (Schmidt, 2001). He found that in his own learning of Portuguese in Brazil he learned and was able to produce only those features that he had consciously noticed in the input of interlocutors, as attested in his learning journal. Combining these personal insights with an examination of the research evidence of 'subliminal' or unconscious perception in learning situations, he reached the conclusion that learners cannot acquire second-language features without some degree of conscious noticing. Or, as he puts it: 'noticing is the necessary and sufficient condition for converting **input** to **intake**' (Schmidt, 1990: 129). This hypothesis has been accepted by most modern writers on the subject of grammar teaching, resulting in a general trend towards the inclusion of conscious language-focused work in English-teaching methodologies.

This trend has been further supported by studies showing that explicit grammar instruction has value for effective learning. A much-cited meta-analysis by Norris and Ortega (2001), for example, examined a number of research studies on types of language instruction and came to the conclusion that the addition of some explicit instruction produces better results than implicit instruction on its own. Similar conclusions have been reached by other researchers and analysts (Dekeyser, 2003; R. Ellis, 2002).

A general move towards the acceptance of a role for explicit grammar teaching has led to a dilemma for syllabus- and materials-designers: how can we include such instruction within the generally accepted communicative approach, whose implementation in practice should surely entail meaning- not form-focused classroom activities? Solutions have been suggested in the shape of various proposals as to how to integrate a temporary focus on grammatical form within a methodology based on communicative tasks. I shall relate here to two of these: *focus on form* and *consciousness-raising*.

4 Focus on Form and Consciousness-Raising

The term *focus on form* means paying temporary attention to a grammatical feature in the course of work on a communicative task (Long, 1991; Long & Robinson, 1998). It is, rather confusingly, contrasted with *focus on forms*, the traditional systematic teaching of grammatical structures according to a predetermined grammatical syllabus. In practice, focus on form may involve 'time out' to talk about a particular grammatical form in the course of an otherwise communicative procedure, or involve paying attention, while focusing on the meaning of a text, to some feature that is salient in its grammar. In any case, it is in principle brief and unobtrusive, and the attention of the learner is to be primarily and consistently on communicative meaning.

Originally, such procedures were intended to include only spontaneous reactions to perceived problems of form. Later writers have, however, interpreted the concept more flexibly. R. Ellis (2001a), for example, draws a distinction between *planned* and *incidental* focus on form. Planned focus on form means that it has been predetermined which feature is to be attended to, usually through text or task design, so a text may contain a large number of exemplars of past progressive forms, or a task may be designed to be based on interrogatives. Incidental focus on form, in contrast, is unplanned and takes place mainly during oral interaction: spontaneous error correction, for example. In practice, what often happens is that the intervention is based on 'planned spontaneity': the text or task may or may not in itself focus on a particular feature, but there is a prior intention, on the part of the teacher or textbook, to exploit some aspect of it for the explicit teaching or review of a grammatical feature at the point where it is encountered in the course of the lesson.

Focus on form has been extensively discussed in the literature, and its interpretation in practice has been very flexible. In Shak and Gardner (2008), for example, grammar activities are suggested under the heading 'focus on form' that involves completing sentences with a correct grammatical form or matching active or passive sentences to a picture. These involve more than a 'brief and unobtrusive' focus on form and are functionally indistinguishable from meaningful grammar practice exercises used within a focus on forms model.

Another model, compatible both with focus on form and task-based learning, but rejecting practice as a useful contributor to learning, is *consciousness-raising* (R. Ellis, 2001b). Consciousness-raising is the deliberate teaching and learning of a grammatical feature, often (though not always) involving the articulation of a rule. It is based on the assumption that the integration of a grammatical feature within the learner's implicit language knowledge system will take place only when the learner is developmentally ready to acquire it and notices it in communicative input. Such noticing may be substantially facilitated by previous conscious knowledge of the feature.

But in general, as shown for example in the Shak and Gardner (2008) article mentioned above, there has been a perceptible recent trend towards a legitimisation of *practice* as a useful component of grammar teaching.

5 Skill-based Learning

The concept of *practice* belongs in principle to skill theory and relies on the assumption that language learning is essentially the learning of a skill, similar to learning to fly an aircraft or play a musical instrument (Johnson, 1996). It involves three stages. First, there is declarative knowledge, where the teacher explains the target behaviour in words, and the learner understands at the level of theoretical or verbalised representation. Second, this knowledge is *proceduralised* through the provision of practice: the learner implements the behaviour that has been explained to him/her and rehearses it through exercises in order to become more skilled. Finally, the learner reaches the point at which the procedural knowledge is *automatised*: he or she can carry out the behaviour rapidly and accurately without thinking about it or referring back to the original explanation. With regard to grammar teaching, then, the first stage implies some explanation of the grammar rule; the second would entail a number of grammar practice exercises; and the third is the stage at which the student becomes able to use the grammar automatically and correctly in his or her own speech and writing.

Essentially, therefore, skill-based language teaching is very similar to 'PPP': 'presentation' resembles the declarative stage; 'practice' relates to proceduralization and 'production' assumes the achievement of automatization.

However, the original objection to 'PPP' – the fact that grammar learned and produced correctly within grammar exercises very often did not transfer to students own speech and writing – remains. This has led to a rethinking of the theory and practice of the concept *practice* by modern proponents of skill-based language teaching (Dekeyser, 2007).

Traditional grammar practice within 'PPP' was limited largely to discrete-point mechanical gapfill, multiple-choice, sentence completion and matching tasks, exercises that could in fact often be done without understanding the meaning of the items (for an example, see Appendix, Exercise 1). The result was that while doing such exercises, the learners' attention was thoroughly focused on getting the grammar right. Given the fact that they had previously been taught the rule, there was no problem completing the exercise: all they had to do was consciously 'proceduralise' the 'declarative' knowledge they already possessed. However, implementing the same rule within a communicative task is a totally different story: in such situations, the learner's attention is not on the declarative knowledge, but on conveying meaning. It is no wonder, then, that if learners' previous experience of using the grammar correctly has been only under optimal conditions – with time and attention to give to the application of declarative knowledge – they fail to do so when such conditions are not present.

The phenomenon of lack of transfer that led Krashen and others to reject practice completely has led others to retain it but with some radical reconceptualisation, leading to a changed implementation in practice (Dekeyser, 2007). What learners need to do, within skill theory, is to become used to using the grammar correctly *when their attention is no longer devoted to it*; hence, practice is a process of progressive de-focus on form (the grammatical rule) (Johnson, 1996). Exercises should therefore not be mechanical, but meaningful, and designed to be progressively more demanding of attention to the conveying of ideas and with correspondingly less and less attention available for focus on form (for examples, see Appendix, Exercises 2, 3 and 4). Learners thus get used to using the grammar for the purpose of communication instead of just to form correct sentences.

The objection remains that any presentation and practice of a particular grammatical feature will be useless to those members of a class who, according to the teachability hypothesis, are not yet ready to absorb it. However, there is some evidence that teaching grammar that is ahead of the learners' developmental level does help them move ahead, even if they still go through the inevitable intermediate stages (Spada & Lightbown, 1999), and that practice can actually accelerate acquisition processes even within the developmental order. True, even with optimally designed practice procedures, there will still be some learners who, because of lack of readiness, will not acquire the target features. This does not, however, negate the validity of practice activities in principle. Its effectiveness has been shown in a number of studies (e.g. Morgan-Short & Bowden, 2006; Salaberry, 1997).

Another difference between the modern skill-theory-based conceptualisation of language teaching and the traditional 'PPP' has to do with the grammatical syllabus and its implementation. The grammatical syllabus has been rejected by many writers (see, for example, Long & Robinson, 1998) as being too rigid and denying a place for the natural development of individual learners in the acquisition of grammatical features. It has been supported, however, by Ellis as part of his 'consciousness-raising' model (R. Ellis, 1993); and it is obviously necessary for a skill-theory based model. In neither case, however, is there any justification for implementing such a syllabus in linear fashion; teaching the items one by one, 'finishing' one before progressing to the next, and not returning to one that has already been taught. On the contrary, although it is accepted by many that there is a place for a syllabus of grammatical points to be taught, it is assumed that this will be used flexibly, and that there will be frequent review and recycling of such points as the need arises.

6 Error Correction

The adoption of implicit models of grammar teaching entailed also the abandonment of error correction: Krashen, for example, claims that error correction only helps learners monitor their own production when they have time and attention available to use explicit knowledge; it does not feed into true 'acquisition', and therefore is of limited usefulness. Truscott (1996, 1999) puts a strong case for abandoning correction of grammatical errors in both speech and writing; he brings some research evidence to show that not only does error correction fail to result in improvement of performance, it may also distress and embarrass students and lead to various negative repercussions. He has been answered by several researchers (notably Lyster *et al.*, 1999) who quote a number of studies where error correction apparently contributed to improvement in the accuracy of learners' oral and written production.

The proponents of a 'focus on form' model use error correction as one of the most useful triggers for occasional discussion of grammar (Long & Robinson, 1998). Altogether, the swing towards an inclusion of explicit procedures within an optimal grammar-teaching model makes the inclusion of error correction inevitable. A discussion of which error-correction strategies are more or less effective is, however, beyond the scope of this chapter.

7 Pedagogical Considerations and Research-based Theory

One of the problems with all the literature on grammar teaching described up to now is that it is based almost exclusively on second-language acquisition research. Such research looks at the mechanisms by which people learn additional languages – in particular, in this case, their grammar – and how teaching can activate these mechanisms most effectively. But it very rarely aims to take into account, let alone examine in detail, pedagogical considerations that come into play in any particular context. Pedagogical factors are those that affect any teaching-learning situation, regardless of the particular subject being taught. These include: students' sociocultural background; the size of a class; student-teacher and student-student relationships; student motivation; student expectations, learning styles and preferences; the influence of stakeholders such as parents, ministries of education, school principals; principles of lesson design and planning; available teaching materials; time available for preparation and assignment-checking; classroom management and discipline; and upcoming exams.

Such factors may, and often do, affect teaching decisions more than insights on grammar acquisition gained through the research or than plausible models of grammar teaching. A teacher may be thoroughly convinced of the effectiveness of a task-based communicative methodology, but decide to use fairly traditional methods because of the preferences of students (or of their parents, by whom he or she is paid). Another may believe in the importance of error correction, but finds that he or she simply does not have time as he or she would wish to correct the written work of a large class. Yet another wishes to emphasise communicative ability and the use of grammar in context, but an upcoming exam includes explicit grammar tests, forcing him or her to spend much of her time rehearsing for the test.

The obvious conclusion from this argument is that anyone attempting to recommend how best to teach grammar has to take into account the wide variety of situations and pedagogical considerations that may affect teaching decisions. No one particular model of those described earlier in this chapter can, therefore, possibly be appropriate for all situations. There is no one 'right' way to teach grammar.

It would be equally misguided, however, to discard all research-based knowledge and teach only according to local constraints and conventions. Insights from research and the thoughtful and informed reasoning that goes into the construction of new models of grammar teaching are of immense potential value for practical classroom teaching. To reject these wholesale as 'impractical theory' is as silly as to adopt any one of them as a monolithic correct model. The thoughtful practitioner needs to use the research literature to inform his or her practice while drawing on personal professional experience and wisdom to select and adapt it to his or her particular teaching context.

8 A Practical Proposal

A practical proposal for a model of grammar teaching, must, therefore, take the shape of a number of options that can be 'mixed and matched' to fit any particular teaching situation. In this section I will attempt to draw together the various theoretical suggestions discussed earlier, express them as practical teaching units and suggest how they may be used in different contexts.

Unit 1: Skill-based methodology

The teaching unit begins with a frank presentation of a grammatical feature, which may be explained by the teacher or textbook and illustrated by examples or elicited from students by inductive reasoning based on exemplars. The presentation is followed by a series of practice exercises, spread over a number of lessons, which progress from those that focus very clearly on accurate forms to those that focus more on the production or reception of meanings (see Appendix).

Unit 2: Focus on form

The teaching unit begins with a communicative task, which may involve the study of a text (usually written). During the course of the task or later, specific grammatical points growing out of either task or text are focused on and discussed. The materials may provide ready-made awareness-raising tasks or exercises that help students to understand and master the target forms and meanings. After a limited time spent on such focused study, learners' attention is drawn back to the content and communicative purpose of the original task.

Unit 3: Communicative task

The teaching unit consists entirely of a communicative task: a discussion, a writing assignment, a listening comprehension or a reading activity. In all of these, the focus is consistently on meanings and purposeful communication, and grammar is not explicitly taught. If or when the students make errors in speech or writing, the teacher may correct them, but will not spend time on discussing the reasons for the error or the underlying grammatical rules.

Unit 4: Consciousness-raising

The unit consists of the clarification of a grammar point. This may be elicited from students by induction from a series of sample sentences, or presented directly by the teacher or textbook. The aim is merely to achieve understanding of the grammatical rule or items; there is extensive discussion, which may be in L1, accompanied by plentiful illustration, and students may also try their hand at some exercises. The aim of such exercises, however, is not to achieve automatisation, but to clarify how the grammar 'works' in context and ensure understanding.

Unit 5: Learning through exemplars

In this unit, students are expected to familiarise themselves, and sometimes learn by heart, texts that contextualise useful grammatical forms. These texts may take the form of dialogues learned by heart, sketches, plays, chants or songs. They may also be passages that the students read, hear and recite repeatedly so that they become very familiar with the text without actually learning it all by heart; for example, they may study a poem and then perform dramatised readings of it.

A programme of language study, one of whose aims is for learners to express themselves using acceptable grammatical forms, will include most if not all of these components, but the weighting and timing will vary according to context.

Let us take, for example, the teaching of English in the first year or two of secondary school in countries where English is not spoken as a mother tongue or official language. Learners are still mastering basic English grammar and will find it helpful to have most of their grammar taught through a traditional skill-based methodology based on a systematic grammatical syllabus. This will be backed up by occasional lessons where the focus is clearly on communication, with the provision of plenty of exposure to written and spoken English, since for many students, this will be the only place where they can get such exposure. Some learning through exemplars will also help, particularly for the younger classes. As they move up the school, there will be more and more lessons organised rather around the focus on form, where texts and tasks provide opportunities for review and use of the previously learned grammatical forms in context.

Another example: a class in academic English for a group of students studying English as a second language in an English-speaking country. Many of these students need to improve their grammatical accuracy, but which particular points they still have problems with cannot be predicted in advance. The main teaching process used here would then be focus on form: the provision of advanced texts and tasks, in the course of which the teacher may take time out to explain or practice specific grammatical features as the need arises. Students learning in this situation do not need very much exposure to informal spoken or written language, as they get this from the out-of-school environment. They are likely, however, to benefit from occcasional 'consciousness-raising' lessons, appropriate for students learning at a high academic level with the capability of understanding grammatical metalanguage, analyzing and abstracting.

9 Implications for Teacher Education

If the theoretical analysis provided in the earlier sections of this chapter, and the practical implementation in a set of methodological options as described above are accepted, then there are clear implications for language teacher education.

9.1 A Moderate Communicative Approach

In many places today, the trend in language teacher education is to promote a strong version of the communicative approach: to discourage explicit teaching of pronunciation, vocabulary or grammar, and to encourage the exclusive use of communicative tasks in the classroom. This is particularly noticeable in teacher-training summer courses run in the UK and attended by teachers from many other countries, but is also seen in national teacher preparation programmes.

The reason often given for this by people planning such programmes is that many teachers are so used to very rigid, traditional 'PPP' presentation of rules and following drills (as they were taught themselves) that it is a good idea for teacher-training methodology courses to stress – perhaps overstress – the importance of using communicative task-based activities. The aim is to convince the teachers of the value of the communicative approach so that, hopefully, they will adopt a methodology that will integrate at least some communicative procedures and lessen the reliance on grammar explanation and mechanical drills.

This may happen. But often the result is counterproductive: teachers realise the total inappropriateness of a strong form of the communicative approach for their home context and reject it completely; or, in some cases, they try to implement it in full on their return, with often negative results. There has been some research on such problems in recent years (Carless, 2003, 2007; Hu, 2002).

A more productive approach is, in my opinion, to encourage teachers to adopt an approach to language teaching that validates both explicit grammar teaching and communicative procedures and helps them to understand how these may be integrated in a balanced programme. In other words, I am advocating here the education of language teachers towards a more moderate communicative approach: the goal is still to teach language for communication, but the means selected to achieve it should take into account what we know about the effectiveness of some non-communicative procedures, including those relating to explicit grammar teaching. A similar approach has been urged with regard to vocabulary teaching (Laufer, 2005).

9.2 Awareness of and a Critical Approach to the Research and its Implications

Another component of English teacher education that may promote effective grammar teaching is courses that update the teachers on research on grammar teaching. It is not enough, however, simply to acquaint the teachers with the content of the latest research articles and books; such theoretical knowledge very often remains 'inert' and does not transfer to practice.

It is necessary, of course, for teachers to understand how research results might be applied in practice, but it is also essential to develop a critical approach. There is, as we have seen above, frequent disagreement on what the 'best way' is to teach grammar, and the best person to resolve this agreement is the practitioner him- or herself.

Courses, therefore, should present the research, but making very clear the controversies and conflicting opinions that exist and encouraging teachers to face the contrasts and make principled decisions about their own approach, based on professional experience and judgment and rational argument, taking into account pedagogical factors such as those referred to earlier in this chapter. Seidlhofer (2003) has suggested that there is a place for courses based on controversies in applied linguistics: it seems to me that teachers would benefit from similar courses relating specifically to grammar teaching.

9.3 Practical Techniques

The third component of language teacher education that needs to be promoted in the context of the promotion of good grammar-teaching is the learning of techniques of explanation, practice, error correction and so on that have been shown to be helpful to learning.

There are, of course, many practical books and articles that can help here; see, for example, Swan (2005b) for a teacher-friendly presentation of how to explain the various grammatical features, and Ur (2009) for a set of meaningful grammar practice activities, as well as an enormous number of internet sources. But there is no substitute for practical hands-on workshops; teachers need to try out such techniques in their own classrooms or use their peers for simulation activities in order to define their own practical principles for classroom procedure design and adaptation. In short, I am here advocating a component of methodology courses that is devoted to such practical work, based on sources available in the literature and on the internet and on teachers' own experiential work.

10 Summary

This chapter has attempted to answer a number of questions, such as: Is there such a thing as correct grammar? Should grammar be explicitly taught? Is there a best way to teach grammar? How can we help teachers to teach it effectively?

None of such questions has a simple answer. On the other hand, to refuse to give any answer on the pretext that the questions are so complex that one can only list the complexities and end up saying 'it depends', is in my opinion unacceptable. The teacher needs an answer, because the teacher needs to teach; we cannot embark on classroom teaching of English grammar without having taken decisions on how we are going to do it.

So this chapter has attempted to answer the questions, but with clearly stated reservations with regard to the applicability of the answers in different contexts.

Yes, I believe that for classroom-teaching purposes, there is such a thing as correct, or acceptable, grammar, and that the acquisition of this grammar is what we are seeking for our learners.

Yes, I believe that explicit teaching of grammar has a place in a balanced programme. This does not mean that all grammar teaching is always based on explanation or conscious practice exercises. It means, rather, that among other procedures such as reading texts, listening, discussion and so on there is also a place for occasional lessons or lesson components that focus on the explicit discussion of a grammatical point.

Yes, there probably is a best way to teach grammar, but this is likely to vary substantially according to the teaching contexts and pedagogical constraints or preferences that apply in any particular situation. A 'best way' is likely to involve at least some explanation, some practice activities, some contextualisation in communicative activities, some incidental relating to grammatical points as they come up and some deliberate teaching of globally learned exemplars (phrases, texts) that exemplify grammatical points. Each of these will be used more, or less, according to the particular teaching situation.

Finally, I have suggested above some ways in which teacher education programmes can promote the effective teaching of grammar: by being willing to compromise and present a moderate form of the communicative approach as a general principled basis for effective teaching; by updating teachers on the research but encouraging a critical and practical response to the different conclusions available and by providing opportunities to acquire a range of different grammar-teaching classroom procedures.

References

Carless, D. (2003) Factors in the implementation of task-based teaching in primary schools. *System* 31 (4), 485–500.

Carless, D. (2007) The suitability of task-based approaches for secondary schools: Perspectives from Hong Kong. *System* 35 (4), 595–608.

Cook, G. (2000) *Language Play, Language Learning*. Oxford: Oxford University Press.

Dekeyser, R.M. (2003) Implicit and explicit learning. In C. Doughty and M. Long (eds) *The Handbook of Second Language Acquisition* (pp. 313–348). Oxford: Blackwell.

Dekeyser, R.M. (2007) Introduction: Situating the concept of practice. In R.M. Dekeyser (ed.) *Practice in a Second Language: Perspectives from Applied Linguistics and Cognitive Psychology* (pp. 1–18). Cambridge: Cambridge University Press.

Ding, Y. (2007) Text memorization and imitation: The practices of successful Chinese learners of English. *System* 35 (2), 271–280.

Ellis, N. (2002) Frequency effects in language processing. *Studies in Second Language Acquisition* 24 (2), 143–188.

Ellis, R. (1989) Are classroom and naturalistic acquisition the same? A study of the classroom acquisition of German word order rules. *Studies in Second Language Acquisition* 11, 305–328.

Ellis, R. (1993) The structural syllabus and second language acquisition. *TESOL Quarterly* 27 (1), 91–113.

Ellis, R. (2001a) Investigating form-focused instruction. In R. Ellis (ed.) *Form-focused Instruction and Second Language Learning* (pp. 1–46). Oxford: Blackwell Publishing.

Ellis, R. (2001b) Grammar teaching – Practice or consciousness-raising? In J.C. Richards and W.A. Renandya (eds) *Methodology in Language Teaching* (pp. 167–174). Cambridge: Cambridge University Press.

Ellis, R. (2002) Does form-focused instruction affect the acquisition of implicit knowledge? A review of the research. *Studies in Second Language Acquisition* 24, 223–36.

Graham, C. (1993) *Grammarchants*. Oxford: Oxford University Press.

Hu, G. (2002) Potential cultural resistance to pedagogical imports: The case of communicative language teaching in China. *Language, Culture and Curriculum* 15 (2), 93–105.

Jenkins, J. (2006a) Current perspectives on teaching world Englishes and English as a lingua franca. *TESOL Quarterly* 40 (1), 157–181.
Jenkins, J. (2006b) The spread of EIL: A testing time for testers. *ELT Journal* 60 (1), 42–50.
Johnson, K. (1996) *Language Teaching and Skill Learning*. Oxford: Blackwell.
Krashen, S. (1999) Seeking a role for grammar: A review of some recent studies. *Foreign Language Annals* 32 (2), 245–57.
Laufer, B. (2005) Focus on form in second language vocabulary learning. *EUROSLA Yearbook* 5, 223–250.
Long, M.H. (1991) Focus on form: A design feature in language teaching methodology. In K. De Bot, D. Coste, R. Ginsberg and C. Kramsch (eds) *Foreign Language Research in Cross-cultural Perspective* (pp. 39–52). Amsterdam: John Benjamins.
Long, M.H. and Crookes, G. (1992) Three approaches to task-based syllabus design. *TESOL Quarterly* 26 (1), 27–56.
Long, M.H. and Robinson, P. (1998) Focus on form: Theory, research and practice. In C. Doughty and J. Williams (eds) *Focus on Form in Classroom Second Language Acquisition* (pp. 15–41). Cambridge: Cambridge University Press.
Lyster, R., Lightbown, P.M. and Spada, N. (1999) Response to Truscott's 'What's Wrong With Oral Grammar Correction'. *The Canadian Modern Language Review* 55 (4), 457–467.
Maley, A. (2009) ELF: A teacher's perspective. *Language and Intercultural Communication* 9 (3), 187–200.
Morgan-Short, K. and Bowden, H.W. (2006) Processing instruction and meaningful output-based instruction: Effects on second language development. *Studies in Second Language Acquisition* 28 (1), 31–65.
Norris, J.M. and Ortega, L. (2001) Does type of instruction make a difference? Substantive findings from a meta-analytic review. *Language Learning* 51 (Supplement 1), 157–213.
Pienemann, M. (1984) Psychological constraints on the teachability of language. *Studies in Second Language Acquisition* 6, 186–214.
Richards, J.C. (2002) Accuracy and fluency revisited. In E. Hinkel and S. Fotos (eds) *New Perspectives on Grammar Teaching in Second Language Classrooms* (pp. 35–50). New York: Lawrence Erlbaum Associates.
Salaberry, M.R. (1997) The role of input and output practice in second language acquisition. *Canadian Modern Language Review* 53 (2), 422–451.
Schmidt, R. (1990) The role of consciousness in SLL. *Applied Linguistics* 11, 129–158.
Schmidt, R. (2001) Attention. In P. Robinson (ed.) *Cognition and Second Language Instruction* (pp. 3–32). Cambridge: Cambridge University Press.
Seedhouse, P. (1999) Task-based interaction. *English Language Teaching Journal* 53 (3), 149–56.
Seidlhofer, B. (ed.) (2003) *Controversies in Applied Linguistics*. Oxford: Oxford University Press.
Shak, J. and Gardner, S. (2008) Young learner perspectives on four focus-on-form tasks. *Language Teaching Research* 12 (3), 387–408.
Skehan, P. (1996) A framework for the implementation of task-based instruction. *Applied Linguistics* 11, 38–62.
Skehan, P. (1997) *A Cognitive Approach to Language Learning*. Oxford: Oxford University Press.

Spada, N. and Lightbown, P.M. (1999) Instruction, first language influence, and developmental readiness in second language acquisition. *Modern Language Journal* 83 (1), 1–22.
Swain, M. (2000) French immersion research in Canada: Recent contributions to SLA and applied linguistics. *Annual Review of Applied Linguistics* 20, 199–211.
Swan, M. (2005a) Legislation by hypothesis: The case of task-based instruction. *Applied Linguistics* 26 (3), 376–401.
Swan, M. (2005b) *Practical English Usage*. Oxford: Oxford University Press.
Truscott, J. (1996) The case against grammar correction in L2 writing classes. *Language Learning* 46 (2), 327–69.
Truscott, J. (1999) What's wrong with oral grammar correction? *The Canadian Modern Language Review* 55 (4), 437–56.
Turnbull, M., Lapkin, S., Hart, D. and Swain, M. (1995) Time on task and immersion graduates' French proficiency. In S. Lapkin (ed.) *French as a Second Language Education in Canada: Recent Empirical Studies* (pp. 31–55). Toronto: The Ontario Institute for Studies in Education.
Ur, P. (2009) *Grammar Practice Activities* (2nd edn). Cambridge: Cambridge University Press.
VOICE (2009) The Vienna-Oxford International Corpus of English. Online at http://www.univie.ac.at/voice/index.php
Wray, A. (2000) Formulaic sequences in second language teaching: Principle and practice. *Applied Linguistics* 21 (4), 463–489.

Appendix

A series of practice tasks on the comparative of adjectives showing the progression from focus on form, through gradual de-focus on form, culminating in focus on meaning.

Exercise 1: Focus on correct forms

Discrete items

(1) A car is .... than a bicycle. (fast)
(2) Chinese is .... than English. (difficult).
(3) A lion is .... than a dog. (big).

Full text

Glenda: I don't know which dress to buy, the red or the green!
Sally: Well, the red one is ....(expensive), the green one is much ...... (cheap).
Glenda: Yes, but the red one is much .... (pretty). Which do you think suits me ....(well)?

Exercise 2: Focus on both form and meaning (cannot be done without understanding)

Compare the people in this family. Use the adjectives big, fat, thin, small, big, tall, young, short, old.

Karen is........................Ben.
Jill is................................
Ben................................ .
....
....
....
....

Ben   Jill

Karen

Exercise 3: Focus on meaning and form (the purpose is mainly the production of meanings, but some attention is paid to form)

Choose one of these pairs of items. How many different ways can you think of comparing them? Use the comparative form of the adjective.

A radio and a computer
A rabbit and a snake
Playing football and reading a book
Harry Potter and Professor Dumbledore

Exercise 4: Focus on communication (the purpose is communication, the comparative of adjectives used incidentally as means to an end)

Performance task

You have enough money to go on holiday abroad. You might:

(1) go skiing in Switzerland
(2) go on safari in Kenya

Prepare a (written or spoken) presentation comparing them. Present the arguments for or against each; decide which you'd prefer and say why.

6 Cognitive + Communicative Grammar in Teacher Education
David Newby

1 Introduction

This chapter focuses on both theoretical and practical aspects of pedagogical grammar. Its aims are twofold: first, to outline some of the principles of what I term Cognitive + Communicative Grammar (see, e.g. Newby, 2002, 2008), an approach that is the focus of my applied linguistic and methodology courses at the University of Graz; second, to consider how students can be encouraged to critically appraise both this approach and other theories of language and of language acquisition and to reexamine the traditional teaching of grammar, which is usually part of their own learning experience.

For students undergoing their initial teacher education, university libraries will offer a plethora of books on linguistic description and language-acquisition theories, some of which will be discussed in linguistics and methodology courses. Yet when students have completed their education, theoretical insights tend to be left behind and do not accompany them into the classroom. One reason for this is that such is the force of traditional methods of teaching, particularly in the area of grammar, that they are unwilling to step outside the familiar didactic framework that they had experienced during their own time as learners. A second reason is that students tend to consume theories but do not digest them; they do not, or are given too little opportunity to *engage* with them, explore their possible applications and assess their validity. Widdowson (2003: 27) has the following to say about the role of theory:

> the value of theory is not that it is persuasive but that it is provocative. You do not apply it, you appraise it. You use it as a catalyst for reflection on your own teaching circumstances, or, to change the metaphor, as a point of reference from which to take bearings on your own practice.

If students are to make this appraisal, however, they need to have access to various theories. If they are to take bearings on their practice, their teacher education must help them to explore how theory can be implemented in pedagogy. In recent years, both language description and language-acquisition theories have been dominated, on the one hand, by Chomskyan generative theories and, on the other, by theories of second-language learning that lean heavily on those of first-language acquisition. Indeed, Birdsong (2004: 83) goes so far as to claim that '[i]n the most general terms, L2A theory tackles the question of the resemblance of L2A to L1A'. Yet how important is this supposed resemblance for secondary school teachers of languages?

Despite the vast growth in the field of second-language acquisition research since the 1980s, very few of its findings seem to be reflected in commonly practiced methodology, school textbooks and teaching materials. The gulf between theory and practice seems very wide. Long (2000: 4-5) comments on this state of affairs as follows:

> The scope of many SLA theories does not extend to the L2 classroom at all. [...] Most SLA theories, and most SLA theorists, are not primarily interested in language teaching, and in some cases not at all interested.

In light of these statements, it is perhaps hardly surprising that in recent years, the arguably trivial theories of Krashen have been perceived as one of the few 'theoretical' straws that teacher educators across Europe could clutch at (see Fenner & Newby, 2006).

It is my view, however, that all this is about to change. A growing interest in the field of cognitive linguistics and the elaboration and refinement of its theories have, in recent years, spawned a number of books by applied linguists that seek to apply cognitive insights to language teaching and learning. Some of these are, in chronological order, Johnson (1996), Skehan (1998), Robinson (ed.) (2001), Hinkel and Fotos (eds) (2002), Dekeyser (ed.) (2007), Achard and Niemeier (2004), De Kop and De Rycker (2008), Robinson and Ellis (eds) (2008), Holme (2009) and Littlemore (2009).

While early cognitively oriented books were concerned with language acquisition but had little to say about language itself – for example, Johnson and Skehan – recent books have been more strongly oriented to language description. Thus, just as Chomsky provides a theoretical framework for both language and language acquisition, cognitive theories are able to investigate both language and learning within similar parameters. Holme and Littlemore, both published in 2009, are two books that, it seems to me, provide insights that clearly show the potential of cognitive linguistics for language teaching.

2 Theory and Pedagogical Grammar

Since grammar is the area of linguistics to which most theoretical attention has been paid and in which most theories and models have been developed, we might expect that some insights from these theories might be discernible in, say, the rules found in pedagogical reference grammars. Yet, following a survey of various pedagogical reference grammars, Chalker (1994: 42) concludes that 'all the books in the survey are concerned with "surface" structure – what is said or written – and not with an abstract theoretical model of grammar'. An earlier survey by Dirven (1990: 8) led him to observe that

> a major assignment for foreign language pedagogy is experimental research into adequate forms of rule formulation and presentation. It is *astonishing* [my italics] that so little research has been carried out in this area.

Swan (1994: 45) does in fact list his own '[d]esign criteria for pedagogic language rules'. Yet these tend to operate at a superficial level and do not address the question of what grammatical meaning actually is. Swan's first criterion – 'rules must be true' – is a rather empty statement if it is not embedded within a more general theory of language that will provide the means for validating their truthfulness.

As Chalker (1994: 31) further points out, there tends to be a tacit assumption among many students, teachers and pedagogical grammarians that there exists what she calls a single, 'God's truth' view of grammar: 'traditional' ways of categorising and describing grammar which focus on formal, rather than semantic, categories. It is my view, based on my work with teachers from many countries, that this traditional view concerning both the nature of grammar and how it should be taught dominates many classrooms across Europe and beyond.

As the above quotations show, as far as pedagogical grammar is concerned, there exists something of a theoretical vacuum; it is the aim of Cognitive + Communicative (C+C) Grammar to fill this vacuum and to provide an alternative to the rather vacuous tenets of traditional approaches.

3 Cognitive + Communicative Grammar

The Cognitive + Communicative (Newby, 2002) axis refers to two separate but complementary aspects of theoretical analysis: language description and language learning. A C+C approach to language seeks to analyse and describe grammar, on the one hand in terms of the mental processes that underlie the use of language (cognitive), and on the other, as an act of communication – a dynamic process in which a speaker's perceptions are encoded by linguistic means into messages (communicative). A cognitive analysis examines initially how the mind is structured and organised to perceive reality and subsequently how cognitive categorisation gives rise to grammar; a communicative analysis embeds the cognitive, semantic and formal categories arising from a cognitive analysis in other aspects of communication such as contextual variables, pragmatic meaning and register. It should be added that the cognitive and communicative categories are inseparable, overlapping and complementary categories, which is why they are always linked by a '+' sign.

The Cognitive + Communicative axis will allow us to explore language description from various perspectives. By adopting a communicative view, we can approach language from a pragmatic, discourse-linked, context-based direction; by adopting a cognitive view, we can approach it from a psychological, mind-based direction. It follows from this that any definition of grammar must reflect what the Council of Europe's Common European Framework of Reference (2001: 9) calls an *action-oriented* conception of language. It must, on the one hand, see grammar as an act of grammaticalisation and, on the other, identify aspects of cognition that steer the grammaticalisation process. As its title suggests, C+C Grammar draws on two theoretical areas, cognitive linguistics and various communicatively oriented theories such as those of Hymes (1964, 1972) and Halliday (e.g. 1978) as well as applied linguists' of the 'communicative' generation, for instance, Widdowson and Wilkins. Brief discussion will be given to some of the main principles of these theories.

3.1 Cognitive Linguistics

Cognitive linguistics was, as Lee (2001: 1) points out, originally motivated by its opposition to the modular view of language, based on the concept of Universal Grammar propounded by Chomsky, and its 'syntactocentric' basis (Jackendoff, 2002: 197). In recent years, theories such as those elaborated by Jackendoff (e.g. 1983) and Langacker (e.g. 1987), complemented by a functional orientation – for example, Halliday and Matthiessen (1999) – have provided a very firm and persuasive theoretical basis.

Two aspects of cognitive linguistics are relevant for the present discussions. The first is the recognition that grammatical competence is not separate from other aspects of the human mind, but is part of an overall system of categorisation that steers human beings' perceptions of the external world. As Jackendoff puts it (1983: X): 'when we are studying the semantics of natural language, we are by necessity studying the structure of thought'. The second is that an analysis of meaning is at the heart of linguistic enquiry. Langacker (1987: 5) states: 'I take it as self-evident that meaning is a cognitive phenomenon and must eventually be analyzed as such. Cognitive grammar therefore equates meaning with conceptualization'.

Croft and Cruse (2004: 1) list three 'major hypotheses as guiding the cognitive approach to language', the third of which points to the potential of a C+C view of language to be applied to learning:

- language is not an autonomous cognitive faculty;
- grammar is conceptualisation;
- knowledge of language emerges from language use.

3.2 Communicative Grammar

In their discussion of the communicative approach to language teaching, Richards and Rodgers (2001: 161) cite four underlying principles:

(1) Language is a system for the expression of meaning.
(2) The primary function of language is for interaction and communication.
(3) The structure of language reflects its functional and communicative uses.
(4) The primary units of language are not merely its grammatical and structural features, but categories of functional and communicative meaning as exemplified in discourse.

All four principles provide support for the 'meaning → form' orientation that is at the core of a process, action-oriented view of language. As far as grammar is concerned, this view lays the basis for a *notional* or meaning-based description of language that can be found in documents such as the Council of Europe's *The Threshold Level* (1977/1991) or Wilkins' *Notional Syllabuses* (1976). However, despite some interesting attempts to implement a meaning-based view of grammar – for example, Doff *et al.* (1983), *Meanings into Words* – nowadays school textbooks tend to use approaches to grammar that could be labelled traditional rather than communicative. Indeed, communicative grammar is a collocation that is rarely heard. For some methodologists, it would appear to mean little more than the desultory use of grammar games or, somewhat perversely, not teaching grammar at all.

One of the reasons for the loss of interest in notional grammar is that the pendulum of applied linguistic research has, in recent years, swung away from a focus on language analysis to a one-sided concern with learning processes. From both a communicative and a cognitive perspective, however, an understanding of language as a use-based system is a prerequisite for researching learning processes: if we do not understand *what* the learner is acquiring, statements about *how* language is acquired and how teachers can facilitate this process will be of dubious validity. It is for this reason that I shall now examine the nature of grammar as part of a system of human communication in some detail.

4 Communicative Events

I shall illustrate fundamental elements of a C+C view of language by means of a 'communication model', a diagrammatic representation of what is termed a 'communicative event', building on the 'speech event', specified by Hymes (1972: 277-278). Following Richards *et al.* (1985: 267), a communicative event will be defined as a 'particular instance when people exchange speech' or as a single unit of communication. This dynamic view is shared by cognitive linguists: Croft and Cruise (2004: 2) state that 'from a cognitive perspective, language is the real-time perception and production of a temporal sequence of discrete, structured symbolic units'. One advantage of representing language in this way is that it stresses that language must be seen both in terms of knowledge and of use; the communication model depicts not only *competence* but also *performance*. Figure 6.1 illustrates some of the main components of a communicative event.

As will be seen from the categories identified in the model, language is seen both as a cognitive phenomenon (cognitive competence, mental context, etc.) and as a communicative process, indicated by the left-to-right arrows and the specification of context. The model attempts to reflect the process by which, when language is used, speakers filter their thoughts about the external world and construct an internal mental representation, in which the perceived components – entities (people and things), actions, properties and circumstances – will be referred to and conceptualised in certain ways that will result in the encoding into lexical and grammatical forms. The theoretical rationale underlying the communication model provides the following definition of grammar:

> Grammar is the process by which speakers encode their perceptions of entities, actions and properties, and the relations between them, into meaningful grammatical form.

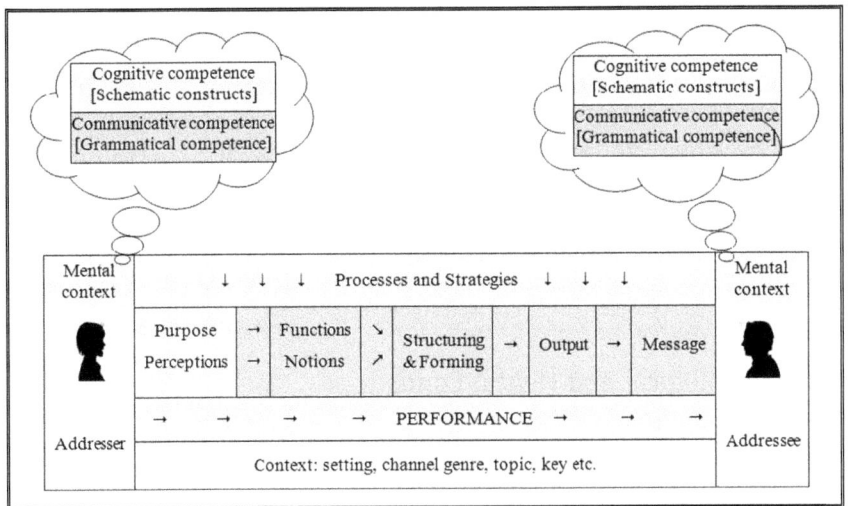

Figure 6.1 Model of a communicative event (adapted from Newby, 2002: 259)

For readers who might wish to reduce this definition to fit on the front of a T-shirt, I can offer the following: *Grammar is marked perceptions*.

Categories identified in the communication model that are most significant for C+C Grammar and for grammar pedagogy will be given brief discussion. Reference will also be made to the Common European Framework of Reference for Languages (CEFR) since it takes a strongly 'action-oriented' approach (2001: 9). An analysis of the CEFR reveals that all the categories, both cognitive and communicative, are identified and discussed. The term 'communicative event' itself occurs 11 times. When teachers and methodologists discuss the CEFR, it is usually the 'communicative' aspects that are referred to – the specification of communicative competence, context, action-oriented, the explicit description of language performance, etc. However, they tend be less aware that language is seen from a strongly cognitive perspective. I shall add some relevant quotations from the CEFR as I proceed.

4.1 Cognitive, Communicative and Grammatical Competence

These terms refer to three complementary and overlapping categories of knowledge that are stored in the brain and that will be activated during communication to aid both the expression and interpretation of messages. *Grammatical competence* is one part of a wider *communicative competence*, and these are, in turn, part of a wider *cognitive competence* (Newby, forthcoming). Cognitive competence can be defined as a stock of *schematic* – i.e. non-linguistic – *constructs* in which systemic – i.e. linguistic – knowledge is embedded. Examples of specifically cognitive categories are *schemata, frames, perspective, scripts,* etc., which will be discussed in Section 5. An example of a specifically communicative category is the *purpose-function* axis. An example of a specifically grammatical category is that of *notions*. The *perceptions* category of the communication model will show how cognitive and grammatical conceptualisation interlock with each other.

4.2 Sociological and Mental Context

All communication takes place in a context. The importance of embedding teaching materials in what I shall term *sociological contexts* has long been recognised in the communicative approach. Contextual variables such as setting, channel, genre, topic, etc. will 'constrain' a speaker's choice of linguistic features such as register, tone of voice, etc. This category is referred to in the CEFR as the 'external context' (2001: 50). From a cognitive perspective, however, it is necessary to add the category of *mental context*. This can be explained as the mental *mindset* of the speaker during communication. Before communication begins and as it proceeds, participants 'set and re-set their mental switches', i.e. activate certain *schematic constructs* relevant to this particular event. *Schematic constructs* may be both *personal*, for example, an individual's knowledge of previous events, attitudes, values, etc. that differ from person to person, or what will be termed *conventionalised* constructs, which are shared by what might be referred to as a *'cognitive community'*, by analogy with speech community. (CEFR, 2001: 160, uses the term 'routinised schemata' in a similar sense.) Conventionalised constructs provide a systematic framework of knowledge in which both language and human behaviour in general are embedded. Since this category is particularly relevant for pedagogical grammar, further discussion will be given in Section 5. Unlike the sociological context, which remains fixed within a specific speech event, the mental context is unstable and constantly changing.

The CEFR also makes use of the term 'mental context' (2001: 50) and explains it as follows:

> As a factor in the participation of a communicative event, however, we must distinguish between this external context, which is far too rich to be acted upon or even perceived in its full complexity by any individual, and

the user/learner's mental context. The external context is filtered and interpreted through the user's:

- perceptual apparatus;
- attention mechanisms;
- long-term experience, affecting memory, associations and connotations;
- practical classification of objects, events, etc.;
- linguistic categorisation.

Both sociological and mental contexts are inextricably bound up with language use. As Widdowson (1998: 8) says, 'Context [...] is no longer *apart* from language but *a part of* it'.

4.3 Perceptions → Notions

Here we are concerned with the process by which speakers filter their thoughts about, and observations of, the external world, reduce them and structure them according to certain operating principles and perceptional categories shared by their cognitive community and map them onto language. The process of filtering, categorising and conceptualising perceptions is at the core of cognitive theories. As Jackendoff (1983: 77) states:

> An essential aspect of cognition is the ability to categorize: to judge that a particular thing is or is not an instance of a particular category. [...] without categorization, memory is virtually useless. Thus an account of the organism's ability to categorize transcends linguistic theory. It is central to all of cognitive psychology.

Clearly, describing the nature of cognitive and linguistic categorisation and the process of conceptualisation is highly complex. Nevertheless, it is a task that must be undertaken by both linguistic and pedagogical grammarians if their descriptions are to have validity. I shall discuss four categories of conceptualisation that form part of C+C theory and explain their relevance for grammatical description.

4.3.1 *Ontological components*

In this category, at its most general level, the perception process will convert what is experienced into what Jackendoff (1983: 5) refers to as 'ontological categories' or 'ontological type' (2002: 316), 'ur-features' such as objects, actions, properties and circumstances. These components form the basis of a *scenario*; i.e. the mental representation of a state of affairs, event or thought that is to be encoded into a proposition. These semantic categories reflect the form classes of form-based grammar – noun, verb, etc.

4.3.2 Global concepts

These are general categories of human thought and experience, which are referred to when language is used. For example, people talk about time and space and make use of tenses and adverbs and prepositions to do so; they express possibility and compulsion using modal verbs or certain adverbs. Global concepts are expressed not only through grammar, but also through lexis. Seeing language as a reflection of 'general notions' is the starting point of a mode of analysis that applied linguists such as Wilkins (1976) undertook in the 1970s and that resulted in the taxonomy of grammatical and lexical notions found in *The Threshold Level* (van Ek, 1977; van Ek & Trim, 1991).

4.3.3 Perceptional options

This can be seen as a system of categorisation by means of which speakers can give detailed information about *how* they perceive global concepts and ontological components in a particular speech event. For example, the ontological component 'action' may be *shaped* as a state, an event or an activity; the global concept 'location' may be perceived as *proximate* or *distant*, etc. This category can be seen as *meaning potentials*, which may influence various grammatical choices. It is cognitive in nature but also shows conceptual structuring that will be reflected in grammatical choices. From the point of view of cognitive linguistics, which claims that language is not modular in the Chomskyan sense but part of a wider system of cognitive classification, it is of considerable interest since it reflects the interface between cognition and language. Since perceptional options are not specifically language-related, they may cut across traditional form classes, as shown in Figure 6.2.

4.3.4 Specific grammatical notions

This is the first specifically language-driven part of the communication model and concerns the semantic meaning of grammar in use. A specific notion will be defined as a single semantico-grammatical concept or a grammatical meaning expressed by a speaker when s/he formulates a proposition and encodes it into form. It is important to distinguish between what *The Threshold Level* (1977) refers to as 'general and specific notions'. To prevent ambiguity, I shall refer to the former as 'global concepts' and reserve the use of 'notion' for the specific sense. To explain this meaning type vis-à-vis the other three categories, it can be said that ontological components are what speakers *refer to*; global concepts relate to what speakers *talk about*;

category	proximate	distant
spatial	here this near	there that far
temporal	now *is* (present tense)	then *was* (past tense)
epistemic reality	You **are** nice.	*If you* **were** *nice.*
identification	*He told me I* **am** *beautiful.*	*He told me I* **was** *stupid.*

Figure 6.2 The perceptional category of proximate versus distant (Newby, 2002: 144)

perceptional options show what grammar *can mean*; specific notions refer to what grammar *does mean* in an actual utterance.

This category is, presumably, the 'surface' meaning referred to by Chalker (1994) and is the type normally described in the rules of pedagogical grammars. Despite her rather dismissive term of 'surface', there are, in my view, two important reasons for focusing analytical attention on notional meaning. First, it provides the 'fine tuning' that is necessary to explain different meanings that the categories provided at the 'perceptional options' level cannot disambiguate. For example, in the two utterances *He can't answer his mobile because he's play***ing** *tennis* and *He can't go to the cinema tonight because he's play***ing** *tennis*, the present progressive meaning shares the same perception categories in both utterances; however, most pedagogical grammars, including my own, state that the present progressive meaning of the respective utterances is different. The conceptual difference between 'referring to a present activity' and 'referring to a future arrangement' requires an additional explanatory meaning level that perceptional options alone do not provide.

The second, and for C + C Grammar more important, reason is that any grammar that takes a dynamic, use-based view of language as exemplified in the communication model needs to specify what it is that the speaker is encoding or what is being grammaticalised. We need to go beyond analysing what grammar *can* mean and describe what grammar *does* mean when it is used in a specific speech event. This meaning level is the focus of 'notional grammar' (see, e.g. Newby, 1991), which seeks to provide a specification of grammatical meaning that fulfils the theoretical criteria of linguistic analysis and to package its findings in pedagogically accessible form.

The following four hypotheses apply to notional grammar (Newby, 2002: 301):

(1) Notions represent the *primary semantico-grammatical unit* of encoding and decoding. Human beings express and comprehend notions.
(2) Notions are *psycholinguistically real*. They represent concepts stored in the 'mental grammaticon' and are utilised in the process of grammaticalisation.
(3) A notion is *an autonomous semantic concept*. Different notions, even if encoded into the same form, express psychologically separate and distinct grammatical concepts.
(4) There is a *systematic relationship* between a specific notion and a form. A notion is always encoded into the same form.

Clearly, a notional approach is not going to come up with completely new categories of grammatical concepts. What it does do, however, is to provide a means (a) for analysing and classifying meaning systematically and (b) for arriving at valid and reliable rules to which there are no exceptions. This might sound like a wild claim, but here I would align myself with the view of Jackendoff (1983: 14), and indeed other cognitive grammarians, who states:

> Under the reasonable hypothesis that language serves the purpose of transmitting information, it would be perverse not to take as a working assumption that language is a relatively efficient and accurate encoding of the information it conveys. To give up this assumption is to refuse to look for systematicity in the relationship between syntax and semantics.

Analysing meaning 'systematically' and arriving at 'valid' rules requires, of course, a theoretical framework and methodology for arriving at these rules. Elsewhere (Newby, 2002: Chapter 11) I have discussed in detail the process of *notion setting*. The concept of 'validity' reflects the design criterion of Swan, quoted earlier, that 'rules must be true'. Let us take one grammatical example to explore the question of how 'true' or valid one of Swan's rules is: the explanation of the meaning of the present perfect progressive, or, in notional terms, the notions which are encoded into this form. My own grammar book lists two notions as follows:

(1) Duration of an activity: *I've been waiting here since two o'clock.*
(2) Recent activities: *I've been watching a Charlie Chaplin film on television.*

According to notional grammar, these represent two autonomous meanings. In Swan's grammar reference *How English Works*, the following statement can be found in the chapter on 'present perfect progressive or simple': 'the present perfect progressive looks at the continuing situation itself; the present perfect simple says that something is completed' and further:

I've been reading your book: I'm enjoying it.
I've read your book. (= I've finished it.)
(Swan & Walter, 1997: 160)

The first utterance seems to express my notion (2) – recent activities. Whilst I would agree that in the second utterance the notion of what I term 'change and completion' is encoded, the 'rule' that the present perfect progressive expresses a 'continuing situation' can soon be 'de-verified'. This could be done simply by changing the lexical item *read* into *finish*, which would give us *I've been finishing your book*. However, I will take two authentic utterances that seem to express the same grammatical meaning, whatever that might be.

At the age of three, my daughter returned home and announced: *I've been feeding the ducks*. Clearly, the activity was 'finished' but in fact whether it was or not was quite irrelevant. What my daughter was referring to and informing me about with this verbal phrase were two notional perceptions: 'recent → present perfect'; 'activity → _ing'. A rather nice example which further de-verifies the 'continuing situation' claim comes from the 19th-century novelist Elizabeth Gaskell in her *Life of Charlotte Brontë*, where she relates how Charlotte confessed to her father that she was the author of *Jane Eyre*:

She informed me that something like the following conversation took place between her and him (I wrote down her words the day after I heard them; and I am pretty sure they are accurate.)
'Papa, I've been writing a book.'
'Have you, my dear?'
'Yes, and I want you to read it.'
'I am afraid it will try my eyes too much.'
'But it is not in manuscript: it is printed.'
(Gaskell, 1975: 325)

Could it be that in fact Charlotte never finished the book? Would Mr Michael Swan urgently contact the Brontë Society...

What Swan has explained is not, in my view, the semantic meaning of the grammar but a possible interpretation of the utterance as a whole. In fact, the finished versus unfinished information is provided not in the grammar but in the two following statements: 'I'm enjoying it' (Swan) and 'it is printed' (Brontë).

Describing grammar from a notional perspective has various advantages:

- It provides a systematic framework for teaching grammatical meaning.
- It provides a specification of meaning-based objectives.
- It provides valid, reliable and exceptionless rules.
- Notional objectives provide a springboard to communicative methodology.
- It permits the specification of grammar in terms of 'I-can' descriptors: 'I can express my intentions using *going to*'; 'I can express the duration of activities using the present perfect progressive', etc.

4.4 Processes

Seeing language as acts of performing entails not only specifying what competence *is*, but also analysing *how* human beings convert their competence into performance. Language processes, as used in the communication model, are well defined by the CEFR as 'chain of events, neurological and physiological, involved in the production and reception of speech and writing' (2001: 10). Processes are, to all intents and purposes, subconscious. Some examples are:

- focusing on, filtering out and categorising salient features from what is perceived, experienced, thought, etc.;
- planning how to conceptualise experience;
- mapping perceptions onto grammatical and lexical notions;
- organising information into a coherent pattern;
- retrieving word forms from long-term memory;
- converting propositions into phonic or graphic form.

The category of language processes is important for foreign-language pedagogy since it stresses the skill element of language processing and use. In order to be able to *perform* with grammar, students need practice in the processes referred to above; first, because the system of concepts in the target language will, to some extent at least, be different from that of the first language and second, because a process such as mapping perceptions onto grammatical notions is a 'real-time' dynamic activity. With exercises that require students to change direct into indirect speech or fill in gaps in sentences, the mapping process has already been done by the teacher or textbook so they do not support grammatical performance.

4.5 Communication Strategies

In contrast to processes, strategies will be defined as largely conscious measures taken by speakers, writers, readers and listeners in order to make communication more efficient or to overcome communication-related problems they are, or expect to be, confronted with. Examples of communication strategies are paraphrasing an unknown word; monitoring the comprehension of the addressee; reformulating an utterance that has not been understood. Some models of communicative competence (e.g. Canale & Swain, 1980, as well as the CEFR) list this category of 'strategic competence' as a central element.

4.6 Structuring and Forming

Structuring refers to the patterning of lexical and grammatical units (syntax); forming refers to the realisation of these units in phonic or graphic form (morphology). Cognitive linguistics will see formal categories as resulting from underlying meaning systems; in this, it differs from generative grammar, which accords centrality to syntax. To quote Halliday (1985: 6): 'Structure no longer occupies the centre of the stage; it enters it because it is one form of the realization of meanings'. Since in C+C Grammar the centre of the stage is occupied by the systems of meanings which give rise to forms, it has little to say about syntax and morphology. This does not mean, however, that they should play no role in pedagogy. Clearly, formal objectives such as irregular past participle forms or syntactically determined word order (S-V-O, etc.) are not excluded from a communicative approach to grammar teaching.

5 Categories of Competence in Pedagogical Grammar

As the author of a reference grammar (Newby, 1989; 1992) and school textbooks (Heindler *et al.*, 1993), one unenviable task I have had to fulfil is to explain, in comprehensible metalanguage, what grammar means. Whilst many linguists may explore and explain underlying semantic categories of language, they tend not to put their cards on the table and say 'this sentence means this'. Making such statements, however, is the bread-and-butter lot of pedagogical grammarians. What they describe and how they describe it will depend to a considerable extent on how they view the nature of grammar – assuming, of course, that they hold any theoretical view at all: virtually all pedagogical grammarians seem quite happy to explain to learners how to change 'direct' into 'indirect' speech despite the fact that this 'pedagogical mathematics' has little to do with grammatical competence and even less with performance.

In this section, I shall consider certain categories – cognitive and grammatical – that are relevant for a pedagogical description of grammar. (A discussion of 'communicative' categories is beyond the scope of this chapter.) Halliday (1978: 28) makes the important point that

> we do not experience language in isolation – if we did we would not recognise it as language – but always in relation to a scenario, some background of persons and actions and events from which the things which are said derive their meaning.

In cognitive terms, language is always embedded in schematic constructs, which will determine the mindset of participants in a speech event. The question then arises as to what mindsets might consist of.

My discussion of this begins with a (true) anecdote. A few years ago, at the beginning of October, a student came to my office for an oral examination. In the course of this exam, I asked her the question: *Have you been to England?* To this, she replied: *No, I've been to Spain* (Figure 6.3). For a moment, communication broke down. From my perspective, she had not answered my question; from hers, she had. As with many misunderstandings, I was, of course, able to repair the breakdown: – *No, I mean, have you ever been to an English-speaking country*. So what went wrong? I shall attempt to explain the misunderstanding with reference to two pairs of cognitive/grammatical categories: *frames and grammatical notions*, and *lexis and schemata*.

5.1 Frames and Grammatical Notions

A frame will be defined as a commonly occurring, generalisable situation with which a speaker and a hearer are familiar or a 'remembered framework' (see Minsky, 1975, cited in Brown & Yule, 1983: 238). Fillmore defines frames in this sense as 'specific unified frameworks of knowledge, or coherent schematizations of experience' (1985: 223 cited in Ungerer & Schmid, 1996: 209). Unlike the sociological context of the external world, frames are set up partly as the result of the speakers' mindset within this context, but may change rapidly within a single context. Frames are what I earlier referred to as conventionalised

Cognitive + Communicative Grammar in Teacher Education   117

Figure 6.3 Present perfect misunderstanding – grammatical and cognitive categories

schematic constructs. The importance of frames for language users and for language learners is that lexical, grammatical and pragmatic meanings are to a certain extent predictable in specific frames. As the CEFR says, 'schemata can free the learner to deal with other aspects of performance, or assist in anticipating text content and organisation' (2001: 160). Moreover, it is possible to identify *'grammatical frames'*, which can be described as a frequently occurring scenario in which specific notions are likely to be encoded.

In the dialogue above, I shall refer to the frame that is part of my mindset as 'examining' and it is within this frame that I express the notion of 'experience' that is encoded into the present perfect form. It is usually the case within a communicative event that common frames will be shared between interlocutors. However, this is not always so, as in the example above. The student has *multiple* frames in her present mindset, one of which she shares with me – 'examining' – but when I ask my question, this triggers a frame switch in her mind to what can be called a 'coming back' frame, and this in turn causes her to misunderstand the grammatical notion expressed through the verbal form of my utterance. Within this grammatical 'coming back' frame, speakers often refer to recent events or activities, using the present perfect simple and progressive, respectively. This is the notion the student erroneously decodes from my utterance and then encodes with her own utterance.

It seems to me that grammatical frames are of considerable significance for language teaching. In an earlier section I referred to my three-year-old daughter, who expressed the 'recent activities' notion in her utterance *I've been feeding the ducks.* It was of interest to me that all three of my children began to use this notion and form at a relatively early stage, despite the fact that in foreign-language teaching it is often considered as a 'difficult' piece of grammar. One reason why native-speaker children acquire this notion quickly may be that the frame in which it occurs is very common within domestic contexts. When a family member comes into one room from another, she might say *I've been watching television.* When a family member comes home, he might say *I've been doing the shopping,* etc. Thus, the acquisition of this grammar is supported and accelerated by the simultaneous acquisition of a common cognitive frame. The pedagogical implications of this are clearly apparent: embedding grammar in commonly occurring frames may well facilitate learning.

5.2 Lexis and Schemata

Schemata are sets of ideas, associations, expectations, etc. that an individual speaker or listener may have in connection with a concept, an object, person, place, action, event, etc. A schematic view of lexical meaning maintains that the actual *sense* or *denotation* or dictionary definition of a word is embedded within a network of related associations. Let us take the word *England* as an example. When, in the above dialogue, I referred to it, it was as a member of a set of 'countries where people speak English'. It could thus be regarded as a synecdoche of 'an English-speaking country'. If the addressee had shared this schematic constellation, then she might have answered *No, but I've been to America.* However, constrained by her 'coming back' frame, she 'interprets' the lexeme as a member of a set of 'foreign countries or holiday destinations one might visit.' Again, this category has important implications for vocabulary learning: learners should be encouraged to engage not only with the sense of a word, but also with its schematic setting.

6 Mediating C+C Grammar in Teacher Education

Despite the abstract nature of the grammatical and cognitive categories discussed in this chapter, I have applied almost all of them in my own grammar pedagogy, as a sample page from my school reference grammar in the appendix shows. Here the entry for the notion of 'recent activities', encoded into the present perfect progressive form, is shown. In keeping with a notional approach, there is no single entry on 'the present perfect'; instead, each notion has its own description and rule. In almost all entries, grammatical explanations are embedded within a communicative event. Also, grammatical rules are presented from a speaker-based perspective: the formulation 'I am referring to' reflects the view that 'grammaticalisation' is an act of referring to perceptions. The 'communicative uses' section includes both frames and a further category of conventionalised schemata: *scripts*. These are, in cognitive terms, chains of frames; in linguistic terms, patterns of discourse. An example occurs in 'communicative use, 1', where the present perfect progressive notion is followed by a statement in the past tense. Various terms are used by the CEFR for this category: 'scripts' and 'interactional schemata' (2001: 160) and 'verbal exchange patterns' (2001: 126).

Yet however promising its theories may be, mediating C+C Grammar in teacher education represents something of a challenge. Some of the hurdles that student teachers need to overcome are:

- the firmly rooted 'God's truth' view of traditional grammar description – students find it difficult to conceive that this has a very weak theoretical basis and that there are other and better ways of describing grammar;
- the fairly radical rethinking involved in approaching grammar through apparently abstract notional categories rather than through the formal categories of traditional grammar;
- the difficulty in distancing themselves from the grammar methodology that they experienced in schools and in seeing this in a critical light;
- the belief, partly enforced through their own studies, that linguistic theory is a purely academic subject that has no relevance for teaching.

Despite these initial hurdles, it is my experience that students undergoing their teacher education show a considerable interest in linguistic and learning theory; however, it must be 'mediated' in certain ways that facilitate their *engagement* with theoretical aspects. If they are, as Widdowson suggests, to 'appraise' and 'apply' theories, they need (a) to have a good understanding of these theories and (b) to be aware of how principles resulting from different theories might impact on their teaching.

At Graz University, two specific courses are offered that seek to mediate C+C Grammar. In a lecture entitled 'Applied linguistics for language teachers', students are confronted with and discuss competing theories of language and of language acquisition. The theories of C+C Grammar are discussed in detail and applications for pedagogy are illustrated. The second course is a hands-on seminar on the teaching of grammar, in which materials and activities based on a C+C rationale are presented. Also, in this course students develop the ability to analyse exercises in school textbooks in a principled way, based on cognitive and communicative criteria, and to design their own teaching materials.

7 Summary

This chapter has been largely concerned with the question of grammatical description. However, it should be noted that the C+C model also provides a comprehensive theoretical framework for language learning, loosely based on Anderson's (1983, 1990) stage model of language processing and learning. O'Malley and Chamot (1990: 217) state that according to a cognitive view, '[l]earning a language entails a stagewise progression from initial awareness and active manipulation of information and learning processes to full automaticity in language use'. The learning stages identified in the C+C model of 'awareness,' 'conceptualisation,' 'proceduralisation' and 'performance' provide a useful and powerful tool for students to analyse grammar exercises and activities in terms of how they might contribute to learning and, moreover, to design their own activities.

References

Achard, M. and Niemeier, S. (2004) *Cognitive Linguistics, Second Language Acquisition, and Foreign Language Teaching*. Berlin: Walter de Gruyter.
Anderson, J.R. (1983) *The Architecture of Cognition*. Cambridge, MA: Harvard University Press.
Anderson, J.R. (1990) *Cognitive Psychology and its Implications* (3rd edn). New York: W.H. Freeman and Company.

Birdsong, D. (2004) Second language acquisition and ultimate attainment. In A. Davies and C. Elder (eds) *The Handbook of Applied Linguistics* (pp. 82–105). Oxford: Blackwell Publishing.
Brown, G. and Yule, G. (1983) *Discourse Analysis*. Cambridge: Cambridge University Press.
Canale, M. and Swain, M. (1980) Theoretical bases of communicative approaches to second language teaching and testing. *Applied Linguistics* 1, 1–47.
Chalker, S. (1994) Pedagogical grammar: Principles and problems. In M. Bygate, A. Tonkyn and E. Williams (eds) *Grammar and the Language Teacher* (pp. 31–44). Hemel Hempstead: Prentice Hall.
Council of Europe (2001) *Common European Framework of Reference for Languages: Learning, Teaching, Assessment*. Strasbourg: Council of Europe, Modern Languages Division/ Cambridge: Cambridge University Press.
Croft, W. and Cruse, D.A. (2004) *Cognitive Linguistics*. Cambridge: Cambridge University Press.
Dekeyser, R.M. (ed.) (2007) *Practice in a Second Language: Perspectives from Applied Linguistics and Cognitive Psychology*. Cambridge: Cambridge University Press.
De Kop, S. and De Rycker, T. (2008) *Cognitive Approaches to Pedagogical Grammar*. Berlin: Walter de Gruyter.
Dirven, R. (1990) Pedagogical grammar: State of the art article. *Language Teaching* 23, 1–18.
Doff, A., Jones, C. and Mitchell, K. (1983) *Meanings into Words*. Cambridge: Cambridge University Press.
Fenner, A.B. and Newby, D. (eds) (2006) *Coherence of Principles, Cohesion of Competences: Exploring Theories and Designing Materials for Teacher Education*. Graz/Strasbourg: European Centre for Modern Languages/Council of Europe Press.
Fillmore, C.J. (1985) Frames and the semantics of understanding. *Quaderni di semantica* 6, 222–254.
Gaskell, E. (1975) *The Life of Charlotte Brontë*. Harmondsworth: Penguin Books.
Halliday, M.A.K. (1978) *Language As a Social Semiotic. The Social Interpretation of Language and Meaning*. London: Edward Arnold.
Halliday, M.A.K. (1985) *An Introduction to Functional Grammar*. London: Edward Arnold.
Halliday, M.A.K. and Matthiessen, C.M.I.M. (1999) *Construing Experience Through Meaning: A Language-Based Approach to Cognition*. London: Cassell.
Heindler, D., Huber, R., Kuebel, G., Newby, D., Schuch, A., Sornig, K. and Wohofsky, H. (1993) *Your Ticket to English*. Vienna: Österreichischer Bundesverlag.
Hinkel, E. and Fotos, S. (eds) (2002) *New Perspectives on Grammar Teaching in Second Language Classrooms*. New York: Lawrence Erlbaum Associates.
Holme, R. (2009) *Cognitive Linguistics and Language Teaching*. Basingstoke: Palgrave Macmillan.
Hymes, D.H. (1964) Toward ethnographies of communicative events. In P.P. Giglioli (ed.) *Language and Social Context* (pp. 21–44). Harmondsworth: Penguin Books.
Hymes, D.H. (1972) On communicative competence. In J.B. Pride and J. Holmes (eds) *Sociolinguistics* (pp. 269–293). Harmondsworth: Penguin Books.
Jackendoff, R. (1983) *Semantics and Cognition*. Cambridge, MA: MIT Press.
Jackendoff, R. (2002) *Foundations of Language*. Oxford: Oxford University Press.
Johnson, K. (1996) *Language Teaching and Skill Learning*. Oxford: Blackwell.
Langacker, R.W. (1987) *Foundations of Cognitive Grammar, Vol. I: Theoretical Prerequisites*. Stanford, CA: Stanford University Press.
Lee, D. (2001) *Cognitive Linguistics: An Introduction*. Oxford: Oxford University Press.

Littlemore, J. (2009) *Applying Cognitive Linguistics to Second Language Learning and Teaching.* Basingstoke: Palgrave MacMillan.

Long, M. H. (2000) Acquisition and teaching. In M. Byram (ed.) *Routledge Encyclopedia of Language Teaching and Learning* (pp. 4–5). London: Routledge.

Minsky, M. (1975) A framework for representing knowledge. In P.H. Winston (ed.) *The Psychology of Computer Vision* (pp. 211–277). New York: McGraw-Hill.

Newby, D. (1989) *Grammar for Communication.* Vienna: Österreichischer Bundesverlag.

Newby, D. (1991) A notional grammar of tense and aspect. Unpublished doctoral thesis, Karl-Franzens Universität Graz.

Newby, D. (1992) *Grammar for Communication: Exercises and Creative Activities.* Vienna: Österreichischer Bundesverlag.

Newby, D. (2002) A cognitive+communicative theory of pedagogical grammar. Unpublished Habilitationsschrift, Karl-Franzens Universität Graz.

Newby, D. (2008) Pedagogical grammar: A cognitive+communicative approach. In W. Delanoy and L. Volkmann (eds) *Future Perspectives for English Language Teaching* (pp. 29–44). Heidelberg: Universitätsverlag Winter.

Newby, D. (forthcoming) Competence and performance in learning and teaching: Theories and practices. In *Proceedings of the 19th International Symposium on Theoretical and Applied Linguistics,* Aristotle University of Thessaloniki, Greece.

O'Malley, J.M. and Chamot, A. (1990) *Learning Strategies in Second Language Acquisition.* Cambridge: Cambridge University Press.

Richards, J., Platt, J. and Weber, H. (1985) *Longman Dictionary of Applied Linguistics.* Harlow: Longman.

Richards, J.C. and Rodgers, T.S. (2001) *Approaches and Methods in Language Learning.* Cambridge: Cambridge University Press.

Robinson, P. (ed.) (2001) *Cognition and Second Language Instruction.* Cambridge: Cambridge University Press.

Robinson, P. and Ellis, N.C. (eds) (2008) *Handbook of Cognitive Linguistics and Second Language Acquisition.* New York: Routledge.

Skehan, P. (1998) *A Cognitive Approach to Language Learning.* Oxford: Oxford University Press.

Swan, M. (1994) Design criteria for pedagogical grammars. In M. Bygate, A. Tonkyn and E. Williams (eds) *Grammar and the Language Teacher* (pp. 45–55). Hemel Hempstead: Prentice Hall.

Swan, M. and Walter, C. (1997) *How English Works.* Oxford: Oxford University Press.

Ungerer, F. and Schmid, H.J. (1996) *An Introduction to Cognitive Linguistics.* Harlow: Addison Wesley Longman.

van Ek, J.A. (1977) *The Threshold Level for Modern Language Learning in Schools.* London: Longman.

van Ek, J.A. and Trim, J.L.M. (1991) *Threshold Level 1990.* Strasbourg: Council of Europe Press.

Widdowson, H.G. (1990) *Aspects of Language Teaching.* Oxford: Oxford University Press.

Widdowson, H.G. (1998) The conditions of contextual meaning. In K. Malmkjaer and J. Williams (eds) *Context in Language Learning and Language Understanding.* Cambridge: Cambridge University Press.

Widdowson, H.G. (2003) Expert beyond experience: Notes on the appropriate use of theory in practice. In. D. Newby (ed.) *Mediating between Theory and Practice in the Context of Different Learning Cultures and Languages* (pp. 23–30). Strasbourg/Graz: Council of Europe Press.

Wilkins, D. (1976) *Notional Syllabuses.* Oxford: Oxford University Press.

Appendix: Grammar as a Speech Event

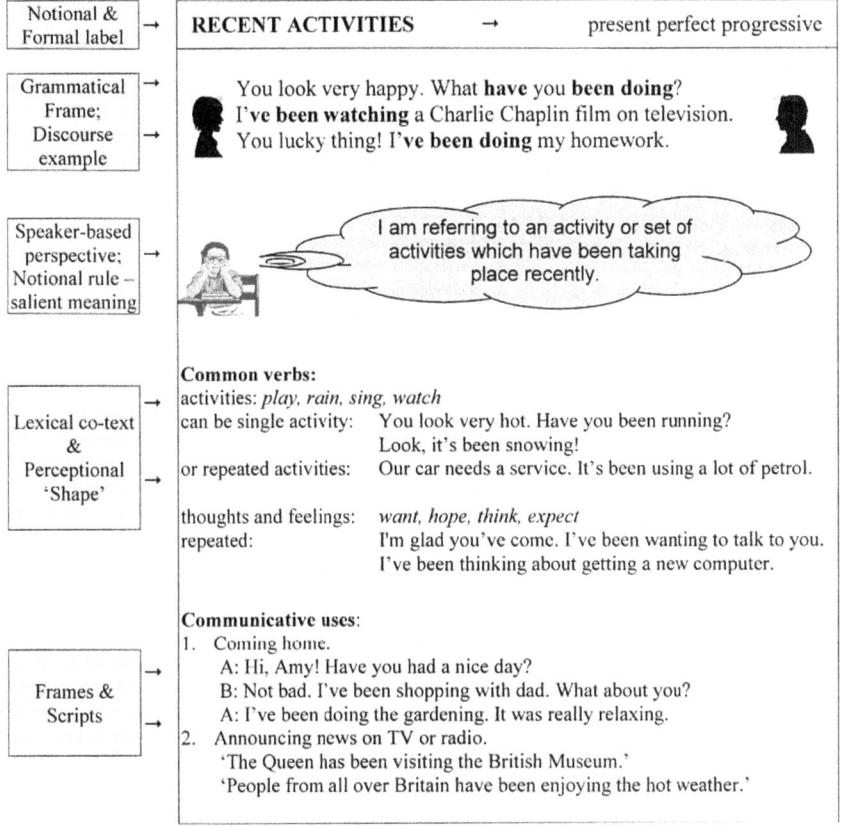

Source: adapted from *Grammar for Communication* (Newby, 1989: 89)

7 Towards a Stronger Intervention: The Role of Literature in Teacher Education
Susanne Reichl

1 Introduction

When it comes to the bridging of gaps between theory and practice that this collection is after, the gap that I have personally identified as one of the most urgent for my work concerns the teaching of literature. As a teacher educator specialising in literature, I have noticed that the student teachers I teach are very critical of the apparent discrepancy between what they are taught in their literature classes and what they perceive as relevant for their future teaching practice. In this chapter I will therefore explore the potential of literature for teacher education. I will start out by discussing some conceptual issues, such as the role of content and pedagogical content knowledge and the way that theory and practice can be seen from a constructivist perspective. I will subsequently discuss the function of literature in the EFL classroom and some suggestions for a more integrative teaching practice within teacher education at the university. As Korthagen *et al.* have recently stressed, 'teacher education [...] only impacts on students if the total ecology of the teacher preparation program is coherently constructed and purposefully conducted' (2005: 107). Taking my cue from this notion of curricular coherence and integration, I will focus on the potential of literature classes to engender reflection on both theory and practice and to strengthen connections between different types of knowledge. There is potential, I claim, for initiating transformative processes that respect what student teachers bring to the learning process and are aimed at their future teaching practice, and my suggestions will attempt to support this claim.

Throughout this chapter, I will be guided by the contextual and institutional constraints of my specific teaching situation and the conviction that, even within structures that are far from ideal, a stronger nexus between subject knowledge and the envisaged teaching practice of student teachers can be established. My aim is to show how this might be achieved in literature classes.

The general framework for my view of learning and teaching is a social constructivist one, based on the notion that individuals learn by constructing their own meanings through negotiating their cognitive resources and new input in social settings (cf. Richardson, 1997: 3). The focus is on the construction of new meaning, on new understandings. This informs my view of the use of literature in the classroom as being guided by a meaning-making paradigm on the one hand (see Section 4 of this chapter), and it frames teacher education as a process of meaning-making, of constructing knowledge, attitudes and values, and of continuously negotiating the old and the new, on the other hand. The focus on meaning construction that is at the heart of a constructivist approach is therefore also at the core of my understanding of the role of literature in teacher education.

2 The Context of Teacher Education at the University of Vienna

For the following arguments, it is helpful to have a little insight into the specific institutional and curricular context that teacher education is embedded in at the English department of the University of Vienna.[1] Student teachers are required to study two school subjects as academic disciplines, and in addition to those, they have to follow a general pedagogical education. The model of teacher education that is currently in operation at the English department at Vienna University could be described as an 'applied science model', following the classification suggested by Wallace (1991: 8): classes focus on teaching methodology, linguistics, literature, cultural studies and language proficiency. The methodology classes and a practice period allow for an element of reflection to enter the learning process. Otherwise, the teaching approach in the subject content classes follows very much a transmission model: the experts in linguistics, literature and cultural studies pass on disciplinary knowledge from their individual research areas, and any connection with a possible teaching practice needs to be established by the students themselves, often at a point in time when they have not yet had any teaching practice at all. It is left to the teaching methodology courses to encourage integration, reflection, and the vital connections between individual fields of teacher knowledge. Except for the methodology classes, all classes are also attended by students aiming for a BA or an MA in English and American studies[2] and most of them are not specifically conceptualised with the target group of future teachers of EFL in mind. This is not necessarily a local characteristic of the Viennese curriculum for students of English, but seems to be a more widespread conception:

> In general, LTE [language teacher education] has been grounded in the dominant technical-rational discourse of teacher education, which maintains that language teaching expertise can be acquired through content-based courses followed by a practicum or school attachment. (Singh & Richards, 2009: 201)

There is plenty that one could argue for and against the prevailing structure, and with an impending new curriculum for future teachers, following a BA and MA structure, these issues will have to be debated anew in the not too distant future. For the purposes of this chapter, though, I will base my assumptions on the current status quo, i.e. on a curriculum that, for its larger part, consists of classes that do not explicitly consider future teachers as their learner target group. By using the word 'explicitly', I want to stress that many of my colleagues are highly aware of the fact that more than half of the students in their classes will be teachers of English, and will undoubtedly take this fact into consideration in their planning of classes or their choice of material. What is missing, however, is a principled way of integrating content knowledge and teaching methodology and a way of creating time and space to reflect on an envisaged teaching practice. This leads to the question of the role of subject knowledge, or content knowledge, in teacher education, and its relationship to more pedagogically relevant types of knowledge.

Shulman, in his 1987 key article, argued for a knowledge-based model of teacher education and devised a categorisation of types of knowledge relevant for teaching, of which I want to focus on only two: content knowledge and pedagogical content knowledge (PCK), the latter defined as 'that special amalgam of content and pedagogy that is uniquely the province of teachers, their own special form of professional understanding' (Shulman, 1987/2004: 92), and as

> the blending of content and pedagogy into an understanding of how particular topics, problems, or issues are organized, represented and adapted to the diverse interests and abilities of learners, and presented for instruction. (Shulman, 1987/2004: 93)

Taking my cue from Shulman, who was keen to point out that the precise categorisation was not the main purpose of his argument (see the criticism by Ball *et al.*, 2008: 389-392; van Dijk & Kattmann, 2007: 889), I will ignore the finer distinctions between the two types of knowledge and instead focus on the basic differences between content knowledge and pedagogical content knowledge, which Ball *et al.* have illustrated for mathematics like this: '[o]ne need only to sit in a classroom for a few minutes to notice that the mathematics that teachers work with in instruction is not the same mathematics taught and learned in college classes' (2008: 404). Along the same lines, for foreign-language learning, Freeman and Johnson (1998) criticised teacher education for pretending that the

> disciplinary knowledge that defines what language is, how it is used, and how it is acquired [...] is the same knowledge that teachers use to teach the L2 and that, in turn, is the same knowledge that students need in order to learn the L2. (quoted in Johnson, 2009b: 22)

With regard to literature as part of the EFL classroom, a teacher's PCK would include issues such as pedagogical canon formation, the ways in which texts can be introduced in an EFL classroom, questions of matching text with task and learner or the ways in which learners can be motivated for certain tasks to do with literature. From this random list it becomes clear that PCK is indeed an amalgamation of various types of knowledge from general pedagogical and methodological areas as well as literature-specific knowledge or competence. The content knowledge that is taught as part of the teacher education curriculum, however, often has little or nothing to do with these realms of knowledge. If we want to close this particular gap, we need to consider the possible transformation processes between the various types of knowledge. I will suggest ways of doing this in literature classes below.

For any exploration of the potential closing of gaps between theory and practice and the transformational processes between the two, it needs to be quite clear just what is meant by practice and its relevant theory. In the following I will attempt to clarify that and provide a possibly idiosyncratic conceptualisation of practice and theory for the purposes of this chapter.

3 Conceptualising 'Practice' and 'Theory' in Pre-service Teacher Education

As Lampert (2010) demonstrates, 'practice' in connection with teacher education can encompass a multitude of meanings. For the purposes of this chapter, 'practice' is not understood as the actual teaching practice of in-service teachers or that of pre-service teachers in their practicum stages.

Rather, following a constructivist paradigm, it is understood as a subjective construct, a mental representation that student teachers create of their future work of teaching while still at university (see Roberts, 1998: 23). In my experience, student teachers, even before they have done any kind of teaching practice, often voice with certainty their ideas of what they will be doing in their teaching practice and judge what they learn in their classes by this yardstick.

Do we need to take this subjective notion of practice into account? I would argue that we do, and support this claim by recent research in teacher cognition, which analyses teachers' and student teachers' knowledge, values, biographies and personal theories. This research is led by the conviction that a student teacher, when s/he comes to teacher education, is not a tabula rasa but brings along a number of conceptions and attitudes that need to be considered in her/his education if it wants to have any effect at all. As Korthagen has argued,

> teachers have spent many years as students in schools, during which time they have developed their own beliefs about teaching, many of which are diametrically opposed to those presented to them in teacher education. (Korthagen, 2004: 81)

Similarly, Dan Lortie's often quoted 'apprenticeship of observation' does not only argue from a quantitative perspective – he claims that an average graduate has spent up to 13.000 hours in the presence of teachers – but also stresses how this consists of meaningful relationships that involve emotion, power and the adoption of particular roles in the process (Lortie, 1975: 61-62).

Beliefs and attitudes, then, that students construct during their time as learners in both secondary and higher education translate into a sense of what their teaching practice might look like. This conception of practice usually surfaces in the negative, when students voice their belief that a text, a topic or a whole class might not be relevant for their teaching practice. Evidently, this is a highly unreliable and idiosyncratic construct, but it is prominent in conversations that I have had with students, and clearly informs their developing identities as student teachers.

Students' conceptualisations, according to Borg (2009: 164), can be fairly persistent and will change gradually rather than promptly through instruction. Borg draws our attention to the fact that, in the literature, pre-service or initial teacher education is often seen as 'a weak intervention' (2006: 40, 62), and that the evidence of the studies on the effect of teacher education is inconclusive, owing to the diversity of contexts and methods used. Following a constructivist view of learning, teacher education logically only has a chance of making an impact if it is based on student teachers' beliefs and values (cf. Borg, 2006: 53). One step towards a stronger intervention seems to me to be a consideration of student teachers' construction of practice.

In the same way that I define 'practice' as a student teacher construct, I suggest regarding 'theory' similarly from the student teachers' perspective. As someone who is involved in teacher education both as a methodology teacher and as a teacher of a subject discipline (i.e. literature), I have found that students tend to categorise what they learn in literature classes as 'theory'. This has nothing to do with the theory of language teaching or language learning, or indeed with literary theory, but with a sense of theory as 'non-practice'. Student teachers seem to construct a binary of theory and practice, and categorise everything that does not fit into their concept of practice as theoretical, i.e. non-practical, non-applied and non-practice-oriented.

The suggestions for bridging the gap between theory and practice in teacher education in Section 5 of this chapter will be based on this binary and will concentrate on how it can be 'bridged' in the literature classroom at university.

4 The Role of Literature in the EFL Classroom

In order to argue with any confidence for the place of literature classes in a teacher education curriculum, we need to be clear of the role that literature plays in the EFL classroom at secondary level. The curricula for the Austrian type of grammar schools (see bm:ukk, 2009) occasionally suggest literary texts explicitly, but most of the time refers to them as one text type or medium among others, such as film or newspaper articles. The position of literature in the curriculum for secondary schools, then, would not in itself justify the prominent role that literature plays in the curriculum for teacher education. Therefore, we need to turn to research into language teaching to support any claims that might be made for the role of literature in the secondary classroom and, as a consequence, the teacher education curriculum. As so often in language-teaching research, the diversity of contexts makes it impossible to overgeneralise on how literature is best used in ELT. Rather, we are presented with a number of arguments that reflect a particular practice and a particular context.

Many experts in the field have written about the benefits and, occasionally, the risks of teaching literature in the foreign language classroom (for two recent reviews, see Carter, 2007; Paran, 2008; for a historical overview, see Kramsch & Kramsch, 2000). From Ur's careful recommendations (1996: 201-202) to Edmondson's rather sweeping polemic against the use of literary texts (1995/96), the arguments, rather than spelling out any reliable evidence for or against literature as such, seem to reflect good or bad practice. As Paran has recently concluded in a review article (2008: 473ff.), the few empirical studies that have been conducted in the field of teaching literature at secondary level indicate that it is the role of the teacher and the kind of task that is set that determine whether literature in the classroom manages to fulfil the learning aims it is expected to. From the studies that Paran reviews, it becomes obvious that a teacher-centred and authoritative approach does not seem to work well with students, whereas when students feel they have more agency in the reading process, the response turns out to be much better (2008: 475). From what is known about learning and the roles of learners and teachers, this should not surprise us much. So, rather than ask whether literature should or should not be used in the classroom as such, then, I will reframe my question as follows: all things being equal, what are the potential learning and teaching aims that literature can fulfil in a foreign language classroom? Also, in what conditions can a literary text unfold the potential that it is often ascribed? I would argue that a literary text lends itself to other learning aims than a non-literary one. In more concrete terms, if a learner is motivated to engage and empathise with a text, the individual perspective on, say, an example of a cultural clash can promote intercultural learning in a way that, say, a newspaper article, an information leaflet for immigrants or a passage from a travel guide, genres that do not usually promote the same kind of identification processes, might not. The clue, however, seems to lie in the practice, not so much in the principle.

The main argument for literature that is often found in the theory is a motivational one: a literary text can be a motivator in itself, as can be seen in the examples of the *Harry Potter* or the *Twilight* series, phenomenally successful novels that caused many young readers to attempt their first extended reading experience in a foreign language because they did not want to wait for the translated versions. In turn, the perceived success of reading a whole novel in a foreign language works as a motivator to read more (see, e.g. De Florio-Hansen, 2003; Hesse, 1997; Küppers, 2001; Weskamp, 2000). In close connection with this, the potential of literature to create empathy, evoke emotional responses and start identification processes in the reader has also been commented on in the literature (e.g. Halász, 1983/1993: 10–11; Holland, 1968: 277-278; Oatley, 1999: 445;

Schneider, 2000: 106-107; Seilman, 1990: 327; Silvia, 2005). With both motivation and empathy, there is no guarantee that the reader will actually feel the anticipated response to any given text. As Edmondson (1995/96: 44) has pointed out, these processes often fall flat, an observation made on the basis of their own experiences with literary texts as learners at the secondary level themselves by many of my students. If these processes do work, however, several language-learning aims can be fulfilled: apart from the very obvious function of promoting extensive reading skills (e.g. Bamford & Day, 2004; Day & Bamford, 1998), literature can promote such learning outcomes as vocabulary acquisition or the recognition of stylistic variety (see Ur, 1996: 201). In this respect, literature works just like other text types, but the learning processes benefit, no doubt, from increased motivation and emotional responses to literary texts.

What, then, are literary texts especially good at for language learners? Kramsch has suggested that literary texts promote a particularly individual kind of understanding: she advocates the use of literature in the EFL classroom because it has 'the ability to represent the particular voice of a writer among the many voices of his or her community, and thus to appeal to the particular in the reader' (Kramsch, 1993: 131). This appeal is not simply an aesthetic or an empathic one; it extends to the area of language learning. The particular voice is one that always strives to articulate itself in its subjectivity: especially fiction for children and teenage readers often revolves around issues of identity formation, growing up or leaving home. The learners can learn, first, to understand a particular voice, its position, perspective, motivation and ideology, and, second, to articulate similar concerns about belonging, growing up and other problems, by using this voice as a means to try out and develop their own.

Literary texts, because they represent particular voices, are ideal for teaching learners about perspective, point of view and ideological position. Especially novels that provide a dialogic experience (see Delanoy, 2008), like *Noughts and Crosses*, in which the same story is narrated from two points of view, can be used to teach students about the contingencies of a subject position, about the individuality of such an experience and about a critical attitude towards the printed word.

What literature is also particularly good at, and I see this as its major asset, is to demonstrate the active role the reader has in the meaning-making process. This provides for endless opportunities for the development of meaning-making skills and strategies in the classroom. Literature is characterised by a potential plurality of meaning that tends to be greater than with a non-literary text, or, in Carter's (1996: 12) words, it 'actively promotes a process of interpretation and [...] encourages a pleasurable interaction with and negotiation of its meanings' (see also Christmann & Schreier, 2003: 272). This meaning potential that is inherent in literature does not have to be seen as something very intellectual or only accessible for very advanced learners who can make use of the metalanguage of literary analysis. We can think of 'meaning-making' as ways of arriving at a personal, subjective meaning, one that does not necessarily need to be articulated. In order to make sense of a picture book like Donaldson and Scheffler's *The Gruffalo* (1999) or Maurice Sendak's classic *Where the Wild Things Are* (1963/91), young learners need to negotiate the fictional nature of the gruffalo or the wild things, figure out the possibility of Max dreaming about the wild things and question maybe why all the animals (including gruffalo and wild things) speak the same language. This, in combination with affective responses (fun, fear, excitement and solidarity with the mouse), results in a meaning that young learners will not be able to articulate in the foreign language, but that engages them in the process of meaning-making in a foreign language.

While stories about wild things and gruffalos might not be the most realistic ones, they do resort to a variety of world schemata that the individual reader brings to the text, such as meeting and greeting people, recognising others, inviting them for a meal or travelling, and these will help him/her understand the text. In the case of picture books, the images aid comprehension, of course, but the same principle applies in school stories from Enid Blyton to the *Harry Potter* series, or any other genre that young readers are familiar with. Readers learn to apply and develop their schematic knowledge in order to understand a text in a foreign language, while at the same time, their range of world schemata is broadened and so, in turn, is their linguistic repertoire.

The function of literature to encourage meaning-making processes is not simply an individual one but an intersubjective one as well. This means that negotiation in a community of readers requires a certain level of language competence, but at the same time provides ample opportunity for the use of a number of discourses in the classroom. Any number of suggestions of how such intersubjective meaning-making activities could be designed in the classroom have been made, ranging from more analytical discussions to the use of creative methods (see, e.g. Nünning & Surkamp, 2006: 65-68). This area of meaning negotiation is where the students' and the teacher's values and beliefs about the function of literature, his/her attitude towards the meaning of a literary text, matter the most and might decide over the success or failure of the use of literature in the classroom.

Whether the benefits of using a literary text call for a conceptualisation of a literary text as a qualitatively different text type, e.g. compared to a newspaper article, which engenders different reception or learning processes in the learner, or whether literature basically has the same effect on the reader as a blog, an article or an informative passage in a coursebook, is a moot point and its answer would require a lengthy discussion into the nature of literature. From a practical view, I would argue that a literary text has the potential, in ideal circumstances, to help reach some language-learning aims faster, more easily or simply with more engagement. How, then, can teacher education cater to the various functions that literature can fulfil in the classroom, especially its meaning-making potential, and how can teacher education research help make the connections between theory and practice apparent?

5 A Way of Bridging the Gap? Reflection in Literature Classes at University

Educational research over the past 20 years has, among other things, provided us with a revised notion of learning and teaching that has at its core the learner's cognitive constructions, her/his attitudes, values, knowledge and personal theories. Based on this, teacher education programmes have begun to place more value on the role of reflection, reflective tasks and reflective practice. Reflection in its broadest sense is one way of facilitating the transformation of content knowledge into pedagogical content knowledge and, as I will argue, can provide for a more integrated curriculum for teacher education.

Research into teacher cognition over the past years has investigated the bundle of influences that makes teachers who they are and what they do (see Johnson, 2009a: 10, Johnson, 2009b: 20), or, in Simon Borg's words, 'the beliefs, knowledge, theories, assumptions and attitudes that teachers hold about all aspects of their work' (2006: 49). Among other things, it has been suggested that it is teachers' values, beliefs and attitudes that inform their teaching practice above all. Viv Ellis (2007) has pointed out the importance of what Banks *et al.*, have called 'personal subject construct' and defined as a 'complex amalgam of past knowledge, experiences of learning, a personal view of what constitutes "good" teaching and belief in the purposes of the subject' (Banks *et al.*, 1999: 95-96; see Ellis, 2007: 47 for a similar definition). Borg, in a review of research into pre-service teachers' cognition, stresses that teacher learning happens 'through the interaction between what trainees bring to a teacher education programme and the experiences and content they encounter on it', and warns that 'ignoring the former is likely to hinder the internalisation by teachers of new ideas they are exposed to and practices they are encouraged to adopt' (Borg, 2006: 54).

Beliefs of all kinds have long played a part in teacher education. Shulman, for instance, includes the following in a long list of what a teacher of English needs to know:

> The teacher also communicates, whether consciously or not, ideas about the ways in which 'truth' is determined in a field and a set of attitudes and values that markedly influence student understanding. This responsibility places special demands on the teacher's own depth of understanding of the structures of the subject matter, as well as on the teacher's attitudes towards and enthusiasm for what is being taught and learned. (Shulman, 1987/2004: 94)

These 'ideas' about literary truths, for instance, reflect for me a belief that relates to the discipline that student teachers need to study but also to the subject they will be teaching. Whereas Borg's 'beliefs' have more to do with pedagogy and methodology, Shulman's 'ideas' concern the place of the subject or discipline within the curriculum and how meaning (or 'truth') is produced, something that for the teaching of literature is very important. It is plausible that beliefs relating to either language teaching or the role of literature interact and work in the same way: they form a crucial basis of learning for the student teachers and need to be addressed and made explicit.

> If we accept the contemporary constructivist position that teacher learning occurs through interactions between prior knowledge on the one hand and new input and experience on the other, ignoring pre-service teachers' prior cognitions is likely to hinder their ability to internalize new material. This is particularly true when these prior understandings of teaching are inappropriate, unrealistic, or naive. For this reason, acknowledging, making explicit, and examining trainees [sic] prior cognitions is an important part of pre-service teacher education. (Borg, 2009: 164)

Implicit beliefs, once made explicit in ways that I will suggest below, provide a first basis on which reflection can take place, even before students' first practice period. The role of reflection in teacher education has long been acknowledged, with a focus on in-service rather than pre-service reflection, and based on the influential work by Dewey (1910) and by Schön (1983) (e.g. Beck & Kosnik, 2006; Burns & Richards, 2009; Burton, 2009;

Farrell, 2007; Postholm, 2008).³ Jon Roberts (1998), summing up the work of a number of thinkers in the area of reflective language teaching, categorises various kinds of reflection by their function and highlights the importance of reflection in pre-service teacher education, as does Jill Burton (2009: 298), who adds that 'it is still not possible to demonstrate precisely what teachers do when being reflective' (2009: 303). Roberts (1998: 53) concedes that reflection is a rather vague term, ranging from self-assessment to casually thinking about one's attitudes towards teaching. To Schön's concepts of 'reflection-in-action' and 'reflection-on-action' (1987; see Farrell, 2007: 4-5), Farrell has added 'reflection-for-action', which is 'proactive in nature' and orientated towards future situations (2007: 6). For the purposes of this chapter, this latter concept seems particularly useful. The kind of proactive reflection that I propose in the following builds on students' constructions of practice (see Section 3) and is more comprehensive in nature than Farrell's suggestion. Rather than restrict itself to students' experiences with language learning and teaching, this kind of reflection is also based on students' own experiences with and attitudes towards reading literature. This bringing together of two different types of reflective thinking has the advantage of providing a broader basis of attitudes, beliefs and experiences that eases the reflective process, and of creating an awareness in students that what they learn at university becomes relevant for their future profession.

With literature, what are these prior cognitions, the values and beliefs that can be valuably reflected on 'for action' and hopefully promote the development of pedagogical content knowledge? We might look at the potential for reflection in literary studies in terms of the WHAT and the HOW of literature, or, in other words, the selection of literary texts and the way that literary texts should or might be dealt with in the classroom. Starting with the WHAT, the selection of texts, one might begin with the kind of literature that student teachers had to read at school. This can take a variety of forms, depending on the class size and type of class, but the main aim is to find out what students experienced as language learners, to draw attention to the fact that this is an experience that will influence their own learning at university and their teaching at secondary level and to alert students to the relevant pedagogical, political, practical and other contingencies of the choices made.

Let us assume as an example that student teachers attend a class on children's literature and are confronted with a reading list of 15 novels to read within a term. For practical reasons to do with timing and the availability of the books, they have not been involved in the pedagogical canon formation that preceded the choice. The teacher now has the opportunity to invite reflection by sharing the generic, historical, gender, national or pedagogical criteria that made him/her arrive at this particular choice and the chain of decisions that eventually resulted in the reading list.[4] This way, student teachers can broaden and integrate their content knowledge, i.e. the theoretical issues of canon formation, with the pedagogical aspects, as well as activate their knowledge of some of the material used, and can see the processes that are involved in pedagogical canon formation at work, processes that they will have to go through in their later teaching careers. Also, this brings in one of the many possible functions of reflection that Roberts has identified: 'become aware of the social and political significance of one's work' (1998: 58) and makes it relevant for the teaching of literature. The discussion of a canon of English literature will inevitably introduce the question of world Englishes, of the postcolonial world and its vast literary production, and of the ideological implications of canon formation. This should raise awareness in the student teachers that the language they are learning and are going to teach is not an 'innocent' language, that it used to be the language of colonialism, and that even today we encounter many examples of colonial and postcolonial discourses and structures. In this respect, too, if student teachers are invited to share and reflect on the teacher educators' decision-making processes, they are more likely to reflect on the way they experienced this at school and on similar choices in their future teaching lives.

I would argue that the way that literature is read and understood, the HOW of literary reading, lends itself very well to the extended kind of reflection that I propose above, in which literature and teaching issues inform the reflective process. The main role of literature that I pointed out in Section 4 is that of a generator of meaning production, and a literary text can be used to demonstrate the agency that the individual learner or reader has in the process. It is evident that a student teacher who is convinced of, say, authorial intention as the only clue to a text's inherent meaning is unlikely to use literature for the purposes of fostering active meaning-making processes in the classroom. Conversely, a student teacher who has reflected on these issues and has experienced the reader's agency in creating meaning from a literary text him- or herself is more likely to adopt such a constructivist paradigm in the EFL classroom as well.

How can such attitudes towards literature be brought to light? Reflective autobiographical writing is one suitable tool for bringing out implicit theories and beliefs (see Borg, 2006: 257-262; Burton, 2009: 303-304) and, at the same time, is easily incorporated in a literature course, which often resorts to reading journals or diaries anyway. One way of engaging student teachers in writing about their assumptions about the reading of literary texts is to ask them to write a short personal piece on their experiences with literature and reading so far. These instructions are intentionally open to allow for very idiosyncratic approaches to the question (see Reichl, 2009: 221-224 for an analysis of metaphors of reading in students' journals). The teacher educator can gain insight into implicit assumptions and challenge those either through written dialogue (if the medium is a dialogue journal) or through class discussion or activities (see Reichl, 2009: 226-235 for some awareness-raising activities).

A questionnaire would be another tool to find out about student teachers' attitudes and beliefs, and one that can be used even in larger classes. Especially with beginning student teachers, questionnaires can reveal interesting attitudes and give the teacher educator a chance to comment on student teachers' beliefs in class and to adjust the activities and instructions accordingly. An example comes from a questionnaire that I asked beginning students to fill in after the first half of an introductory course in English literature and that was mainly aimed at finding out about students' main problems with texts and their sense of agency and problem-solving capacities (for details, see Reichl, 2009: 192-193 and 247). It contained the question '[d]id you find any of the texts particularly difficult to understand?', which most students answered, rather globally, with 'poems' and 'Shakespeare'. The next question asked was '[w]hat about the text did you find difficult to understand and why do you think it was?' Here, students on the whole displayed very little awareness of problem-solving strategies and a generally very passive notion of reading, with little responsibility on their part to solve problems, as well as a great reliance on the teacher to provide solutions. One student, for instance, answered '[w]ell, they are poems. I think poems are often difficult to understand' and in response to the next question, '[w]hat would have helped you to understand the text better?', the answer was 'no idea. Maybe if I had spent more time on it.' In the following classes, I could not only discuss these underlying assumptions, but could also make sure to focus more on concrete reading strategies that showed students their agency in the meaning-making process.

As an anecdote, I would like to report an episode in a lecture on children's literature that shows how the attitudes towards literary reading and those more closely related to teaching merge in practice: in a discussion of the *Harry Potter* series, one of my students suggested that the character of Dumbledore was quite obviously homosexual. Most of the other students disagreed, and in the ensuing discussion, students said things like 'but it's in the book', 'but Rowling said so herself', or 'of course he is not gay, it's a children's book'. I then interrupted the discussion and confronted them with what they claimed as evidence for 'true' meaning. This gave me a chance to remind students of some basic concepts in literary studies, such as intentional fallacy or the overreliance on text-inherent meaning. Here again, students had a chance to contradict (and reflect on their beliefs and personal theories about literary meaning), and I had a chance to demonstrate that a reader has much more agency in the reading process if he/she does not need to speculate on authorial intention or the exact inherent meaning of a text, and that this made a crucial difference to their notion of reading and, later, teaching literature.

6 Conclusion and Outlook

Literature is part of the education for teachers of English as a foreign language in Austria, and it seems to me to be a very valuable part. But literature has, in the past, been taught in the teacher education programme at university with a view to an accumulation of knowledge about periods, text types and formal analysis, with less regard to the processes involved in meaning-making or to beliefs about where meaning can be located. It is these processes that make literature so valuable for the EFL classroom, and unless some trace of it can be found at university, student teachers are unlikely to make any connections between the 'theory' they have been taught at university and their conception of practice.

Teacher education research, however, has provided us with insights and approaches that can be fruitfully taken up by teacher educators across the curriculum. By inquiring into student teachers' cognitions, providing opportunities for reflection and sharing pedagogical decisions with students, the necessary connections can be established between content knowledge and pedagogical content knowledge. My suggestions do not only work for literature classes, of course, but may equally be applied to other fields. This would produce a more interconnected curriculum, would give student teachers the opportunity to identify larger portions of their studies with their future profession and might eventually lead to a point at which pre-service teacher education at university is no longer a 'weak intervention'. Indeed, the benefits of such an approach can be far-reaching: if student teachers are introduced to this kind of reflection outside their methodology classes, too, they might understand it as an integral part of a teacher's professional identity, and are more likely to develop from reflective student to reflective teacher, which is one of the prime goals in teacher education.

Despite this optimism, a few caveats are due: the first regards the feasibility of a great amount of reflection in literature classrooms. Roberts points out the importance of a positive setting for reflection to take place generally (1998: 59), and this might not always be achieved in a literature classroom in which students know they are eventually going to be assessed. Moreover, not all university teachers of English literature see themselves as teacher educators, and since teaching qualifications at university are only beginning to matter (see Schendl, 2006: 262), it is indeed possible for university teachers not to be particularly interested in teacher education or teaching itself, even at a tertiary level.

Another argument to hold against my suggestions is that student teachers should be receiving all these opportunities for reflection in their methodology classes rather than their content-knowledge classes, and that there are usually between one-third and one-half of students in the classroom who do not want to be teachers in the future. The kind of introduction of reflection that I have advocated is very much concerned with the teacher educator laying open beliefs, convictions and decisions, reflecting openly on his/her own position as a learner, a reader, and a teacher and making certain mediation processes transparent. Anyone studying a language, who will be, in one way or another, concerned with ways of mediating this language to other people, will profit from the transparency of processes that I propose. Learning to evaluate a pedagogical situation also has to do with observation, with knowing your beliefs about education, with critical thinking and with creative problem-solving and decision-making. Surely such learning is profitable for anyone and should not be restricted to future EFL teachers.

It is to be hoped, then, that the constructivist principles that have been suggested by experts in learning theories and in teacher education will find increasing acceptance at university, not just on a meta-level in the methodology classrooms but in classes across the teacher education curriculum. As for future research, Simon Borg (2009: 169) has pointed out how there is as yet no direct connection between teacher cognition and student learning, and this bridging of gaps is certainly a desideratum. Even though my suggestions have been tried and tested on a small scale, a great deal of research is still needed in a broad range of contexts to establish the potential of literature in the classroom. Also, a large number of university teachers need to be convinced of the need to focus on teacher education across the curriculum. Such an integrated curriculum should find more acceptance with student teachers and help bridge the gap between students' subjective constructs of theory and practice.

Notes

(1) See also Mehlmauer-Larcher (this volume) and Hüttner and Smit (this volume).
(2) For details of these curricula, see http://anglistik.univie.ac.at/studium-studienservices telle/studien/uf-englisch/.
(3) See also Mehlmauer-Larcher (this volume).
(4) For a study on what they call 'explicit modelling', which is all about the sharing of pedagogical decision-making processes, see Lunenberg et al. (2007). See also Loughran and Berry (2005).

References

Ball, D.L., Thames, M.H. and Phelps, G. (2008) Content knowledge for teaching: What makes it special? *Journal of Teacher Education* 59 (5), 389–407.
Bamford, J. and Day, R.R. (eds) (2004) *Extensive Reading Activities for Teaching Language*. Cambridge: Cambridge University Press.
Banks, F., Leach, J. and Moon, B. (1999) New understandings of teachers' pedagogic knowledge. In J. Leach and B. Moon (eds) *Learners and Pedagogy* (pp. 89–110). London: Open University Press.
Beck, C. and Kosnik, C. (2006) *Innovations in Teacher Education: A Social Constructivist Approach*. Albany, NY: State University of New York Press.
bm:ukk (Bundesministerium für Unterricht, Kunst und Kultur) (2009) Lehrpläne für Allgemein Bildende Höhere Schulen. Online at http://www.bmukk.gv.at/schulen/unterricht/lp/lp_abs.xml.
Borg, S. (2006) *Teacher Cognition and Language Education: Research and Practice*. London: Continuum.
Borg, S. (2009) Language teacher cognition. In A. Burns and J.C. Richards (eds) *The Cambridge Guide to Second Language Teacher Education* (pp. 163–171). Cambridge: Cambridge University Press.
Burns, A. and Richards, J.C. (2009) Introduction. In A. Burns and J.C. Richards (eds) *The Cambridge Guide to Second Language Teacher Education* (pp. 1–8). Cambridge: Cambridge University Press.
Burton, J. (2009) Reflective practice. In A. Burns and J.C. Richards (eds) *The Cambridge Guide to Second Language Teacher Education* (pp. 298–308). Cambridge: Cambridge University Press.
Carter, R.A. (1996) Look both ways before crossing: Developments in the language and literature classroom. In R.A. Carter and J. McRae (eds) *Language, Literature, and the Learner: Creative Classroom Practice* (pp. 1–15). London: Longman.
Carter, R.A. (2007) Literature and language teaching 1986–2006: A review. *International Journal of Applied Linguistics* 17 (1), 3–13.
Christmann, U. and Schreier, M. (2003) Kognitionspsychologie der Textverarbeitung und Konsequenzen für die Bedeutungskonstitution literarischer Texte. In F. Jannidis (ed.) *Regeln der Bedeutung: Zur Theorie der Bedeutung literarischer Texte* (pp. 246–285). Berlin: Walter de Gruyter.
Day, R.R. and Bamford, J. (1998) *Extensive Reading in the Second Language Classroom*. Cambridge: Cambridge University Press.
De Florio-Hansen, I. (2003) Lesemotivation und Lesekompetenz: Techniken und Strategien für das Leseverstehen. *Fremdsprachenunterricht* 47 (56:6), 403–408.

Delanoy, W. (2008) Dialogic communicative competence and language learning. In W. Delanoy and L. Volkmann (eds) *Future Perspectives for English Language Teaching* (pp. 173–188). Heidelberg: Winter.
Dewey, J. (1910) *How We Think*. Boston: D.C. Heath and Co.
Donaldson, J. and Scheffler, A. (1999) *The Gruffalo*. London: Macmillan.
Edmondson, W. (1995/96) The role of literature in foreign language learning and teaching: Some valid assumptions and invalid arguments. *AILA Review* 12 (Applied Linguistics across Disciplines), 42–55.
Ellis, V. (2007) *Subject Knowledge and Teacher Education: The Development of Beginning Teachers' Thinking*. London: Continuum.
Farrell, T.S.C. (2007) *Reflective Language Teaching: From Research to Practice*. London: Continuum.
Freeman, D. and Johnson, K.E. (1998) Reconceptualizing the knowledge-base of language teacher education. *TESOL Quarterly* 32, 397–417.
Halász, L. (1983/1993) *Dem Leser auf der Spur: Literarisches Lesen als Forschen und Entdecken. Zur Sozialpsychologie des Literarischen Verstehens*. Trans. Reinhold Viehoff. Braunschweig: Vieweg.
Hesse, M. (1997) Aktuelle Englische Jugendbücher für deutsche Jugendliche. *Der Fremdsprachliche Unterricht Englisch* 5, 10–18.
Holland, N.N. (1968) *The Dynamics of Literary Response*. New York: Oxford University Press.
Johnson, K.E. (2009a) *Second Language Teacher Education: A Sociocultural Perspective*. New York: Routledge.
Johnson, K.E. (2009b) Trends in second language teacher education. In A. Burns and J.C. Richards (eds) *The Cambridge Guide to Second Language Teacher Education* (pp. 20–29). Cambridge: Cambridge University Press.
Korthagen, F.A.J. (2004) In search of the essence of a good teacher: Towards a more holistic approach in teacher education. *Teaching and Teacher Education* 20 (1), 77–97.
Korthagen, F.A.J., Loughran, J. and Lunenberg, M. (2005) Editorial: Teaching teachers – studies into the expertise of teacher educators. *Teaching and Teacher Education* 21, 107–115.
Kramsch, C. (1993) *Context and Culture in Language Teaching*. Oxford: Oxford University Press.
Kramsch, C. and Kramsch, O. (2000) The avatars of literature in language study. *Modern Language Journal* 84 (iv), 553–573.
Küppers, A. (2001) Von Harry Potter lernen heißt: Lesen lernen. Von den Erkenntnissen der Lesesozialisationforschung und deren Bedeutung für den Fremdsprachenunterricht. *Fremdsprachenunterricht* 5, 324–331.
Lampert, M. (2010) Learning teaching in, from and for practice: What do we mean? *Journal of Teacher Education* 61 (21), 21–34.
Lortie, D.C. (1975) *Schoolteacher: A Sociological Study*. Chicago: University of Chicago Press.
Loughran, J. and Berry, A. (2005) Modelling by teacher educators. *Teaching and Teacher Education* 21, 193–203.
Lunenberg, M., Korthagen, F.A.J. and Swennen, A. (2007) The teacher educator as a role model. *Teaching and Teacher Education* 32, 586–601.
Nünning, A. and Surkamp, C. (2006) *Englische Literatur Unterrichten: Grundlagen und Methoden*. Seelze-Velber: Kallmeyer/Klett.

Oatley, K. (1999) Meeting of minds: Dialogue, sympathy, and identification, in reading fiction. *Poetics* 26, 439–454.
Paran, A. (2008) The role of literature in instructed foreign language learning and teaching: An evidence-based survey. *Language Teaching* 41 (4), 465–496.
Postholm, M.B. (2008) Teachers developing practice: Reflection as key activity. *Teaching and Teacher Education* 24, 1717–1728.
Reichl, S. (2009) *Cognitive Principles, Critical Practice: Reading Literature at University.* Göttingen: Vienna University Press.
Richardson, V. (1997) Constructivist teaching and teacher education: Theory and practice. In V. Richardson (ed.) *Constructivist Teacher Education: Building a World of New Understandings* (pp. 3–14). London: Falmer Press.
Roberts, J. (1998) *Language Teacher Education.* London: Arnold.
Schendl, H. (2006) Lehrerinnenausbildung und Hochschuldidaktik: Versäumnisse und Chancen. In S. Hochreiter and U. Klingenböck (eds) *Literatur Lehren Lernen: Hochschuldidaktik und germanistische Literaturwissenschaft* (pp. 255–268). Wien: Böhlau.
Schneider, R. (2000) *Grundriß zur kognitiven Theorie der Figurenrezeption am Beispiel des Viktorianischen Romans.* Tübingen: Stauffenburg.
Schön, D.A. (1983) *The Reflective Practitioner: How Professionals Think in Action.* New York: Basic Books.
Schön, D.A. (1987) *Educating the Reflective Practitioner: Toward a New Design for Teaching and Learning in the Professions.* San Francisco: Jossey-Bass.
Seilman, U. (1990) Readers entering a fictional world. *SPIEL* 9 (2), 323–342.
Sendak, M. (1963/1991) *Where the Wild Things Are.* London: Harper Collins.
Shulman, L.S. (1987/2004) Knowledge and teaching: Foundations of the new reform. In L.S. Shulman *Teaching as Community Property: Essays on Higher Education* (ed. P. Hutchings) (pp. 84–113). San Francisco, CA: Jossey-Bass.
Silvia, P.J. (2005) Emotional responses to art: From collation and arousal to cognition and emotion. *Review of General Psychology* 9 (4), 342–357.
Singh, G. and Richards, J.C. (2009) Teaching and learning in the course room. In A. Burns and J.C. Richards (eds) *The Cambridge Guide to Second Language Teacher Education* (pp. 201–208). Cambridge: Cambridge University Press.
Ur, P. (1996) *A Course in Language Teaching: Practice and Theory.* Cambridge: Cambridge University Press.
Van Dijk, E.M. and Kattmann, U. (2007) A research model for the study of science teachers' PCK and improving teacher education. *Teaching and Teacher Education* 23, 885–897.
Wallace, M.J. (1991) *Training Foreign Language Teachers: A Reflective Approach.* Cambridge: Cambridge University Press.
Weskamp, R. (2000) Können wir nicht einmal das lesen, was die gerade in England lesen? Fremdsprachlicher Literaturunterricht, autonomes Fremdsprachenlernen und das Internet. *Praxis des neusprachlichen Unterrichts* 47 (1), 34–44.

Part 3

Assisting Language Teachers' Knowledge Construction

8 Supporting the Transfer of Innovation into Foreign-Language Classrooms: Applied Projects in In-Service Teacher Education

Sandra Hutterli and Michael C. Prusse

1 Introduction and Purpose of the Study

The discussion of the frequently perceived gap between the theory taught to pre-service teachers in the course of their education and the practice of teaching foreign languages in classrooms has been continuing for some time. The phenomenon as such is neither new nor does it lack in controversy. The theory-practice gap has been widely described in its various aspects and is regularly addressed in books, articles and at conferences. Moreover, the relationship between theory and practice is clearly of a complex nature and is influenced by a variety of factors (Newby, 2003: 14). To set theory and practice in opposition frequently results in an unfortunate misrepresentation of both of them (Widdowson, 2003: 6).

This chapter is not going to outline the whole range of circumstances linked to this issue, but we would merely like to state at this point that the ensuing discussion will attempt to exemplify one particular possibility – an in-service teacher training module that involves network learning – as a potential solution of how theory and practice can successfully be blended when providing continuing education for in-service teachers of *foreign languages*. These last two words are significant since our research in a particular Swiss context does not exclusively focus on the education of English teachers but on the education of foreign-language teachers in general. Hence, the in-service teachers we refer to in this study are either English teachers or French teachers, and they include a number of educators who teach both. The findings presented here are based on the first implementation of a Certificate of Advanced Studies (CAS) course in foreign-language teaching that was developed and run at the Zurich University of Teacher Education.

1.1 Background

The teachers of foreign languages in state schools in the Canton of Zurich, Switzerland, are confronted with a number of challenges in the present climate of change and innovation that results from new developments in at least three different spheres, namely on a European level (concerning the Council of Europe's Common European Framework of Reference for Languages [CEFR], 2001, and the European Language Portfolio [ELP][1]), on a national level (concerning the introduction of standards by the Swiss Conference of Cantonal Ministers of Education [n.d. a]) and on the local level (due to the introduction of English as a new subject at primary school). All these innovations are intended to have a positive, long-term impact on the teaching of foreign languages and, as a result of the changes in classrooms, to raise the standard of foreign-language learning and teaching in the Canton of Zurich. In the following we will provide a brief overview over the various initiatives that have an influence on the teaching of foreign languages.

National and cantonal strategies of a number of ministries of education in Switzerland pursue a range of projects that intend to enhance foreign-language education (see the Swiss Conference of Cantonal Ministers of Education [n.d. b]). One consequence of these strategies can be perceived in the launching of a number of research projects within both international and national frameworks, such as the IMPEL project for the implementation of the ELP in Europe, supported by the European Centre for Modern Languages (ECML) in Graz (Bosshard, 2007), and national research projects supported by the Swiss National Science Foundation (SNSF), which target key objectives regarding the 'diversity of languages and language competences' (Haas, 2010). On a national level, empirically validated tests, such as Lingualevel (Lenz & Studer, 2007), have been developed. Lingualevel is a web-based testing system for English and French as foreign languages that is linked to the descriptors of the ELP and assesses foreign-language competences of fifth to ninth graders.

On the local level, i.e. in the Canton of Zurich, new teaching materials have been created or are in the process of being created. The new series of English coursebooks, Explorers (Achermann & Sprague, 2006) and Voices (Stotz & Suter, 2009), are suitable for pupils from fourth to ninth school grade and are characterised by a focus on task-based and action-oriented language-teaching methods. In addition to this, there are in-service teacher education programmes that offer a wide range of courses to supplement the teachers' repertoire of language-teaching methodology, help to implement new teaching materials and inform about the educational strategies and ongoing projects regarding the teaching of foreign languages.

1.2 Challenges

This flurry of activities, however, results in a number of problems that appear to accentuate the concerns addressed in this collection, namely the gap between theory and practice. The most decisive challenge concerns the fact that many teachers are not acquainted with governmental educational strategies (as surveys of further education courses show [PHZH, 2007]). They also do not know about current teaching methodologies or, if they have been informed, they resist adopting them (as written feedback after hands-on training sessions has clearly stated). A decisive factor in this resistance against new methodologies is the teachers' almost instant rejection of new methodologies as not suitable for their practice (Hutterli & Keller, 2006). Some teachers actively oppose educational decisions and refuse to implement new instruments (Hutterli, 2011). Again, others fail to keep up with changes as a result of not being used to reading research literature or because there is a lack of readily accessible theoretical texts. Those who do embrace innovation are often frustrated when adopting new methods in their classrooms. This results from the discovery that the other staff members do not support their endeavours – a phenomenon that has also been observed by Robinson and Latchem (2003: 239):

> New teaching methods tend to become established only when they have been proven in practice and adopted by a critical mass of teachers who, together, reinforce each other's beliefs, reduce the risks of innovation and eventually change the culture of teaching. Shared goals, a supportive headteacher and a collaborative atmosphere are needed for this.

Finally, a large proportion of in-service teachers in the Canton of Zurich do not attend any postgraduate courses in foreign-language teaching at all (as we know from the internal statistics of the department of continuing education at the Zurich University of Teacher Education).

A further element that has to be kept in mind is the significance of time in any process of innovation. Clearly it takes time for innovation to take root and to transform practices in classrooms. Depending on the school system, effective innovation might require a whole generation of teachers to be replaced by the subsequent generation. Time may also prove to be a hindrance when innovation is introduced into classrooms. Since the new element 'will involve changes in teachers' attitudes and practices, it will often involve an increase in teachers' workloads, and it will almost always involve time, cost and evaluation' (White, 1987: 211). Since teachers in the Canton of Zurich are faced with innovation in a wide range of contexts *not* connected with the teaching of foreign languages, they are extremely sensitive with regard to any novelty that looks as if it were time-consuming. Since the implementation of all this innovation is resolutely decreed by the relevant ministry of education, the resulting top-down process has to be managed circumspectly. Clearly, the teachers who are to adopt the new methodologies and instruments have to be guided carefully into accepting the novelties as part of their own teaching practice.

2 Possible Solutions for In-service Teacher Education

In this volatile environment, a traditional transfer of knowledge by means of strategic decisions by educational authorities, research papers, teaching materials and individual courses is no longer sufficient to bridge the gap that teachers perceive between theory as taught at universities of teacher education and the actual practice in their classrooms throughout the Canton of Zurich (similar effects are reported from other locations as well). However, the process of change – direct change regarding the curriculum and indirect change by means of new teaching materials as well as new methodologies – certainly entails

> a need for teacher learning, i.e. opportunities for teachers to learn about the rationale for the new form of teaching, to critically evaluate it and understand how to get the best out of it. (Waters & Vilches, 2001: 137)

If one accepts that traditional models of continuing education of in-service teachers fail to succeed in such a context, the need for new forms of teacher education is self-evident. Such new forms of teacher development will guide teachers towards innovation and simultaneously enable them to develop a culture of cooperative network learning in their schools. Network learning is perceived as an efficient means of effecting positive outcomes whereby teachers may fruitfully blend theory and practice.

3 The Setting

Our empirical case study provides a new design for change that has already been put into practice. It is based on three factors that are directly linked to each other: theoretical input, biographical learning and implementation by means of projects. It is assumed that change cannot be realised by any individual but by individuals with process competences, i.e. the competence to adapt information and decisions at each step of the process to local school conditions and to the abilities of the teaching staff. Doppler and Lauterburg (2005: 155) speak of 'dynamic interactions' and underline that the main reason for problems can be traced back to dysfunctions in interaction. In order to implement new findings from research effectively in the classroom or to spread the use of new tools such as the ELP, teachers must accept them as consistent with their teaching practice and any instruction must guide them towards putting such new tools to good and appropriate use in their daily context. The process of introducing innovation in the teaching of foreign languages must consider the following aspects and their influence on the teachers concerned:

- How they learned foreign languages themselves.
- How they were educated to become language teachers.
- How they have taught the foreign language up to now.
- Subjective theories/mindsets (regarding the learning of foreign languages).
- Findings from relevant research.
- The institutional context and its scientific background.
- Opportunities of instructional development.

Wedell (2005: 639) postulates a list of rather similar considerations. Effective reception of research results among practitioners cannot be achieved by means of information supplied to individuals; instead, it is crucial to set up a professional learning network. In order to put this successfully into practice, two distinct aspects have to be considered: on the one hand, the incorporation of a learning network within the teacher development unit and, on the other hand, gaining access to staff at the different schools of a community in view of creating an additional, local network. This particular design corresponds in many respects to Wedell's analysis of cascading training into the classroom, in particular when he refers to the need of continued 'coaching', first of the experts and later of the experts and practitioners within the schools (Wedell, 2005: 645-646). We will first look at the network within the CAS (Certificate of Advanced Studies)

Teaching Foreign Languages and then proceed to an analysis of the spin-off networks within the schools that delegated a teacher into this CAS programme.

3.1 A Learning Network within the CAS Programme

Regarding the learning network within the teacher development course, the following aspects have been taken into consideration in the planning phase:

- The participants in the teacher development course come with a background of teaching at different levels and of teaching different foreign languages. This heterogeneity of backgrounds results in a comprehensive discourse on the processes of foreign-language teaching and acquisition in the classroom (horizontal and vertical coherence are thus a constant issue).
- Insights from theoretical input are adapted to the teacher's own lessons and, in the course of a project that involves at least one other member of the teaching staff at the participant's school, these insights are transferred into the classrooms. The lecturers running the CAS course provide support for the participants' work on the project (a) by coaching them in project management and (b) by acting as consultants when the project is put into practice.
- Participants may exchange texts, materials and experiences on a web-based platform where they also form new project teams.
- Local school authorities from the schools in which the participants are employed as teachers are regularly invited to attend selected sessions of the course in order to enable the participants to set up learning networks within their schools and/or communities. The school principals have to approve of the projects and provide them with the necessary resources such as time or a platform and support in staff meetings.

3.2 Schools and Communities as Networks

Schools and communities as networks play a further crucial role, as the following illustrates: Since schools in the Canton of Zurich (and elsewhere) have been provided with more autonomy in recent years, they need to redefine the roles of the various members of the teaching staff. In as many schools and communities as possible there ought to be a teacher who is a specialist in teaching foreign languages and who is familiar with current theories and state-of-the-art methodologies in foreign-language teaching.

This teacher is also characterised by both the capability and the desire to keep his or her knowledge up-to-date by reading up on the latest trends or by attending further in-service education programmes. Moreover, this specialist teacher has been trained in applying project-management procedures to processes of innovation regarding the teaching of foreign languages. This teacher acts as a contact person for fellow staff members when they have queries regarding the teaching of foreign languages. Together with the principal and the head teachers, he or she implements innovative projects within the team.

The local education authority nominates this teacher as an official expert and coach in foreign-language teaching within the community where the school is situated. Furthermore, he or she is the contact person for representatives of the ministry of education and for lecturers in methodology at universities of teacher education when further innovative projects are planned or launched at cantonal level. The teaching load of the participating teachers is eased so that they are enabled to successfully tackle such tasks and projects.

4 Rationale for Innovation in Teacher Development Courses

The design of the CAS programme that was developed at the Zurich University of Teacher Education to meet these challenges is based on the notion that opposing innovation releases a lot of energy among the teachers in question. As early as 1988, Kennedy rightly noted that disagreement does not necessarily mean 'resistance and opposition rather than something positive which can be built into the project plan' (Kennedy, 1988: 335). If this energy could be channelled into a useful course, new findings in research and innovation in foreign-language teaching might successfully be introduced into classrooms by means of network learning. As Newby (2003: 17) asserts, the

> theory-practice interface could be seen as a filtering process, in the course of which principles and certain elements of theory which have practical applications are filtered out, modified and implemented in teaching and learning procedures, materials and activities.

The metaphor of the filter results in the recognition that ultimately theories can very well also be informed by practice, in particular when teachers are not only seen as consumers of theories, but also as possible protagonists of change that is inspired by their daily practice. Maciel (2008: 125-126) sums this up neatly by stating that innovation processes may be sparked by impulses from above (top-down) or by needs in certain situations where teachers attempt to find a response (bottom-up). In the case of the Canton of Zurich, new methodologies and instruments are mostly introduced in a top-down process and, hence, the management of the introduction of innovation has to be handled with particular care.

5 Models for the Transfer of Innovation

Waters and Vilches (2001: 134) outline a model that provides suitable procedures for projects in ELT innovation, which are supported by a clear rationale. They suggest four distinct stages to ensure the successful introduction of innovative practices in ELT. First of all, teachers need to be 'properly familiar with the innovation situation' (Waters & Vilches, 2001: 134; see also Wedell, 2005: 639). This first encounter, usually by means of input in the form of continuing teacher education, has to be followed up by socialisation, i.e. 'the model at this phase of its development is checked for its match with the prevailing sociocultural educational preconceptions' (Waters & Vilches, 2001: 134). The ensuing step is concerned with monitoring and supporting the process by means of which teachers test the contextualised innovations 'in such a way that the necessary level of personal, practical understanding and expertise is built up' (Waters & Vilches, 2001: 134). At the topmost level,

> scope should be given for the innovation to become the personal 'property' of the users, through its further development, in ways determined as far as possible by the users' individual priorities. (Waters & Vilches, 2001: 134)

The procedure selected for the programme in the Canton of Zurich recognises the significance of these four stages. It has been slightly modified to take into consideration aspects of organisational learning. As already mentioned above, the success of an effective implementation of innovation relies not only on individual learning, but also on the learning of the entire staff of a school. Nonaka and Takeuchi (1997: 87) define four sequences of transfer from individual knowledge to organisational knowledge, which they perceive as sequences that form a continuous cycle:

(1) Socialisation: Individuals learn by practicing and observing; this knowledge is implicit and limited to experience.

(2) Externalisation: By means of communication and reflection this knowledge becomes explicit and accessible to others.
(3) Combination: The externalised knowledge can now be combined with existing and theory-based knowledge. New knowledge will be generated or existing knowledge will become palpable.
(4) Internalisation: This new or palpable knowledge is transferred into action. In the course of this process, the applied knowledge becomes an automatic part of the repertoire inherent in the members of the organisation.

Both the four steps postulated by Waters and Vilches as well as the sequence, also in four steps, of organisational learning as defined by Nonaka and Takeuchi form the basis of the model applied in the CAS programme, which has been put into practice in the setting of in-service teacher continuing education at the Zurich University of Teacher Education.

6 The CAS 'Teaching Foreign Languages'

After the extensive analysis of teachers' needs, the answer to the critical points listed above is a design that equips progressive in-service teachers with continuing education to bring them up to the current state-of-the-art in the teaching of foreign languages. In addition, they are provided with tools and tasks. The most important tool is an introduction to project management in the context of the local school organisation in the Canton of Zurich with the specific purpose of initiating innovative practices in foreign-language teaching; the predominant task is to work with volunteers within their schools and to establish small projects that will spread the knowledge about innovations in foreign-language teaching within the school in which they are based. All in all, the participants in this course format have to set up three projects as part of their course assignments. These projects aim at three core goals of the CAS and focus on the following areas:

(1) Introduce new methodologies into the foreign-language classroom.
(2) Implement the use of the ELP and Lingualevel.
(3) Improve vertical coherence between different school levels (for example, by establishing continuity at the interface of primary and secondary school).

Next, we would like to show briefly what such a project might entail when put into practice. The teacher in question decided to focus on developing the methodological repertoire of his fellow staff members and opted for task-based language learning (TBL). He outlined a project plan and had it reviewed both by his local school management and the lecturers responsible for the continuing education programme. Next, he briefed two colleagues who volunteered to participate in his project about the theoretical background of this method. In the following step, the three teachers prepared task-based lesson plans and carried out the lessons with their classes. The task they gave their students was to create a *fotoromanzo* ('photo story'); this firstly involved writing a script; secondly, the pupils had to shoot the photos to illustrate their narrative and, thirdly, they inserted the dialogue and speech bubbles into their photo story. When this task was completed, the photo stories were printed out and read by the various groups within the class and later presented to other classes, teachers and parents. The three teachers then reflected upon their experience of task-based language learning and decided that they felt sufficiently confident to continue with further tasks. The teacher who participated in the sessions of our continuing education programme and whose project was monitored and supported by the lecturers responsible for the CAS then wrote a final report about his project, which was handed in as part of the course assignment.

Once the participants in the CAS Teaching Foreign Languages at School have completed three compact projects of this kind (the first phase of the further education course), they will select one of these projects and extend it into a larger project that might, for example, involve all of the staff that teach foreign languages within their school or community (which constitutes the second phase of this CAS programme). This more ambitious project is coupled with a thorough grounding in theory and is written up in a thesis, which, once accepted, concludes this postgraduate qualification programme for in-service teachers. This specific design of the CAS course programme is the result of the two rationales outlined in further detail below.

6.1 Rationale I: Theoretical Input as an Integral Part of a Comprehensive Teacher Education Context

Theoretical input is always presented as a part of the entire teaching context. Essentially the in-service teachers work out which elements of the theory they may directly link to their daily practice and which aspects demand a change in their habits. Only once this process of acculturation has taken place can they begin to adapt the new input to their own teaching needs.

The structure of the courses combines models of biographical learning (Fröhlich & Finger, 1990; Gautschi, 1995) with results of research in change management (Doppler *et al.*, 2002; Fullan, 2001) and with studies of mindsets (Dweck, 2000). In setting up the course, the lecturers paid particular attention to the following five aspects: Firstly, clear sets of questions guide the teachers when reflecting their practice and they are always provided with the necessary time to deal with questions that are still unanswered and expectations or needs that have not been fulfilled. These explicit exercises in raising consciousness – consciousness of their own principles when in the classroom – help the teachers to become aware of questions that have not been answered and also to recognise where they might still have gaps or require further information.

Secondly, the theoretical input has a twofold function, namely to increase their knowledge on the processes involved in the teaching of foreign languages and, at the same time, to bring them up-to-date with current theories of language learning and teaching. Widening the teachers' repertoire in foreign-language teaching methodology is one of the central concerns of the course, which is designed to lead to the practical application of these methods in the classrooms of those schools that delegate representatives to this particular certificate course at the Zurich University of Teacher Education.

Thirdly, a particular aim is to make sure that the theoretical input is part of the teachers' context so that they recognise that the changes are definitely relevant and they become convinced that the innovation is indeed necessary.

Fourthly, when the teachers on the course compare their own subjective theories with the results of empirical research, they may acknowledge and overcome hurdles that prevent their own learning and may actually rethink their own role models.

Finally, the transfer and changes that result from an innovative project conducted in their own teaching environment makes teachers aware of the practicability of introducing innovations that are based on findings from research into the classroom and convinces them of their value. Waters and Vilches (2001: 138) stress that the 'need for the innovation development strategy to include a *school-based* teacher learning element' is a key factor of success in school innovation. Furthermore, school boards that actively support such a project by offering incentives to the teachers certainly provide an additional and essential stimulus. Taken together, these two aspects work in favour of creating the necessary 'harmony' between the goals of the innovation and the teachers' immediate working environment (Wedell, 2005: 642).

6.2 Rationale II: Organisational and Network Learning as a Basis of Course Design

When designing the course, the relevant factors of organisational and network learning were considered (Doppler *et al.*, 2002; Doppler & Lauterburg, 2005; Fullan, 2006; Senge & Sterman, 1994). It is assumed that if learning networks within a further training course are to work, the following aspects are relevant:

- The participants' backgrounds, i.e. the fact that they teach different foreign languages at different levels, is used for an approach that results in encompassing discussions and supports horizontal and vertical cohesion. Whenever there are tasks that need to be resolved in groups, the requirements of the course aims and the needs of the participants are carefully assessed and then either homogenous or heterogeneous groups are formed.
- Insights that result from theoretical input are adapted to each teacher's classroom needs and put into practice by means of a project that involves at least one further member of staff in his or her school. The course instructors support the work on the project by training the participants in project management and by coaching them when they work on concrete projects.

The following concrete support measures have been introduced:

- The Web platform ILIAS provides the space for the exchange of texts, materials and experiences of the participants and, moreover, serves as a repository for final project reports.
- The school principals are invited at two relevant stages in the course, namely when the participants first set up their projects and, most importantly, at the final presentation of the results of the various projects.
- The cantonal ministry of education supports communities by sponsoring 50% of the total cost per participant in the CAS in order to provide these communities with experts in foreign-language teaching. To provide further incentive for the teachers to participate in the programme, the local school authorities cover the remaining 50% of the costs for the course.

7 The Case Study and its Results

The course design was evaluated by means of the following three instruments: firstly, the course participants filled in questionnaires.

Secondly, the lecturers teaching the course evaluated the written biographical reflections that the participants handed in. Thirdly, the final project reports, which were also evaluated by the course lecturers, offered a wealth of insights into the processes that resulted from the course design. The limitations of the study are self-evident: the sample is rather small, as only 14 participants enrolled in the pioneering CAS course. The participating teachers were recruited from the following (Zurich) school levels:

- four teachers from lower primary level (first to third grades)
- three teachers from upper primary level (fourth to sixth grades)
- four teachers from secondary level I (seventh to ninth grades)
- three teachers from secondary level II (tenth to twelfth grades)

As a consequence of the limited numbers of teachers participating in the project, the results should be regarded as an illustration or as indicators of a possible trend rather than hard evidence.

7.1 Results Relating to Rationale I: Theoretical Input as an Integral Part of a Comprehensive Teaching Context

Regarding the first rationale, the following results can already be emphasised: Teachers are more willing to change or adapt their regular practice once they have truly understood their own language-learning biography and have been enabled to put novel theoretical input into relation with their own past experiences. A quotation from the initial questionnaires, filled in after an in-depth analysis of the participants' language-learning biography and a detailed revision of the theory of (foreign) language acquisition, will serve to illustrate this point:

> I now understand the influence of my own learning on my teaching. Just because I learned the language in a certain way doesn't mean it is the appropriate learning method for my class. I will, from now on, offer my pupils a range of learning opportunities to choose from.[2]

This message might sound banal and its content already well established among those who manage innovation in education systems. And yet, it is crucial to understand that only by means of such eye-opening experiences regarding their own learning do individual teachers exhibit a true willingness to change their own teaching practice. This has certainly been shown to be the case in the subsequent projects.

Teachers who introduce innovation in the teaching of foreign languages into classrooms by means of projects might have a dual benefit: firstly, they perceive the relevance of these adjustments to their former practice and secondly, they discover the practicability of such innovative forms. Yet again, this process may be substantiated by an insight that is provided in one of the questionnaires:

> For the first time, I have understood how to teach properly using this course book. Up to now I have changed almost every exercise in it because I didn't understand its methodological concepts. Now I do – and, best of all: it works.

Since the new methodologies and instruments are implemented in a communal procedure by all the staff working together as a team in one school or one school district, the individual teacher feels supported in his or her sense of achieving meaningful accomplishment. One of the participating teachers wrote in her questionnaire that the team effort proved to be thoroughly worthwhile:

> I would never have organised a parents' information evening on this topic. Thanks to this project we have done so in a team of staff from three different schools. We were able to support each other in the preparation. The feedback from parents as well as from participating teachers was positive.

7.2 Results Relating to Rationale II: Organisational and Network Learning as a Basis of Course Design

The second rationale is confirmed by reference to two exemplary cases. The first instance refers to the fact that the participants use the further training course itself as a learning network in different ways: they share information and materials on the e-learning platform ILIAS, they prepare projects together with some of the other participants and then implement them individually in their own schools; furthermore, they also plan projects in cooperation across different school levels. One example of this is the introduction of the European Language Portfolio (ELP). It was introduced to both teachers at secondary schools (grades seven through nine) and teachers at grammar schools (grades 10 through 12) in the same course. The main focus was on demonstrating to them how the continuity and coherence of the language-learning process can be supported by making use of the ELP at all school levels. Teachers from different school grades cooperated in order to plan the use of the ELP in a coherent way. The resulting networks helped them to better understand the process of language acquisition at the different ages of their pupils. At the same time, these networks made sure that the ELP was established in a coherent and continuous fashion in the foreign-language classrooms across the different grades.

The second instance concerns those teachers who have set up networks within their own schools and communities. The more they feel supported by their local education authorities, the more effectively they achieve their objectives (see also Wedell, 2005: 644). This motivates the teachers to develop further projects for their school team and to assume responsibility for the management of innovation in foreign-language classrooms. Again, this process will be illustrated with one exemplary case: a local school authority has recently appointed a primary school teacher who participates in the CAS course as a consultant for foreign-language teaching. As a result of this appointment, she could choose whether she wanted to be dispensed from teaching for one lesson per week or whether to have one week off per year to plan a series of projects that aim at improving foreign-language teaching in her community. The primary teacher chose the exemption from one teaching lesson per week and started to plan an annual programme with graded priorities to implement change in foreign-language teaching in her school. She has come up with one major project (the implementation of the beginners' version of the ELP), which is linked to an official implementation programme of the Swiss canton she works in. Furthermore, she has planned some small projects that are linked to the general development also in other subjects at her school, such as the information of parents and the coordination of learning strategies across the subjects as well as across school levels. It is self-evident that this slight reduction in the teaching load permits only a limited amount of activities and can merely be seen as a first step towards more professional specialisation among foreign-language teachers. More decisive steps will have to follow if the school management and the local education authorities are serious about effectively implementing innovation in foreign-language teaching.

Further evidence of the effectiveness of the design was furnished in the course of the presentations that the participants delivered at the end of the CAS in front of an audience consisting of their peers and some school principals. The presence of the school principals was a key factor with regard to organisational learning and in order to safeguard further developments within the schools. The presentations of the participants offered insights into one of the three projects they carried out while enrolled in the course and documented quite a few instances of success and, although rarely, also the odd example of a project that failed to live up to expectations, and, fortunately, only one case of a complete failure. Focusing on the success stories, one teacher presented a whole set of portfolios filled in by pupils at lower and upper primary levels. These portfolios provided ample evidence for the methodological creativity the two teachers brought to bear on the task of introducing the ELP into the classrooms of their school. Such accounts of accomplishment more than balanced out the one distinct failure, which arguably resulted from the lack of support given by the principal and by fellow staff members. The presentation of good practice yet again served as an externalisation of newly gained implicit knowledge, which could then be combined with experiences from colleagues and feedback from the CAS trainers. The circle of transfer from individual learning to organisational learning (Nonaka & Takeuchi, 1997: 87) turned into a continuous process as each teacher chose one of the projects to implement within their school and/or community. Ultimately, it was the positive impression left by these presentations and the equally positive outcomes scrupulously documented in the project reports that we feel permit the qualification of the course design as a success. Nevertheless, we are well aware of the fact that further research and a larger sample of results are required in order to provide more valid data and to permit us to confirm the effectiveness of the course design.

8 Conclusion and Prospects for Future Research

We would like to end by saying that in-service teacher education by means of projects and learning networks (within the course itself as well as within the school community) definitely helps to overcome the gap teachers perceive between theory and practice and actually results in blending theory and practice. However, there still remain a number of aspects that need to be developed further. First and foremost, it is critical to ensure that the teachers selected for the role of expert in foreign-language teaching feel accepted by the other staff, both with regard to their competence and their role as genuine delegates, to whom the transfer of innovation in the teaching of foreign languages into a community's classrooms is entrusted. Teachers need time to get accustomed to their new roles as specialists. Furthermore, they have to accept the fact that in their role as individual teachers, they are no longer responsible for keeping up with developments in all the subjects in the curriculum. Until certain opportunities for teachers to assume specialist roles were introduced in the Canton of Zurich as a result of a new law for compulsory schooling (2008), most teachers – with the exception of secondary level II (grades 10 through 12) – were 'generalists' and were faced with the Herculean (and impossible) task of keeping abreast of developments in all subjects they taught. A second significant aspect of the outcome of the first CAS concerns the fact that greater weight must be given to the role of principals and school leadership in general. In particular it is essential to make the school management aware of how relevant and indeed decisive the impact of coaches in foreign-language learning and their respective networks can be for the further development of their schools. This finding ties in with other studies that have stressed the need for local support if change is to be achieved successfully (Wedell, 2005: 644). With regard to project management, there must be an even greater emphasis on dealing with resistance and opposition in staff teams and on clarifying the various roles and positions within a learning network. There is also an urgent need for case studies, such as the one outlined in this chapter, to be evaluated by an external body and, if this is not possible, at least by the researchers responsible for the study. Criteria for the evaluation of the effects resulting from the innovation ought to be transparent and will help readers and anybody else involved in the management of change within an educational setting to draw accurate conclusions (cf. May Yin, 2009: 546).

What is clear at this intermediate stage, however, is that developing an approach both for teacher training and for the management of innovation will be a matter of continuing interest to anyone who is concerned with the theory and practice of foreign-language teaching at school. And, as Wedell (2009: 398) rightly argues, seeing how much educational authorities are willing to invest in innovation in the teaching of foreign languages in some parts of the world, it is vital to focus in more detail on what innovation theory offers with regard to successfully implementing change in classrooms than has often been the case in the past.

Notes

(1) In Switzerland there exists a coherent series of ELPs: the Portfolino (four to seven years), the ELP I (seven to 11 years), the ELP II (11 to 15 years) and the ELP III (15+); the use of ELPs is part of the national and regional language strategy.
(2) This statement (as well as the other statements by participants in the course) has been translated from the original German into English by the authors of this study.

References

Achermann, B. and Sprague, K. (2006) *Explorers*. Zürich: Lehrmittelverlag des Kantons Zürich.
Bosshard, H.U. (coord.) (2007) *ELP Implementation Support/Soutien à la Mise en Oeuvre du PEL*. Strasbourg/Graz: Council of Europe/European Centre for Modern Languages. Online at http://archive.ecml.at/mtp2/impel/html/IMPEL_E_Results.htm

Council of Europe (2001) *Common European Framework of Reference for Languages: Learning, Teaching, Assessment*. Online at http://www.coe.int/T/DG4/Linguistic/Source/Framework_EN.pdf

Doppler, K. Fuhrmann, H. Lebbe-Waschke, B. and Voigt, B. (2002) *Unternehmenswandel gegen Widerstände: Changemanagement mit den Menschen*. Frankfurt/New York: Campus.

Doppler, K. and Lauterburg, C. (2005) *Changemanagement: Den Unternehmenswandel gestalten*. Frankfurt/New York: Campus.

Dweck, C. (2000) *Self-theories: Their Role in Motivation, Personality and Development*. Philadelphia: Psychology Press.

Fröhlich, E. and Finger, M. (1990) Biografische Methode und Erwachsenenbildung. *Berichte der Akademie für Erwachsenenbildung* 1, 2–16.

Fullan, M. (2001) *Leading in a Culture of Change*. San Francisco: Jossey-Bass.

Fullan, M. (2006) *Quality Leadership <=> Quality Learning: Proof Beyond Reasonable Doubt*. Toronto: Brosna Press.

Gautschi, P. (1995) Biografische Arbeit in der Lehrerbildung als Möglichkeit der Ausbildung von 'Reflektierenden Praktikern' – Ein Erfahrungsbericht. *Beiträge zur Lehrerbildung* 3, 293–300.

Haas, W. (ed.) (2010) *Do you speak Swiss? Sprachenvielfalt und Sprachkompetenz in der Schweiz*. Nationales Forschungsprogramm NFP 56. Zürich: NZZ Libro.

Hutterli, S. (2011) *Beurteilung der Sprechkompetenz in einer Fremdsprache. Theorie und Praxis der Einführung neuer Verfahren in einem schweizerischen Schulsystem* (Fallstudie). Bern: Peter Lang Verlag.

Hutterli, S. and Keller, R. (2006) *Beurteilung fremdsprachlicher Kompetenzen in Ausrichtung auf internationale Standards: Beurteilung der Schreibkompetenz in Englisch und Beurteilung der Sprechkompetenz in Französisch*. Zürich: PHZH.

Kennedy, C. (1988) Evaluation of the management of change in ELT projects. *Applied Linguistics* 9 (4), 329–342.

Lenz, P. and Studer, T. (2007) *Lingualevel: Instrumente zur Evaluation von Fremdsprachenkompetenzen; 5. bis 9. Schuljahr*. Bern: Schulverlag BLMV.

Maciel, R.F. (2008) Innovation in language teaching: A theoretical contribution. In R.F. Maciel, V. Araujo and V. de Assis (eds) *Ensino da Língua Inglesa: Contribuições da Lingüística Aplicada* (pp. 123–145). Campo Grande: Editora UNAES.

May Yin, T. (2009) Innovation and change in English language teaching: over a decade of shared perspectives. *Language Teaching* 42 (4), 536–547.

Newby, D. (2003) *Mediating Between Theory and Practice in the Context of Different Learning Cultures and Languages*. Graz: ECML.

Nonaka, I. and Takeuchi, H. (1997) *Die Organisation des Wissens*. Frankfurt: Campus.

PHZH (2007) Internal Report of In-service Teacher Education. Zurich: Department of continuing education at the Zurich University of Teacher Education.

Robinson, B. and Latchem, C. (2003) *Teacher Education through Open and Distance Learning*. London: Routledge.

Senge, P.M. and Sterman, J.D. (1994) Systems thinking and organizational learning: Acting locally and thinking globally in the organization of the future. In J.D.W. Morecroft and J.D. Sterman (eds) *Modelling for Learning Organizations* (pp. 195–216). Portland, OR: Productivity.

Stotz, D. and Suter, C. (2009) *Voices*. Zürich: Lehrmittelverlag des Kantons Zürich.

Swiss Conference of Cantonal Ministers of Education (EDK) (n.d. a) *HarmoS* website, accessed 10 January 2011. Online at http://www.edk.ch/dyn/11659.php

Swiss Conference of Cantonal Ministers of Education (EDK) (n.d. b) *Sprachenunterricht*, website, accessed 10 January 2011. Online at http://www.edk.ch/dyn/11911.php

Waters, A. and Vilches, M.L.C. (2001) Implementing ELT innovations: A needs analysis framework. *ELT Journal* 55 (2), 133–141.

Wedell, M. (2005) Cascading training down into the classroom: The need for parallel planning. *International Journal of Educational Development* 25, 637–651.

Wedell, M. (2009) Innovation in ELT. *ELT Journal* 63 (4), 397–399.

White, R.V. (1987) Managing innovation. *ELT Journal* 41 (3), 211–218.

Widdowson, H.G. (2003) The theory of practice. In H.G. Widdowson (ed.) *Defining Issues in English Language Teaching* (pp. 1–18). Oxford: Oxford University Press.

9 Developing Student Teachers' 'Pedagogical Content Knowledge' in English for Specific Purposes: The 'Vienna ESP Approach'

Julia Hüttner and Ute Smit

1 Introduction

For roughly the last 40 years, one of the biggest areas in English-language teaching has been English for Specific Purposes (ESP), and English courses for academic and occupational purposes are flourishing around the globe. This is true also for the Austrian context, with the majority of upper-secondary pupils attending vocational colleges, which focus on ESP as their English foreign-language provision. Despite its strong presence, English-language teacher education in Austria has so far not taken ESP much into consideration, making it one of its challenges to prepare student teachers to become professional and versatile pre-service ESP teachers.

Teaching ESP is characterised by diversity, but all ESP teaching shares the characteristic of basing the choice of particular teaching methods firmly on established learner needs, which are as varied as the fields of expertise requiring English-language proficiency. What these needs generally have in common is the ability to comprehend and produce particular texts required within the profession, such as case briefs, contracts, lab reports or scientific articles to name just a few, and teachers must be able to understand the workings of these text types and their underlying conventions. This required ability often instils worry in the prospective (or even practicing!) ESP teachers as to their required level of subject knowledge, especially of relevant language knowledge related to text types or genres as mentioned above. While the larger areas of ESP, such as business or law, benefit from commercial publishers' interest and so teachers have a good selection of up-to-date and fairly accurate materials at their disposal, many smaller or emerging areas of ESP still require teachers to develop their own materials and to be able to familiarise themselves quickly with new text types. This blends in with the problem facing ESP teacher educators that it is impossible to predict the genres that future ESP teachers might be teaching in the next 40 years of their professional lives and is, to our minds, a clear reason for adopting an approach that goes well beyond mere teacher training (cf. Widdowson, 1983: 23-28). In fact, ESP teacher education must enable the future practitioners to autonomously analyse any ESP genre with a view to teaching it to learners who themselves are not necessarily familiar with the conventions of their future discourse communities.

Austrian teacher education is generally organised in an 'applied science model' (Wallace, 1991: 8 ff.), that is to say, student teachers are first introduced to theoretical knowledge in, e.g. literature and cultural studies, applied linguistics, general linguistics, education and subject didactics, which they are expected to mediate to their teaching practice at some point in the future. In spite of a prevailing applied science model, there is some space devoted to teaching practice during the undergraduate degree, creating potentials for reflective practice.

This article presents the core elements of an innovative educational module, the Certificate of Teaching ESP (CerTESP), which addresses the need of preparing Austrian student teachers for the teaching of relevant written ESP genres and for developing the necessary skills of analysing unfamiliar genres and developing materials for specific settings. We will attempt to show how this aids student teachers in developing their 'pedagogic content knowledge' (Shulman, 1986; 1987)[1].

2 Pedagogical Content Knowledge

One of the recurring (semi-)public debates on teachers relates to the very essence of their professional expertise and knowledge, a matter apparently answered with greater ease for other professions, like lawyers or medical doctors. In answering the question of what the knowledge base of teachers incorporates, Shulman (1987: 8) identified the following eight categories as the minimum:

- content knowledge;[2]
- general pedagogical knowledge [...];
- curriculum knowledge [...];
- pedagogical content knowledge, that special amalgam of content and pedagogy that is uniquely the province of teachers, their own special form of understanding;

- knowledge of learners and their characteristics;
- knowledge of educational contexts [...];
- knowledge of educational ends, purposes and values and their philosophical and historical grounds.

Shulman (1987: 15) went on to clarify pedagogical content knowledge (PCK) as 'the capacity of a teacher to transform the content knowledge he or she possesses into forms that are pedagogically powerful'. In the original conceptualisation, Shulman (1987) views PCK as distinct from content knowledge, but both as essential elements of a successful teachers' knowledge base, a view followed by later researchers like Grossman (1990) or Magnusson et al. (1999), whereas Marks (1990), Fernandez-Balboa and Stiehl (1995) and Koballa et al. (1999) view content knowledge as integrated into PCK. In her review of models of PCK, Kind (2009) found that the majority favoured an integration of subject matter knowledge into PCK. Gess-Newsome (1999) termed the former 'transformative' models and the latter 'integrative' models. Integrative models differ quite profoundly from Shulman's original proposal in removing the transformational element from PCK and considering PCK as a conglomerate of all teacher knowledge. For the purposes of this chapter, we follow a transformative view of PCK. One reason for doing so is conceptual: if PCK is no longer distinguished clearly from subject matter knowledge, it becomes difficult to define the type of knowledge uniquely the province of teachers. Another reason is more practical and relates to our roles as teacher educators of – mostly – novices, namely the need to give guidance to student teachers as to the nature and the possible development of their PCK. In integrative models of PCK, the risk arguably is that subject matter knowledge takes precedence and a transmission model of teaching is retained, especially as in applied science models of teacher education, the teaching of subject content enjoys great curricular prominence.

The applicability and perceived usefulness in capturing teachers' expertise have made PCK a successful concept in teacher education over the last 25 years, despite justified criticism of its elusive nature and vague definition (Kind, 2009: 171). Especially, the focus on the development of new knowledge through transformation of subject matter knowledge into PCK and the dynamic nature of PCK (Abell, 2008: 1407–1408) are amenable to exploitation in teacher education. As PCK is by definition subject-specific (cf. Abell, 2008: 1414), it is well suited to be the prime focus of subject didactic teachers, and in our case also of applied linguists, i.e. those educators focusing on aspects of ESP teaching.

The focus of this contribution lies in developing student teachers' PCK, a matter that in the constraints of our overarching teacher education structure is a little difficult. Kind (2009: 186–187) identified three contributing factors to the development of PCK in her overview of existing research: firstly, good subject matter knowledge, secondly, classroom experience and finally, emotional attributes, including building student teachers' self-confidence and providing supportive and collaborative working environments. Especially the second aspect, classroom experience, is difficult to provide in our context, so we attempted to develop another means of creating realistic tasks that would encourage student teachers to transform their subject matter knowledge into PCK, or at least to raise their awareness of a need for such transformation.

If we consider the nature of ESP teacher education, we can see that the content knowledge of the linguistic conventions of ESP genres needs to be transformed into the PCK of how to make these language practices relevant and achievable to learners. In our local context, where student teachers have little access to practical teaching sessions, the designers of the CerTESP decided on trying to develop student teachers' PCK by making them relate their linguistic analyses to envisaged teaching situations that involve materials development.

Materials choice and development is in general a rather neglected area in teacher education, possibly due to the existence of many high-quality language teaching materials for general purposes, and often pre-service and in-service teacher education focus only on developing some very general guidelines for choosing materials. Canniveng and Martinez (2003: 485) show how materials development can and should be seen as the result of an interaction between theoretical knowledge, teacher cognition and teacher experience. It is also, we would argue, a task typically requiring PCK. We would add that this genuine task of creating materials for ESP settings, usually in areas that might be so small or newly emerged that no published commercial materials are available, requires specific content knowledge of language – often underestimated in teacher education – in the area of materials development. This is important, given the findings of genre and discourse analysis, which highlight the importance of knowing genre-specific conventions, including features of lexico-grammar, phraseology and multimodality. The act of choosing aspects of such analysis in the teaching materials for an envisaged group of learners provides an opportunity of showcasing for student teachers how to transform their linguistic content knowledge into PCK. The means of developing the PCK of small-scale materials development is thus used as a bridge between the two banks of applied linguistics as content knowledge and anticipated teaching practice in ESP.

More precisely, the process of developing materials allows student teachers to develop experiential knowledge about the nature of ESP teaching. While, at the onset, ESP student teachers worry mostly about the required level of specific content knowledge, working on materials for specific ESP genres allows them to realise the importance not of simply expanding their content knowledge related to the text types or genres in question, but especially of their PCK of making this accessible to learners.

3 Analysing ESP Texts for Materials Development

Embedded in the applied science model of pre-service teacher education in Austria and many other countries, ESP student teachers need education rather than training (cf. Widdowson's distinction, 1983: 23–28). That is to say, they need to be prepared for handling future teaching demands of their roughly 40 teaching years that cannot be anticipated in detail at the time of their pre-service education. Therefore, what is needed is theory-informed and mediated principled education. When keeping in mind the centrality as well as the diversity of genres to be learnt and taught in ESP (a good proportion emerging and not linguistically or pedagogically described), student teachers need to be made familiar with principles and tools with the help of which they can approach any new genre in the future. Based on such considerations, the 'Vienna ESP approach' has been developed by a group of experts in language teaching and applied linguistics at the English department at the University of Vienna, and tested and found useful by a large number of participants in the CerTESP (Certificate in Teaching ESP) Module (cf. also Hüttner *et al.*, 2009; Smit, 2005; Smit & Hüttner, 2006).

3.1 The 'Vienna ESP Approach'

The CerTESP Module consists of four one-semester courses of 30 contact hours each and is intended to be completed within one to two years, as a complementary strand of the regular EFL teacher education programme (cf. Department of English, 2004). Given that a good majority of the student teachers have not had any previous experience in English used for specific purposes, two language courses are designed to familiarise learners with selected areas of ESP such as commerce and economy, technology, medicine or law. To substantiate this initial training in specific English registers and styles, the two remaining courses are dedicated to the actual educational process of introducing the learners to the principles of ESP genres, to analysing such genres and using the resulting insights and knowledge for material development. More precisely, the first course,

'Approaching ESP Texts', focuses on 'teaching-oriented corpus-based genre analysis' (Hüttner et al., 2009: 104–105), while material development based on such analyses, pedagogic applications and implications for the classroom are dealt with in the second course, 'ESP Methodology'. In terms of the transformative view of PCK, these 'core' courses for teaching ESP provide subject matter knowledge in terms of applied linguistic theories and methodologies, and, most crucially, knowledge on how this knowledge can be transformed into pedagogical content knowledge. This transformation is primarily achieved by student teachers undertaking a genre analysis in relation to a specific teaching scenario and, contingent on the respective teaching purposes, develop related teaching materials.

As will be argued in the following, the core courses allow for such knowledge construction and transformation because of the underlying approach of 'the investigative procedure of teaching-oriented corpus-based genre analysis' (Hüttner et al., 2009: 106). As illustrated in Table 9.1, the procedure consists of seven steps, of which the first and last (A and G) function as pedagogical frame and orientation, while the central five describe the analytical processes of teaching-oriented genre analysis, comprising genre description (B), corpus compilation (C) and genre analysis (D) with the help of analytical methods taken from corpus analysis (E), phraseology and multimodality (F).

Table 9.1 The investigative procedure of teaching-oriented corpus-based genre analysis (further developed from Hüttner et al., 2009: 106)

(A)	Selection of genre and description of the teaching situation envisaged (incl. the imagined group of learners)
(B)	Description of the genre (communicative purpose/s + potential discourse community)
(C)	Collection of exemplary texts and compilation of the mini-corpus
(D)	Description of the 'moves' on the basis of the texts included in the mini-corpus
(E)	Lexico-grammatical analysis: comparison of mini-corpus with reference corpus (*BNC*) with the help of WordSmith Tools
(F)	Analysis of textualisations: connection investigative steps (D) and (E) and integrating multimodal analysis
(G)	Interpretation of the results with reference to the teaching and learning situation, developing teaching materials

From a student teacher's perspective, step A actually entails two preparatory steps: firstly, some personal experience with ESP, which, for instance, can be gained in the CerTESP language courses, and, secondly, some knowledge of the general characteristics of specific-purpose texts as well as of the basic tenets of genre analysis as described in Swales (1990; 2004) and Bhatia (1993; 2004). Information on genre analysis is provided at the beginning of the first core course. Based on such established knowledge, every student teacher chooses a genre for a (hypothetical) teaching scenario (Step A) and describes its use and communicative purposes (Step B). With the basics established, they can then collect a few sample texts, combine them into a mini corpus (Step C) and undertake a purpose-oriented analysis of the building blocks ('moves') that are relevant to the genre in question (Step D). Once the communicative functionality of the genre and its parts is described, the focus turns to the micro-level of lexico-grammar and phraseology. Supported by the methodological possibilities of corpus analysis, Step E allows for a detailed description of the linguistic resources typically employed in the genre in question. So, while Step D is concerned with the 'why' of genres, Step E deals with the 'how' of verbalisation. Analysing the 'how' more generally, Step F focuses on larger textual patterns that characterise the genre in question. This analytical step draws on the preceding steps and, additionally, pays tribute to the relevance of multimodality, i.e. the fact that genres draw on more semiotic modes than the verbal one and rely centrally on the meaning potential of other modes such as colour, still or moving image or hypertext (for more information, see 3.4). With the genre analysis finalised and their experiential applied linguistic knowledge lastingly enriched, the student teachers turn to the pedagogical application (Step G). Here, again, established knowledge on ESP teaching and materials development is provided, with the help of which student teachers can enter the creative process of developing materials. Although student teachers have an obligatory teaching practice in an ESP context, they cannot always use the materials they have developed as they need to adhere to the demands of the classes they are teaching. However, both the process of creating materials and – whether linked or not – the actual teaching experience are intended to help student teachers further develop their PCK.

In view of the relevance allotted to specific kinds of content knowledge, pre-service ESP teacher education is well served to appraise, adapt and operationalise the relevant (applied) linguistic and pedagogical theories and methodologies in a process of mediation between applied theories and classroom practices (Widdowson, 2003: 23). As argued in detail in Hüttner *et al.* (2009), such central applied linguistic areas are genre analysis and corpus linguistics, which, in combination, allow for a corpus-based genre analysis (Tribble, 2001). Put briefly, this model combines the ESP genre approach to describing the functions and forms of texts (Bhatia, 1993, 2002; Swales, 1990, 2004) with corpus analytic methods (Adolphs, 2008; Sinclair, 1997), thus allowing for a mixed-methods analysis of largely written genres relevant to specific groups of experts (for more details, see 3.2). In view of the relevance of the semantic and semiotic characteristics of a specific genre, we will enrich this 'model of mediated corpus-based genre analysis' (Hüttner et al., 2009: 102) by taking on board considerations of phraseology (3.3) as well as multimodality (see 3.4).

3.2 Corpus-based Genre Analysis

Informed largely by the 'ESP approach' to genre analysis, *genre* is defined here as

> a class of communicative events, the members of which share some set of communicative purposes. These purposes are recognized by the expert members of the parent discourse community and thereby constitute the rationale for the genre [, which] shape[s] the schematic structure of the discourse. (Swales, 1990: 58)

The prominence given to 'communicative purpose' as defining criterion is of particular relevance in teaching contexts since it allows learners and teachers to go beyond mere surface features in trying to capture the essentials of a text. At the same time, the centrality given to 'purpose' proves to be somewhat problematic for actual analyses as, firstly, it is debatable whether to prioritise the analyst's or the genre users' (intuitive) understanding of 'purpose' (Hüttner, 2007: 27). Secondly, a detailed description of a communicative purpose often turns out to be an iterative process, with analyses requiring 're-purposing' (Swales, 2004: 72) the genres in question, potentially running the risk of circularity. Despite such partly unresolved issues, the ESP approach offers a well described step-by-step procedure (e.g. Bhatia, 1993: 22 ff.) with which unfamiliar genres can also be analysed (Hüttner, 2007: 101–113). Basically, the analysis rests on two pillars: the 'situational concerns of the discourse community and their evaluations of generic purpose and structure' (Hüttner et al., 2009: 102) and, centrally, the linguistic analysis that combines focusing on lexicogrammatical features, patterns of textualisation and the genre-structuring 'moves', i.e. 'discoursal or rhetorical unit[s] that perfor[m] coherent communicative function[s]' (Swales, 2004: 228). While the two analytical pillars complement each other, it is the latter that is particularly insightful for second-language learners as it produces detailed information on what should be communicated and how this could be done.

> The move [structure] need[s] to be [manually] defined through researchers' careful analysis of the entire texts with an aim of capturing all functional elements, and by taking into account some linguistic cues in the decision of move boundaries. [...] It does not set out to find particular moves, but tries to identify stretches of text that fulfil a function recognisable to users of the genre. (Hüttner, 2010: 204)

As concerns the analysis of lexico-grammatical features, the insights and tools offered from corpus linguistics prove particularly helpful. Language corpora serve as collections of actual language use (Kaltenböck & Mehlmauer-Larcher, 2005: 70–71). As the recent literature shows, language patterns, such as typical choices of words and their frequencies or appropriate use of collocations, can be extracted quickly and easily with the help of any text analysis software available nowadays, e.g. WordSmith Tools (© Mike Scott). As regards ESP genres, however, published corpora such as the British National Corpus (BNC), the International Corpus of English (ICE) or the Corpus of Contemporary American (COCA) have their limitations. Despite being impressively large, they have usually been compiled to represent a language in its generality and not to contain substantial exemplars of the many ESP genres available at present. Additionally, the definition of genre used in these corpora tends to be more general, for example, 'formal letter', than the one proposed here, following Swales (1990, 2004) and Bhatia (2004), that classifies letters of recommendation or academic abstracts as individual genres. Therefore, Tribble (2001) suggests compiling genre-specific mini-corpora by collecting electronic exemplars of the genre in question. Such corpora can then be analysed by corpus linguistic methods, including statistically substantiated comparisons with one of the large corpora of general English that serves as a reference corpus (for illustrations, see 4).

3.3 Phraseology/Lexico-grammar

While a largely manual move analysis provides insights into the required and purposeful parts of any given genre, extracting information on the lexico-grammatical profile of any genre is particularly interesting with a view towards creating materials helpful to foreign-language learners. One of the areas where a corpus-based analysis yields most relevant results regards formulaic phrases or chunks of language. The issue of the appropriate use of idiomatic or formulaic language has received much attention in the research literature over the last few years (Schmitt, 2004; Skandera, 2007; Wray, 2002), and increasingly the focus has shifted from idiomaticity in the sense of proverbs or opaque phrases like *to kick the bucket*, to the more typical combinations encountered with particular words, where other combinations at first glance seem equally possible but are simply not typical and often appear somewhat 'un-English', even if the reader cannot specify quite what is wrong with them. An example of this would be the phrase *major catastrophe*, which is used typically rather than, e.g. *serious catastrophe*, *big catastrophe*, although there is little apparent difference in meaning (Wray, 2002: 206 ff). For learners of unfamiliar genres, the appropriate use of such idiomaticity is one part of the learning process that ought not to be neglected. An additional analytical strategy in this context is to compare the mini-corpus in question with a large reference corpus, such as the BNC. With the help of concordancing software, it is a fairly simple procedure to identify lexemes that appear significantly more or less frequently than in the large and general reference corpus, thus identifying what seem to be typical words and word combinations of the genre in question. On the basis of such statistically identified 'keywords' of the genre, learners can be made aware of a genre's key phrases and phrases that support the textualisation of particular communicative purposes.

Overall then, linking the discourse-oriented study of genre to a corpus-based lexico-phraseological analysis takes on board the benefits of both fields of enquiry; it incorporates the context-driven nature of genre analysis but also uses the advantages of quantitative corpus analysis in order to avoid reliance on intuitions or on (possibly atypical) single examples. The creation of a corpus focused on a single genre ensures that the lexico-phraseological profile established is relevant to teaching that particular genre.

3.4 Multimodality

Understandably, most of the literature as well as the CerTESP Module have focused almost exclusively on the verbal mode, both in regards to gaining familiarity with specific ESPs as well as the underlying approach sketched so far. Lately, however, more and more new and emerging genres are substantially linked to the internet and its complex, non-linear and partially fleeting structure (Crystal, 2006: 203 ff.). Manual pages for electronic devices, for instance, are increasingly available on the internet, thus making use of hypertext amongst other features absent from printed leaflets. While hypertext is prominent as an internet-contingent structuring device of texts and genres, there are also other modes that genres draw on in diverse ways and that a purely verbal analysis ignores, arguably to the detriment of fully disclosing their specificities.

A 'mode' in this context is understood in the social semiotic way as a 'socially shaped and culturally given resource for making meaning' (Kress, 2010: 79) and refers to a variety of 'forms of communication' (Bezemer & Jewitt, 2010: 183), such as (moving) images, layout, gesture, speech or writing. In this understanding, modes and their meaning potentials are culturally and socially shaped, but draw on their specific 'affordances', i.e. 'the material "stuff" of the mode (sound, movement, light and tracings on surfaces, etc.)' (Kress, 2010: 80). Sound, for instance, unfolds in time; the resulting sequentiality is integral to speech and contrasts with the non-sequential affordance of marks on paper and the consequent non-fleeting nature of writing (Bezemer & Jewitt, 2010: 184). Actual meaning potentials, however, are not only dependent on the material limitations of modes, but also on their sociocultural conventionalisation, and thus are continuously changing and developing. Furthermore, the meaning of one mode is always dependent on other modes, with the interaction between modes making meaning as well. For instance, both images of museum exhibits and verbal texts describe museum collections, but the interaction between the two will allow for additional meaning-making potentials in terms of what the museum representation reveals to potential visitors.

The interrelatedness of modes to the meaning-making process also comes to the fore in the social semiotic understanding that 'representation and communication always draw on a multiplicity of modes' (Bezemer & Jewitt, 2010: 183). In other words, the meaning potential of a text and of the genre it exemplifies do not rely solely on the verbal mode, but integrates all the relevant modes. To illustrate this point, let us consider a hotel brochure that combines verbal text, images and, above all, layout. This brochure can be expected to describe the hotel verbally and by the images chosen, but equally important is the layout, i.e. the positioning and framing of the texts and images and the kind and degree of salience given to them with the help of features such as (font) size or colour (Kress & van Leeuwen, 2006).

Given the focus of genre analysis on communicative purposes, genre-based teaching approaches are arguably well advised to take on board the insights gained through multimodal analysis. So far, however, multi-modality has been largely ignored, most likely because of the pedagogical focus of ESP teaching on the verbal mode. While this focus is fully understandable and also well founded in terms of the limited time resources in view of the (language) learning aims that need to be met, the relevance of the non-verbal modes should not be completely sidelined, especially as this might lead to a misrepresentation of the textualisations typical of certain genres in meeting their communicative purposes. As already hinted at above, hotel descriptions can hardly do without images, internet-based manual pages need hypertext, annual business reports require graphs and tables and all of them draw on layout in its sociocultural conventionalisation. It is for this reason that the CerTESP core courses also integrate considerations of multimodality into genre analysis as well as the ensuing materials development (for illustrations, see below).

4 Examples

Given that the aim of this contribution is to argue for the approach presented so far as a way to engage student ESP teachers in developing their PCK, even when confined to an applied scientific teacher education system, it seems particularly important to turn to the student projects themselves and exemplify how these can be considered as evidence of growing PCK. As the basic specificities of the corpus-mediated genre-analytical approach have been exemplified in Hüttner et al. (2009), we shall confine the discussion here to three projects undertaken by students of the CerTESP Module. Each of the three sample projects is meant to illustrate in particular one of the additional resources, i.e. phraseology, multimodality and materials development.

4.1 Internet-based Package Inserts

Based on a corpus of 22 package inserts of non-prescription drugs, downloaded from the websites of pharmaceutical companies, Semmelrock and Steiner (2006) identify the overall communicative purpose as 'on the one hand to inform and to advise the customer and on the other hand to promote the product' (12) as well as outlining a set of obligatory and optional moves that give the package inserts a relatively uniform structure overall (see Table 9.2).[3]

Especially as regards the two obligatory moves 'Indicating' and 'Warning', the detailed phraseological analysis reveals a wealth of important formulations, partly hinging on specific verbs (*to reduce, to prevent, to relieve*) and partly foregrounding particular clause constructions, such as *if* clauses or the use of the imperative (for some examples, see Table 9.3).

Table 9.2 Move structure (based on Semmelrock & Steiner, 2006: 11–12)[4]

Obligatory moves	Optional moves
1. Naming product	
2. Visualising package	2b. Ordering possibilities by hyperlink
3. Introducing product by describing functions and ingredients	
	4. Informing on package size
5. Giving active ingredients	5b. Adding inactive ingredients
6. Indicating use and purpose	
7. Warnings	
8. Directions on usage and dosage	
9. Instructing on safety and storage	
	10. Providing contact possibilities

Based on their project work, the student teachers identify different findings as particularly relevant to the various potential teaching scenarios they envisaged (Semmelrock & Steiner, 2006: 3):

- Lay people travelling in English-speaking countries 'would surely benefit most from enlarging their vocabulary and practicing their passive skills (reading and listening)' in understanding typical word fields, such as symptoms and side effects or different measuring systems.
- Medical professionals will also need to acquire productive knowledge and 'get the content and meaning across to patients or customers'. Thus, additionally to the lexis, ESP teaching should also focus on typical grammatical patterns, e.g. imperative constructions and *if* sentences.
- Employees of pharmaceutical companies would need 'to gain knowledge about the overall structure of packages inserts and product marketing' and would thus need to learn about the move structure as well.

4.2 Press Releases of IT Companies

Based on an initial analysis of 40 press releases of IT companies, Kraus and Schmid (2010: 3) describe the relevant communicative purpose as 'to inform the press and ultimately the public of any kind of new developments in the company. At the same time, their aim is to persuade potential

Table 9.3 Phrases typical of the moves Indicating and Warning (Semmelrock & Steiner, 2006: 1–619)

temporarily effectively	relieves	nasal allergy/cold symptoms minor aches (sinus) pain pains of joints nasal/sinus congestion itching (of the nose and throat) nausea diarrhoea
	reduces	fever redness inflammation
prevents relieves	symptoms	associated with XY
if	symptoms pain	worsen/s persist/s clear/s up get/s worse
if	sleeplessness sore throat	persits
if you	get	nervous dizzy
can may	cause	a severse allergic reaction liver damage problems in the unborn child
Do not	use	unless directed by a doctor for ... if ...
ask	a doctor a doctor or pharmacist	before use before use if ... before taking this product

customers/investors of investing in the company'. Contrary to the preceding genre, this one was found to be structured rather loosely, with the 16 obligatory, core and optional moves appearing in changing sequencing (Table 9.4). The distinction between obligatory, core and optional moves is

Table 9.4 Move structure (based on Kraus & Schmid, 2010: 5-6)

Obligatory moves	Core moves	Optional moves
1. Press release/logo		
2. Title		
3. Synopsis		
4. Abstract (place, date, introducing topic)		
	5. What is innovative	
		6. Who benefits
	7. Advantages of product	
		8. Data of product
	9. Where to get additional info	
		10. Providing info on past and future events
		11. Pricing and availability
	12. Info on partners	
13. Info on company		
14. Press contacts		
15. Note to editors		
		16. Related resources

based on frequencies, with obligatory moves appearing in 90 to 100% of all sample texts, core moves in more than 50% and optional moves in less than 50% (cf. also Hüttner, 2007: 110).

While the lexico-grammatical analysis reveals interesting verbal patterns, the authors also stress the relevance of multimodality by singling out some non-verbal modes, such as layout, hyperlinks, tables and graphs and in some cases also visual images. Made possible by the internet, some press releases include still or moving images in support of the communicative purpose 'to persuade the reader of the positive aspects of the product or event in question' (Kraus & Schmid, 2010: 9). Interestingly, however, company logos play a minor role as identifier of the originator of the texts. Tables and graphs are regularly used to provide additional, numerically based information such as quarter results. This, the authors point out convincingly, 'improves the readability of the press releases and thus enables the readers to find relevant information more quickly' (Kraus & Schmid, 2010: 9). Hyperlinks are also a standard feature, allowing readers to move on directly to other websites related to the product or the company. Interestingly, the function of moving between (parts of) texts is sometimes also fulfilled by asterisks or footnotes, i.e. cross-referential features of printed rather than online texts. As regards layout more generally, the student teachers identified salience markers, such as bulleting and paragraphing, employed to foreground key words and important information and bold print as marker of (sub)headings.

As to potential teaching scenarios, Kraus & Schmid (2010: 17) imagine either upper secondary teenagers or a specialised adult learner group, both at a minimum competence level of B1+ according to the Common European Framework of Reference for Languages. The student teachers also suggest some tasks for teaching materials, mainly based on the move and lexico-grammatical analyses. While the multimodal findings have been sidelined in the admittedly brief section on possible teaching tasks, most likely reflecting the (student) language teachers' overpowering focus on the verbal mode, they should definitely be included in an integrative teaching approach. For instance, the different meaning potential of cross-referencing in printed and online modes would require a task focusing on the use of hypertext.

4.3 Letters of Recommendation

With learners in a business communication course in mind, Mayer and Müller-Reim (2010) focus on how the genre of letters of recommendation could be taught to 'professionals in the field of technology [...] [on] an upper-immediate level of English or above' (Mayer & Müller-Reim, 2010: 3). In their roles as managers, such learners would need to write letters recommending either individuals or other businesses. Given that such learners would need to learn about the 'what', 'why' and 'how' of such letters, the authors collected 25 sample texts available on the internet as JPEG or PDF files and thus assumed to be genuine. Based on an analysis of this mini-corpus, the communicative purposes of this genre are described as 'to reveal information (such as achievements, performance, qualities of the recommended person or company) and to persuade potential employers or business partners to work with the recommended company or to employ the recommended person' (Mayer & Müller-Reim, 2010: 2). Similar to the

Table 9.5 Move structure (based on Mayer & Müller-Reim, 2010: 5–6)

Obligatory moves	Core moves	Optional moves
	1. Emblem of recommender	
	2. Date	
	3. Headline	
	4. Salutation	
	5. Contextualisation	
6. Description of previous work		
	7. Praise of skills	
8. Reassurance		
		9. Willingness to provide further info
	10. Greeting	
	11. Signature, name, position	11a. Contact information

preceding example, the move analysis distinguishes obligatory, core and optional moves based on frequency of usage (for an overview, see Table 9.5).

Enriched by detailed lexico-grammatical and textual analyses (steps E and F in Table 9.1), Mayer and Müller-Reim (2010: 16–19) transform their content knowledge of genre analytical findings into the PCK of developing teaching materials for their hypothetical teaching scenario. To begin with, learners would be made aware of the basic threefold structure of the letters (opening – body – closing) by an exercise that allows learners to assemble a sample letter from jumbled building blocks.

With the overall structure thus established, the teaching unit would focus on the body of the letters, to be precise on two moves in particular, i.e. 'Description of previous work' and 'Praise of skills'. These are argued to be essential in terms of the communicative purposes of the genre. As regards both moves, learners would be exposed to sample paragraphs in order to identify their purposes, but also to prefabricated phrase banks. Exercises based on the lexico-grammatical findings should not overlook the potential need to revise some grammatical issues, such as the use of tenses. More importantly, however, teaching time would focus on collocations and phrases provided in worksheets. Here, the authors offer a few examples,

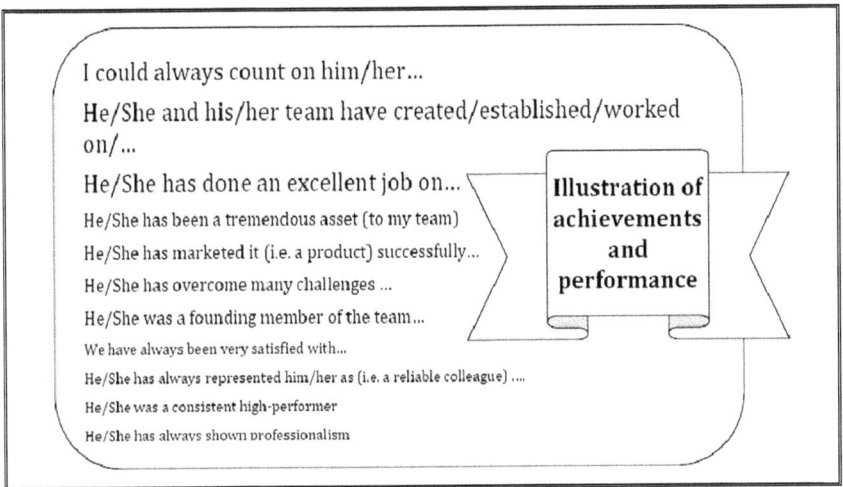

Figure 9.1 Worksheet of phrases useful for 'Description of previous work' (Mayer & Müller-Reim, 2010: 18)

such as the one given in Figure 9.1, where the font size is chosen indexically and indicates frequency of usage in the mini-corpus.

In relation to move 7, learners' attention needs to be drawn to what Mayer and Müller-Reim (2010: 18) fittingly call 'coded language', i.e. overtly appreciative language used to 'indicate a certain degree of recommendation'. While recommendations make exclusive use of affirmative formulations, the degree of praise chosen reveals the recommender's stance towards the abilities and strengths of the recommended individual or company. It goes without saying that such subtle linguistic ways of expressing evaluations are very central to newcomers to that genre and need explicit teaching and practicing. The worksheet given in Figure 9.2 provides an overview of the respective language items and would be used for activities that could help learners to 'actively use the relevant lexical expressions themselves' (Mayer and Müller-Reim, 2010: 19).

Overall then, the three examples introduced here illustrate the different but generally fruitful ways in which student teachers manage to transform the received applied linguistic and pedagogical knowledge they are exposed to in the core CerTESP courses into PCK as regards mediated corpus-based genre analysis and use this knowledge to develop genre-specific ESP teaching materials. While the limitations of the teacher education programme rarely allow actual ESP teaching, the 'Vienna ESP approach' provides ample opportunities for Kind's (2009) three contributing factors to developing PCK.

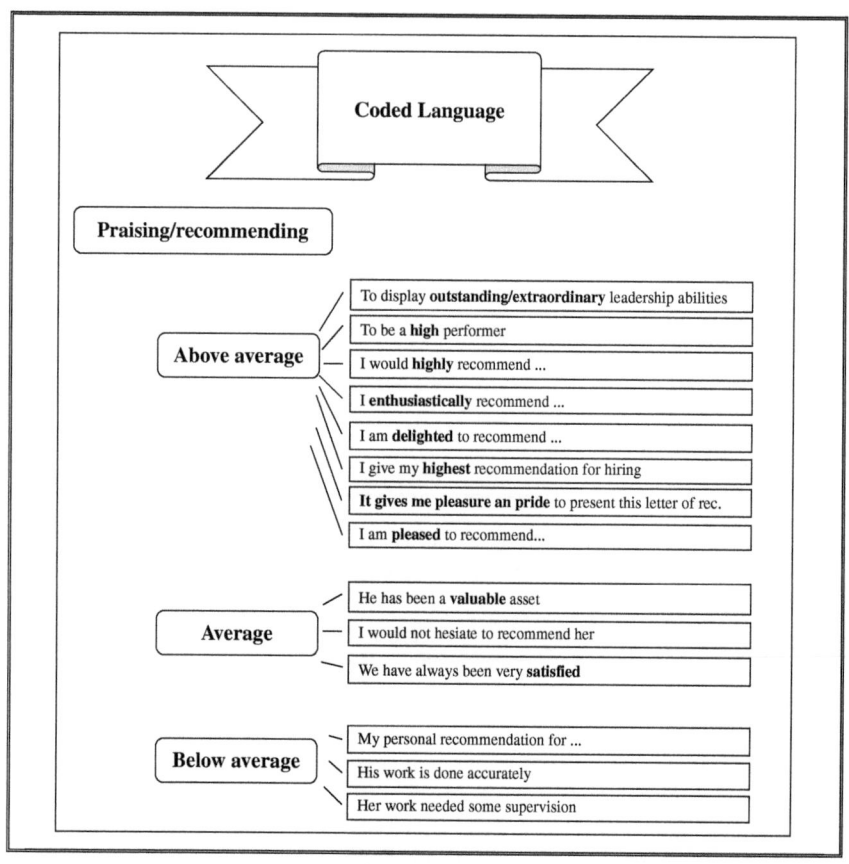

Figure 9.2 Worksheet on 'coded language' useful for 'Praise of skills' (Mayer & Müller-Reim, 2010: Appendix)

As supported by course outcome and student feedback, the CerTESP holders have built good subject matter knowledge and experience their self-confidence and other relevant emotional attributes as strengthened. Finally, the student-centred and directed project work resulting in pedagogically oriented genre description and materials development helps student teachers in transforming their content knowledge into relevant PCK for future ESP practice.

5 Conclusions

Pedagogical content knowledge (PCK) is a powerful construct to describe the aspect of the professional knowledge base that is uniquely the domain of teachers and as such seems a prime area for student teachers to develop in their teacher education. The concrete project described here aimed at addressing the dilemma of novice ESP teachers' apparent lack of PCK and our wish as teacher educators to provide opportunities for its development, despite some structural obstacles, such as the temporal and emotional distance to the actual teaching practice.

The CerTESP module and its 'Vienna ESP approach' were developed with the aim of providing a framework to foster student teachers' development of PCK in the area of ESP teaching and so to improve the rather problematic situation of preparation for ESP contexts among our graduates. Despite the problem of an overarching applied science model of teacher education and thus highly limited classroom practice, we believe the CerTESP succeeds in some degree in providing an opportunity for transforming content knowledge in applied linguistics into PCK for ESP. It does this mainly through focusing on materials development, which forces student teachers at the planning stage of designing or even just deciding on teaching materials to consider the potential learning difficulties of their envisaged learners, considered by Shulman (1986: 9) as an essential part of PCK. The actual analyses carried out by the student teachers are, as has been shown above, sophisticated and, at times, better and more pedagogically adequate than published materials, which do not exist for all genres and which sometimes have a lower degree of overlap with the actual genres as used and understood by their discourse communities. Thus, the materials produced by our student teachers are frequently more recognisable and thus more genuine. We would suggest that the realistic nature of the task – after all, most materials developed are for internet-based and/or emerging genres where no materials exist – helps develop student teachers' PCK. Thus, their ability to make use of fairly sophisticated applied linguistic methods and tools *in order to* apply these to a teaching situation aims to help them engage in the process of transforming this content knowledge into PCK.

Clearly, the CerTESP can only start a process of student teachers' developing their PCK, but if an awareness of this type of knowledge required for teaching grows among student teachers, ideally it will feed into their future teaching practices and should limit a 'one-size-fits-all' attitude to teaching ESP. The success of the CerTESP evidenced both in the responses of student teachers and in the quality of final student projects should serve as encouragement to other teacher educators in similar situations and with similar constraints.

Notes

(1) On PCK, see also Mehlmauer-Larcher, Reichl, and Tsui (all this volume).
(2) Often termed subject matter knowledge.

(3) Interestingly, the second obligatory move draws on a non-verbal mode, thus indicating the relevance of a multimodal approach.
(4) Defining criteria of what makes a move either obligatory or optional are not given in the student paper.

References

Abell, S.K. (2008) Twenty years later: Does pedagogical content knowledge remain a useful idea? *International Journal of Science Education* 30 (10), 1405–1416.
Adolphs, S. (2008) *Corpus and Context: Investigating Pragmatic Functions in Spoken Discourse*. Amsterdam and Philadelphia: John Benjamins.
Bezemer, J. and Jewitt, C. (2010) Multimodal analysis: Key issues. In L. Litosseliti (ed.) *Research Methods in Linguistics* (pp. 180–197). London/New York: Continuum.
Bhatia, V.K. (1993) *Analysing Genre: Language Use in Professional Settings*. Harlow, UK: Pearson Education.
Bhatia, V.K. (2002) Applied genre analysis: Analytical advances and pedagogical procedures. In A.M. Johns (ed.) *Genre in the Classroom: Multiple Perspectives* (pp. 279–283). Mahwah, NJ: Lawrence Erlbaum.
Bhatia, V.K. (2004) *Worlds of Written Discourse: A Genre-Based View*. London: Continuum.
Canniveng, C. and Martinez, M. (2003) Materials development and teacher training. In B. Tomlinson (ed.) *Developing Materials for Language Teaching* (pp. 479–517). London/New York: Continuum.
Crystal, D. (2006) *Language and the Internet* (2nd edn). Cambridge: Cambridge University Press.
Department of English, University of Vienna (2004) CerTESP – Certificate in Teaching English for Specific Purposes. Online at http://anglistik.univie.ac.at/esp
Fernandez-Balboa, J-M. and Stiehl, J. (1995) The generic nature of pedagogical content knowledge among college professors. *Teaching and Teacher Education* 11 (3), 293–306.
Gess-Newsome, J. (1999) Pedagogical content knowledge: An introduction and orientation. In J. Gess-Newsome and N.G. Lederman (eds) *Examining Pedagogical Content Knowledge* (pp. 3–17). Dordrecht: Kluwer Academic.
Grossman, P. (1990) *The Making of a Teacher*. New York: Teachers' College Press.
Hüttner, J. (2007) *Academic Writing in a Foreign Language: An Extended Genre Analysis of Student Texts*. Frankfurt: Peter Lang.
Hüttner, J. (2010) The potential of purpose-built corpora in the analysis of student academic writing in English. *Journal of Writing Research* 2 (2), 197–218.
Hüttner, J., Smit, U. and Mehlmauer-Larcher, B. (2009) ESP teacher education at the interface of theory and practice: Introducing a model of mediated corpus-based genre analysis. *System* 37 (1), 99–109.
Kaltenböck, G. and Mehlmauer-Larcher, B. (2005) Computer corpora and the language classroom: Forced marriage or perfect match? On the potential and limitations of computer corpora in language teaching. *ReCall* 17 (1), 65–84.
Kind, V. (2009) Pedagogical content knowledge in science education: Perspectives and potential for progress. *Studies in Science Education* 45 (2), 169–204.
Koballa, T.R., Gräber, W., Coleman, D. and Kemp, A.C. (1999) Prospective teachers' conceptualisations of the knowledge base for teaching chemistry at the gymnasium. *Journal of Science Teacher Education* 10 (4), 1529–1562.
Kraus, N. and Schmid, S. (2010) Genre analysis of press releases of IT companies. Unpublished student paper, University of Vienna.

Kress, G. (2010) *Multimodality: A Social Semiotic Approach to Contemporary Communication*. London: Routledge.
Kress, G. and van Leeuwen, T. (2006) *Reading Images: The Grammar of Visual Design* (2nd edn). London: Routledge.
Magnusson, S., Krajcik, J., and Borko, H. (1999) Secondary teachers' knowledge and beliefs about subject matter and their impact on instruction. In J. Gess-Newsome and N.G. Lederman (eds) *Examining Pedagogical Content Knowledge* (pp. 95–132). Dordrecht: Kluwer Academic.
Marks, R. (1990) Pedagogical content knowledge: From a mathematical case to a modified conception. *Journal of Teacher Education* 41 (3), 3–11.
Mayer, K. and Müller-Reim, A. (2010) 'To whom it may concern' Analyzing and teaching letters of recommendation: A project report. Unpublished student paper, University of Vienna.
Schmitt, N. (ed.) (2004) *Formulaic Sequences*. Amsterdam/Philadelphia: John Benjamins.
Semmelrock, N. and Steiner, B. (2006) Genre analysis: Package inserts available on the internet. Unpublished student paper, University of Vienna.
Shulman, L.S. (1986) Those who understand: Knowledge growth in teaching. *Educational Researcher* 15 (2), 4–14.
Shulman, L.S. (1987) Knowledge and teaching: Foundations of the new reform. *Harvard Educational Review* 57 (1), 1–22.
Sinclair, J.M. (1997) Corpus evidence in language description. In A. Wichmann, S. Fligelstone, T. McEnery and G. Knowles (eds) *Teaching and Language Corpora* (pp. 27–39). London/New York: Longman.
Skandera, P. (ed.) (2007) *Phraseology and Culture in English*. Berlin: de Gruyter.
Smit, U. (2005) Applied genre analysis in pre-service ESP teacher education: A report on a recently developed applied linguistics course. *Vienna English Working Papers (VIEWS)* 14(2), 72–83.
Smit, U. and Hüttner, J. (2006) Das Potential fachsprachenspezifischer Minikorpora: Analyse und Evaluierung einer innovativen Lehrveranstaltung im Rahmen der Lehramtsausbildung Englisch. In B. Kettemann (ed.) *Planing, Gluing and Painting Corpora: Inside the Applied Corpus Linguist's Workshop* (pp. 233–256). Frankfurt: Peter Lang.
Swales, J.M. (1990) *Genre Analysis: English in Academic and Research Settings*. Cambridge: Cambridge University Press.
Swales, J.M. (2004) *Research Genres: Exploration and Application*. Cambridge: Cambridge University Press.
Tribble, C. (2001) Small corpora and teaching writing: Towards a corpus-informed pedagogy of writing. In G. Mohsen, A. Henry and R. Roseberry (eds) *Small Corpus Studies and ELT* (pp. 381–408). Amsterdam/ Philadelphia: John Benjamins.
Wallace, M. (1991) *Training Foreign Language Teachers: A Reflective Approach*. Cambridge: Cambridge University Press.
Widdowson, H.G. (1983) *Learning Purpose and Language Use*. Oxford: Oxford University Press.
Widdowson, H.G. (2003) 'Expert beyond experience': Notes on the appropriate use of theory in practice. In D. Newby (ed.) *Mediating between Theory and Practice in the Context of Different Learning Cultures and Languages* (pp. 23–30). Strasbourg: Council of Europe Publishing.
Wray, A. (2002) *Formulaic Language and the Lexicon*. Cambridge: Cambridge University Press.

10 The EPOSTL (European Portfolio for Student Teachers of Languages): A Tool to Promote Reflection and Learning in Pre-Service Teacher Education

Barbara Mehlmauer-Larcher

1 Introduction

Within the European educational context there is a movement towards harmonising educational programmes; additionally, those programmes should become more transparent, thus increasing the quality and the comparability of acquired qualifications. In many European countries, educational authorities and institutions have formulated outcome-oriented competences as well as educational standards, which are further indications of an education policy with a strong focus on quality control and a demand for greater accountability. This demand for greater accountability and consequently the specification of required competences has also reached the field of foreign-language teacher education and led to the publication of two influential documents, namely the *European Profile for Language Teachers* (Kelly & Grenfell, 2004) – an EU document compiled at the University of Southampton – and most recently the so-called EPOSTL (European Profile for Student Teachers of Languages) (Newby *et al.*, 2007) initiated by the European Council. The EPOSTL follows the design of a competence-oriented self-assessment tool aimed at supporting language teachers in their critical reflection on their teacher learning processes and the development of language teaching competences.

Whereas the debate on and the demand for quality control and a higher degree of accountability within language teacher education programmes has recently been brought to the field of language teacher education from the outside, researchers, course designers of teacher education programmes as well as practitioners within the field have been occupied with re-examining and reconsidering the required knowledge and skill base of language teachers and consequently the instructional approaches applied in various language teacher education programmes (cf. Richards, 2008).

One of the issues discussed not only by researchers in the field of language teacher education, but in all fields of teacher education is the actual impact that teacher education programmes have on the behaviour of novice teachers in classroom settings. Several studies (e.g. Cochran-Smith & Zeichner, 2005; Grossman, 2008; Wideen et al., 1998) carried out in a variety of settings point toward the danger that instructional approaches might not have a satisfactory level of impact on student teachers' learning and their teaching practice during field experience phases and after their graduation when they start their professional careers.

Given the danger of a so-called divide between theory and practice, designers of pre-service teacher education programmes are faced with the challenge of developing carefully designed instructional approaches to overcome (or at least to minimise) the gap between the theory level of university-based coursework and research and student teachers' actual teaching practice. Korthagen (2010: 99) points out that specifically designed approaches to teacher education can have the potential of helping to reduce the divide between theory and practice.

In this chapter, an innovative instructional design for teacher pedagogy will be discussed, namely the implementation of the above-mentioned EPOSTL in the pre-service language teacher education programme at the Centre for English Language Teaching (CELT) at the University of Vienna. The EPOSTL, a recently developed reflection and self-assessment tool, has been implemented into the course programme for various purposes. One of the more general aims of its implementation has been to contribute to the reduction of the theory-practice-divide within the programme. Furthermore, this document has a potential influence on the definition and clarification of the knowledge and skills base of future language teachers.

Given the prominent role of reflection and its centrality in teacher education programmes aiming at a mediation between theory and practice, a brief analysis of the concept of reflection and its various modes in the context of teacher learning will be provided. This analysis will be followed by a more detailed description of the recently developed implementation scheme of the EPOSTL for the language teacher education programme at the CELT at the University of Vienna. In addition to this description, some initial results of an investigation into the impact the EPOSTL can have on aspects of teacher learning will be presented.

2 Some Challenges of Pre-Service Teacher Education

Traditionally, many teacher education programmes at universities have been based on an 'applied science' model (Wallace, 1991: 8 ff.). The underlying assumption of this model is that academic knowledge acquired in university courses can and will be directly applied by teachers in their language classrooms.

Widdowson (1990: 31 ff.) has pointed at one of the many problematic aspects of this kind of approach to teacher education, namely the inherent 'one-way structure' of such a model, based on disciplinary knowledge just being passed down to the (student) teacher who is supposed to apply it in her/his classroom setting. In his model of mediation between (applied) linguistics and language pedagogy, Widdowson stresses the importance of agency on the (student) teacher's side and the underlying two-way structure of his mediation model. Widdowson's model offers an empowered role of the teacher, who is the one to decide on the relevance of findings from validated theories for her/his classroom, and it is the teacher who decides on the application, operationalisation and (empiric) evaluation of these findings applied in the language classroom.

A further step away from the traditional applied science model is the plea for a distinction between subject matter knowledge and pedagogical content knowledge (cf. Freeman & Johnson, 1998; Johnson, 2009; Shulman, 1987) and subsequently a closer look at the nature, the relevance and the development of pedagogic content knowledge within programmes of teacher education.[1] Pedagogical content knowledge is the knowledge used by teachers 'to make the content of their instruction relevant and accessible to students' (Johnson, 2009: 22). This does not mean that language teachers do not need the disciplinary subject knowledge any longer, but that they need both types of knowledge (Johnson, 2009: 22). Consequently, language teacher educators are required to develop teacher education programmes and instructional approaches that enable student teachers to develop pedagogical content knowledge. Moreover, student teachers should be provided with ample opportunities to apply their newly developed pedagogical content knowledge in classroom settings in order to help overcome the theory-practice divide so often criticised with many teacher education schemes.

In parallel to an increasing interest in pedagogical content knowledge, a so-called reflective model of language teacher education was developed by Wallace (1991, see also Schön, 1987) that was meant to replace the applied science model of teacher education. One of the main features of this model is the integration of actual and continuous teaching experiences into teacher education programmes. As its name already indicates, in this model reflection is an important cognitive activity and is regarded as essential for teacher learning processes. Furthermore, reflection plays a vital role in this model as regards the challenge of bridging the gap between knowledge and concepts provided by validated theories and their application and operationalisation in an actual teaching context. Additionally, reflection is regarded as a prerequisite for improvement and increased effectiveness of classroom teaching as well as continuous teacher learning leading to professional development (cf. Wallace, 1991).

In the following section, the central role of reflection in processes of teacher learning will be discussed. According to Burton (2009: 298), reflection is a recognised axiom within language teacher education. However, the actual meaning of this cognitive activity is often not clearly defined. As criticised by Noffke and Brennan (2005), the term 'reflection' has frequently become a kind of popular and unquestioned slogan; consequently, a closer look at the concept of reflection seems necessary (cf. Mehlmauer-Larcher, 2010).

2.1 The Concept of Reflection as an Integral Part of Teacher Learning

The American educational philosopher John Dewey (1910: 6) was the first one to deal with the term reflection in the context of education and defined reflection as:

> active, persistent, and careful consideration of any belief or supposed form of knowledge in the light of the grounds that support it, and the further conclusions to which it tends [...] it includes a conscious and voluntary effort to establish belief upon a firm basis of evidence and rationality.

According to Dewey's understanding of reflection, this cognitive activity involves thinking that is intentional, goal-directed and closely related to processes of evaluation and can be initiated and supported by formal education (cf. also Moon, 1999: 12). For Dewey, reflection is usually triggered by some kind of unexpected incidence interrupting the usual course of events (cf. also Roberts, 1998: 48).

According to Dewey (1910), reflection is the prerequisite for personal and professional development and growth because reflection enables us to distance ourselves from a one-sided perspective on problematic issues. In this context, Dewey (1910: 68 f.) coined the term of 'reframing', which refers to a multi-perspective view of problems.

Dewey's concept of reframing is similar to Eraut's (1994) term of 'metaprocessing', which defines a type of control knowledge. According to Eraut (1994: 115), metaprocessing involves 'evaluation of what one is doing and thinking, the continuing redefinition of priorities and the critical adjustment of cognitive frameworks and assumptions'.

Bartlett (1990: 204 f.) also refers to reflection as the key to continuous professional development of language teachers. Similarly to Zeichner and Liston (1996), for Bartlett reflection should not be limited to the assessment of one's knowledge and teaching practice, but, in the sense of a *critical* reflection, the historical and sociocultural setting of any teaching practice needs to be considered as well.

Freeman (2002) stresses the necessity for teacher education to teach reflectivity. At the same time, Freeman requires student teachers to be provided with the terms and expressions of their discourse community in order to be able to reflect and talk about their experiences. Freeman (2002: 11) argues that '[w]e need to understand that articulation and reflection are reciprocal processes. One needs the words to talk about what one does, and in using those words one can see it more clearly'.

2.2 Types of Reflection

Beside theoretical considerations, in his article *Reflections on Reflection* Akbari (2007) also stresses the importance of practical aspects of reflection in the context of language teacher education when he argues that the actual purpose of reflection ought to be 'better student learning and more efficient teacher performance' (Akbari, 2007: 204). Consequently, Akbari (2007: 195) pleads for a careful typology of reflective processes in the context of language teacher education.

As regards the time level, traditionally the focus of reflection is on teaching events in the past. This kind of backward-oriented reflection is referred to as 'retrospective reflection' (Akbari, 2007: 193, 197). Reflection that is directed towards the future and closely related to the planning of teaching and possible innovations is referred to as 'prospective' or alternatively as 'creative' or 'innovative reflection'. These types of reflection directed towards future events are often neglected as the focus of interest is usually on retrospective reflective processes (Akbari, 2007: 192). Similarly, Farrell (2007: 6) uses the term 'reflection-for-action', referring to reflective activities concerned with future actions and describes this kind of reflection as 'proactive in nature'.

Jay and Johnson (2002) suggest another useful typology of reflection in connection with teaching activities. They distinguish between three reflective steps: description, comparison and critique. First, the problem area that the reflection is focusing on is described; second, the problem is analysed from various perspectives and the results of this analysis are compared with the aim 'to discover meanings we might otherwise miss' (Jay & Johnson, 2002: 78). In the final phase, possible solutions to problems are being evaluated critically, and new insights are integrated into the existing knowledge base with the aim of reaching a decision.

With regard to the interaction format within which reflection takes place, one distinguishes between 'monologic' and 'dialogic reflection'. Monologic reflection refers to a cognitive process that can also be considered as an 'inner monologue', whereas dialogic reflection includes the interaction with others. In this context, Kemmis (1985: 140) points out the social aspect of reflection that he sees is not limited to some sort of an inner monologue. According to Kemmis, reflection at some point also requires exchange and communication with others.

With reflection taking up a central role in language teacher education, designers of study programmes are faced with the challenge of providing opportunities for structured reflection within teacher education courses and, in particular, in connection with integrated field experiences of student teachers.

3 The EPOSTL: Context, Aims and Structure

The EPOSTL, with its main section of 'I-can' descriptors, provides a well-structured and concise overview of the main pedagogical content knowledge required by a practicing language teacher whose aim is to help her/his learners develop communicative competence. At the same time, the descriptors not only represent a survey of pedagogical content knowledge, but can also be used for inquiries into the underlying disciplinary knowledge of linguistics, applied linguistics, SLA research, cultural studies, learner psychology and general pedagogy.

The EPOSTL was developed by an international team of experts, led by David Newby, at the European Centre for Modern Languages (ECML) at Graz (Austria). At present, the document is available in nine languages.

The EPOSTL is the fourth document within a series of official documents at the European level dealing with standardisation and the definition of required competences within the fields of language teaching and learning. One of these documents is the *European Profile for Language Teacher Education: A Frame of Reference* (Kelly & Grenfell, 2004), which is a reference tool for curriculum developers, teacher educators and institutions involved in the education and development of language teachers. The main purpose of the document is to provide an overview of the required knowledge base as well as a comprehensive and systematic list of essential competences and skills required of future language teachers. In addition, this overview of required knowledge and these lists of competences are meant to increase transparency with regard to content and quality of teacher education programmes. Moreover, the profile can be seen as a kind of checklist for institutions offering teacher education programmes when they need to plan curricula and their course programmes (cf. Kelly & Grenfell, 2004: 3).

Both the EPOSTL and the European Profile provide lists of required competences and skills. However, in contrast to the European Profile, whose target groups are primarily teacher educators and curriculum planners of teacher education programmes, the EPOSTL has as its target group student teachers, practicing language teachers and teacher educators. Hence the EPOSTL provides a kind of 'bottom-up perspective', whereas the perspective of the European Profile can be called a 'top-down perspective'. In principle, the EPOSTL is closely related to the Common European Framework of Reference for Languages (CEFR) in so far as it lists the knowledge, competences and skills required of language teachers so that these teachers are enabled to teach the competences and skills required of language learners by the CEFR (cf. Newby, 2007: 24).

Both documents, the European Profile and the EPOSTL, represent efforts of the EU and the European Council to introduce cross-nationally accepted standards for language teacher education in order to improve the quality of teacher education programmes and to meet the demand for higher accountability. With these documents and their descriptions of the knowledge, skills and competences required of graduates, European education policy clearly aims at higher levels of transparency and comparability across the multifarious language teacher education programmes and approaches in Europe.

Structure and Aims of the EPOSTL

The EPOSTL consists of three main parts: (1) the personal statement, (2) the self-assessment part and (3) the dossier. In addition to these three main parts, it has an introduction, an index, a glossary and a users' guide.

The personal statement is meant to initiate with student teachers a process of reflection on their teacher education programme and their future profession. The second and main part of the EPOSTL comprises a list of more than 190 'I-can' descriptors. This main part should serve student teachers and teachers as a tool for reflection and self-assessment with regard to their language-teaching competences. Furthermore, this part of the EPOSTL provides student teachers with a good overview of the necessary basic competences a language teacher needs to acquire. Darling-Hammond et al. (2005: 398), stress the importance for student teachers to 'understand the bigger picture [which] allows them to locate what they are learning'.

In the third part, the so-called dossier, users of the EPOSTL are supposed to collect material they have produced for their teaching practice, such as lesson plans and teaching material. These documents should serve as evidence of the development of teaching competences (cf. Newby, 2007: 24).

The second and core part of the EPOSTL is the self-assessment section with its 'I-can' descriptors for the assessment of specific subject didactic competences. The descriptors are divided into seven categories: context, methodology, resources, lesson planning, conducting a lesson, independent learning and assessment of learning. The authors of the EPOSTL view the list of descriptors not as a prescriptive list but rather as a collection of competences to be acquired by language teachers during their teacher education programme and later during their professional lives. The focus is on the process of acquiring these listed competences. This process of competence acquisition is regarded as a continuous process starting during pre-service teacher education and continuing during the whole professional life of a teacher (Newby et al., 2007: 7).

The following descriptor taken from the category 'methodology: speaking/spoken interaction' should serve as an example: 'I can evaluate and select meaningful speaking and interactional activities to encourage learners of differing abilities to participate' (Newby et al., 2007: 21). Under each descriptor there is a bar for the user to indicate her/his competence level at a given time. On the right side, the bars have arrows that indicate the continuous and infinite quality of the process of competence development.

In Figure 10.1, the user has indicated her supposed level of competence twice, each time the date of self-assessment was entered into the bar. In this case, the user assumes that she has already acquired some basic level of competence; however, the user seems to see some need for further development.

Figure 10.1 Descriptor and bar indicating the competence level

In contrast to the European Language Portfolio (a self-assessment tool for language learners), the authors of the EPOSTL decided against a numerical quantification because teacher learning and development is seen as a non-linear process and as difficult to quantify; additionally, the process of competence development should be in the foreground as opposed to the actual results of such a process. Moreover, some of the listed didactic competences can only be developed after some years of teaching practice (cf. Newby, 2007: 25).

One of the main aims of the EPOSTL is to encourage and support student teachers to reflect on their learning process and to assist communication amongst student teachers and between student teachers and their mentors or their teacher educators. The EPOSTL aims at initiating student teachers' as well as practitioners' reflection on their didactic knowledge and didactic skills. As a result of this reflective process, the users of the EPOSTL should be enabled to assess their didactic competences and chart their progress. Furthermore, the dossier part of the EPOSTL assists its users in recording their teaching experiences (Newby et al., 2007: 5).

In the context of field experiences, the EPOSTL can assist in the exchanges between student teachers and mentors. Additionally, the EPOSTL can help mentors offer systematic and structured feedback to their mentees before and after a held lesson or micro-teaching unit (cf. Newby, 2007: 24). The EPOSTL can also serve as a starting point for reflective talks following a teaching practice phase between student teachers and their mentors or teacher educators.

As opposed to the European Language Portfolio, which is meant to be a 'showcase' as well as a 'process portfolio', the authors of the EPOSTL regard it as a process portfolio that is meant to stay with its owner and not to be used for any kind of grading or assessment (cf. Newby, 2007: 26).

4 Implementing the EPOSTL in a Pre-Service Teacher Education Programme

4.1 The EFL Teacher-Education Programme at the University of Vienna

Shortly after the publication of the EPOSTL in 2007, this reflection and self-assessment tool was implemented in the EFL teacher education programme at the Centre for English Language Teaching (CELT), which is situated at the Department of English at the University of Vienna. The ELT study programme offered at the Department of English lasts for nine semesters and is an integrative programme including courses in anglophone literatures, cultural studies, linguistics and applied linguistics, language education, EFL teaching methodology and general pedagogy (the latter one is offered by the faculty of education). In addition to these courses at university and some short field experiences offered in conjunction with methodology classes, students take part in two practicum phases, a general pedagogic one and a subject-specific one (English as a foreign language) during their study programme at university.

Considering these various parts of the EFL teacher-education programme, the EPOSTL as a reflection and self-assessment tool for didactic competences is predestined to be used in connection with EFL methodology classes and the subject-specific practicum phase. The EFL methodology programme consists of two introductory classes to be followed by the subject-specific practicum at a secondary school. During this practicum, the student teachers also attend a practicum tutorial at university accompanying the practicum (after the practice phase, another four EFL methodology classes need to be taken). Two of the main aims of this tutorial accompanying the subject specific practicum are to provide a closer link between the two involved institutions, namely the university and secondary schools, and to help minimise the often quoted 'gap' between theory and practice.

Apart from the main aims of this practicum tutorial (PT) mentioned above, the tutorial is also meant to support and assist students in their preparation of observation tasks and in their planning of teaching units for the practicum. At the end of this course, the teacher educator leading the tutorial asks students individually to a final reflective talk with the main purpose of reflecting critically on the experiences gained during the school placement phase.

The PT with its focus on critical reflection was chosen for an intensive use of the EPOSTL because of its potential to initiate and support reflection. Further reasons for the use of the EPOSTL in this course is the fact that the EPOSTL is an instrument to assist students with the self-assessment of their didactic competences and that it can help to function as a springboard for discussions among student teachers as well as between student teachers and their teacher educators. Helping student teachers build up a critical and reflective attitude towards their teaching, as well as offering students opportunities for exchange with colleagues are important aims of the PT.

4.2 Implementing the EPOSTL in the Practicum Tutorial (PT)

The PT comprises three phases; in the first phase before the practicum, observation tasks specifically relevant for language teaching are dealt with alongside with various language teaching approaches and methods. In this first phase, selected descriptors of the EPOSTL are being discussed. For a successful learning process to happen at this basic level of the education programme, when student teachers are in their third year of their four and one-half year pre-service programme, it is essential that teacher educators help students to split complex competences into sub-competences and revise in an interactive process the underlying knowledge base of selected and particularly relevant basic language teaching competences. This detailed analysis of a few basic descriptors from the EPOSTL has been termed as 'deconstructing the descriptors' by the CELT team to make explicit the twofold aim of this instructional mode: firstly, to help student teachers become aware of the underlying knowledge base and conceptual frameworks of a particular descriptor and, secondly, to build up a repertoire of possible teaching enactments of a descriptor for different kinds of target groups.

Working on selected competences before the practicum aims at making students once again aware of the basic required competences, helping them assess their competences together with colleagues or on their own and, finally, encouraging them to formulate attainable learning objectives for their practicum. In addition to these more general aims, students are also prepared more specifically for observation tasks they have to carry out during their practicum. In groups they discuss possible enactments of competences and how these enactments can be observed via focused observations of their mentor and other experienced teachers at the educational institution where they carry out their practicum.

During the second phase, when students actually teach at secondary schools, they are supposed to continue work on relevant descriptors ideally in cooperation with their mentors. During the second phase of the PT, student teachers discuss their lesson plans in groups with their colleagues and the teacher educator in charge of the tutorial. The lesson plans presented during this second phase need to refer to relevant EPOSTL descriptors. Until the next and third phase of the tutorial, student teachers choose a basic descriptor they are particularly interested in or they regard as especially relevant for their practicum and read up on relevant theory underlying their chosen descriptor. In the third phase of the tutorial, they present and sum up the results of their background reading for their colleagues. After the practicum phase has ended, the EPOSTL serves as a springboard for the reflective talks between each individual student teacher and the teacher educator in charge of the PT at university. Student teachers bring their EPOSTLs to the reflection talk and together with the teacher educator they discuss selected descriptors and try to work out their strengths and weaknesses and devise an individual plan for further development (cf. Mehlmauer-Larcher, 2011).

5 Researching the Impact of the EPOSTL: Initial Results

As mentioned in 4.2 the EPOSTL is used in the PT (tutorial accompanying the practicum phase) at the Centre of English Language Teaching (University of Vienna) to initiate and foster student teachers' reflection processes. With the purpose of continuous quality development and control parallel to the implementation of the EPOSTL, a research project was started to analyse the potential of the EPOSTL as a tool for reflection and self-assessment in pre-service language teacher education. So far, 124 questionnaires have been filled in by student teachers after the practicum tutorial. Additionally, 11 reflective talks between student teachers and their teacher educators were recorded and 13 semi-structured interviews (lasting about half an hour) were held with individual students after they had finished their practicum and their PT. First results of the collected quantitative and qualitative data will be presented.

The responses to two of the more general questions from the questionnaire point at a satisfactory acceptance of the EPOSTL, as Table 10.1 below illustrates. In Question 1, students were asked how they would describe their experience of using the EPOSTL on a Likert scale from one to six, with one indicating a positive and six indicating a general negative experience. In question two, students, in a similar way, indicated their agreement/disagreement concerning the potential of the EPOSTL with regard to helping them plan their development as student teachers in a more concrete and effective way.

The standard deviation for both questions being more than one indicates a fairly varied and broad spectrum of answers provided by students concerning these two questions. On the whole, the more specific the questions are, e.g. with regard to the EPOSTL's potential to foster reflection, the more positive the answers given by the students.

A closer look at some of the qualitative data presented below concerning the EPOSTL's potential to promote reflection demonstrates that students

Table 10.1 Student teachers' acceptance of the EPOSTL

N = 124	Mean	SD
Question 1: general attitude to the EPOSTL	3.14	1.13
Question 2: potential of the EPOSTL to support student teachers' professional development	3.05	1.29

appreciate the EPOSTL as a tool to assist their teacher learning processes and voice their thoughts on the various types of reflection which the EPOSTL promotes. Following Akbaris' (2007) typology of reflective processes, the analysis of student interviews revealed some interesting results. Regarding the time level of their reflections as well as the interaction format, student teachers made the following statements:[2]

Example 1: Prospective/retrospective reflection:
You can use the EPOSTL again and again, well, you can use it for planning (...) so if you want to hold a similar lesson again, for example, you can try to remember, right (...), how was it when I first held this lesson?

Example 2: Monological/dialogical reflection:
I think, at the beginning, you should discuss things together with colleagues, I am sure later on you can work on your own on it [collection of descriptors of the EPOSTL] and make your own entries (...) when you have become used to it [EPOSTL], you can just use it yourself, that's no problem (...) but you can always use it as a springboard for discussions.

The first comment made by a student teacher indicates the EPOSTL's strong potential to initiate reflective processes before and after teaching practice, whereas the second comment refers to the possibility of using the EPOSTL individually or together with colleagues as a springboard for discussions, as suggested by the main author of the document (cf. Newby, 2007: 24).

Further interesting and very positive comments were made by teacher students with regard to the EPOSTL's potential to provide a structure for reflection:

Example 3:
Well, it really is a kind of stimulus to think about various things and not just act in a kind of intuitive way, but you have something to look at and are able to structure things. And then, in case something goes wrong you need not rely only on your intuition and react accordingly.

Example 4:
Also this kind of self-assessment is sometimes really helpful. There are always situations when I think, well, I haven't really thought about that, or (...) you know (...) I had to think carefully, did I take

everything into consideration, (...) ok (...) you know, it [EPOSTL] really made me think.

Example 5:
For my second subject we don't have anything like this [EPOSTL] (...) there, things are less structured (...) you just look and take notes (...) there is no structured reflection in such a way.

Example 6:
With these descriptors you know what you have to concentrate on when you reflect; they help you stay focused.

Example 3 points at the potential of the EPOSTL to help students reframe a certain teaching situation they experienced by looking at this event from different perspectives. In this context, the EPOSTL also seems to support a kind of structured and rational analysis of a critical teaching incidence instead of just an intuitive reaction to a problematic experience. Both comments are in line with Dewey's definition of reflection (see Section 2.1) as a cognitive activity characterised by rationality and, furthermore, a process that enables us to reframe important instances and to look at these instances from a variety of perspectives. Comments 4, 5 and 6 may serve as exemplifications for the potential of the EPOSTL to support and initiate structured self-assessment and reflection processes. In these comments, students quite explicitly stress their need for and the importance of a structured way of reflection, which they see provided via their work with the EPOSTL.

Beside the many positive comments on the EPOSTL, some students also point to problems they have with the main part of the EPOSTL, namely the self-assessment section with its huge number of more than 190 'I-can' descriptors. The following comments refer to some of the problematic aspects of self-assessment:

Example 7:
I found it difficult to indicate my level of competence on these descriptor bars, as it's really hard to assess oneself. I think no one actually has a 100%, but it's hard to decide at which level one is.

Example 8:
Particularly at the beginning I found it difficult to assess myself with the help of these 'I-can' do descriptors. I believe that I just don't have enough teaching experience to assess myself properly and realistically.

Comments 7 and 8 illustrate the problem students have with assessing themselves with the help of the bars below the 'I-can' do descriptors in the EPOSTL and can also be seen as an indicator of a general problem with self-assessment. One of the reasons for these problems might be that, apart from the recently introduced European Portfolio for Language Learners, students in the Austrian education system are not really used to working with self-assessment instruments. Additionally, student teachers frequently mention their lack of teaching experience as a general problem at the beginning of their teacher education programme and regard it as one of the reasons for their difficulties with realistic self-assessment processes.

Despite the two main challenges expressed by many students in the interviews, namely on the one hand their difficulty with self-assessment and on the other hand their strongly felt lack of sufficient teaching experience, the following comments (9 and 10) confirm the strong motivational potential the EPOSTL can have for student teachers of languages even at the beginning of their practical education:

Example 9:
The use of the EPOSTL before, during and after the practicum shows that I really make progress. I find this very motivating!

Example 10:
Using the EPOSTL before, during and after teaching at school made me realise I was actually making some progress. I found this so motivating.

These positive comments might also be interpreted as an indication for the successful integration of the EPOSTL into the earlier described practicum tutorial accompanying the subject-specific practicum in the department of English at the University of Vienna.

6 Implementing the EPOSTL: Implications and Limitations

The EPOSTL should help initiate processes of reflection, serve as a starting point for dialogues and assist students in the self-assessment of their didactic competences. All three activities, namely reflection, dialogue and collaboration with colleagues as well as self-assessment, are nowadays regarded as essential aspects of teacher learning and the development of professionalism (cf. Richards, 2008; Johnson, 2009).

This is the reason why immediately after its first publication, a conceptual plan was developed to integrate the EPOSTL into the existing teacher education programme at the CELT.[3] After using the EPOSTL for several semesters, this reflection and self-assessment tool has become an integral part of the teacher education programme at the CELT. Initial results of this research project clearly demonstrate the strong potential the EPOSTL has to initiate and to support discussion and collaboration among students and teacher educators as well as processes of reflection and self-assessment. The data analysis clearly illustrates that the EPOSTL initiates various types of reflective activities among student teachers, referring to past teaching experiences they had as well as to further teaching activities planned in the near future. Moreover, student teachers repeatedly report that this reflection tool supports a definitely more focused and well-structured approach to the different kinds of reflections either carried out on their own, in groups with their peers or with their teacher educators, e.g. in their final reflective talks after the practicum phase described above.

The data analysis has not only demonstrated the strong potential of the EPOSTL, but also the challenges pre-service student teachers at an early phase of their study programme experience in connection with the use of this reflection and self-assessment tool. It is the self-assessment in particular that student teachers report as difficult because of a lack of field experience many of them have at this early phase of their education programme. Another reason for this frequently articulated challenge felt in connection with self-assessment might also be a general absence of a tradition of self-assessment in the Austrian education system. It is to be hoped that with the increasing use of the European Language Portfolio and similar self-assessment tools for other school subjects in the Austrian secondary school system in the future, student teachers will come to university with a higher awareness of the importance of self-assessment in connection with effective and successful learning processes.

In future, the application of the EPOSTL needs to be further developed in order to minimise problems and challenges in connection with its use. A crucial step will be a more intensive collaboration with the practicum mentors who work with the student teachers during their practicum phase. In workshops, mentors need to be informed about the aims, potentials and underlying principles of the EPOSTL, so that it will not only be used in the practicum tutorial accompanying the practicum, but that mentors working with student teachers at schools will also be motivated to make use of the EPOSTL for the pre- and post-teaching conference sessions with their mentees.

On the one hand, these new plans for a wider application and dissemination of the EPOSTL require a coherent, well-designed and clearly structured application procedure, while on the other hand, a more intensive and varied application of the EPOSTL provides the opportunity to carry out further research on the potential of the EPOSTL in terms of initiating and supporting reflection and self-assessment amongst student teachers of languages. One of the many crucial research questions will be whether a more intensive and varied application of the EPOSTL can further help to reduce the divide between theory and practice in early pre-service language teacher education.

Notes

(1) See also the discussions of pedagogic content knowledge in the chapters by Hüttner and Smit, Reichl, Tsui and Vodopija-Krstanovic in this volume.
(2) Talks and interviews were originally held in German. For this chapter, the transcripts were translated into English by the author.
(3) Thanks go to my colleagues G. Dirnberger, S. Katzböck and D. Weitensfelder for their many ideas and the enthusiastic support they have provided for the implementation of the EPOSTL at the CELT.

References

Akbari, R. (2007) Reflections on reflection: A critical appraisal of reflective practices in L2 teacher education. *System* 35, 192–207.
Bartlett, L. (1990) Teacher development through reflective thinking. In J.C. Richards and D. Nunan (eds) *Second Language Teacher Education* (pp. 202–214). Cambridge: Cambridge University Press.
Burton, J. (2009) Reflective practice. In A. Burns and J.C. Richards (eds) *The Cambridge Guide to Second Language Teacher Education* (pp. 298–307). Cambridge: Cambridge University Press.
Cochran-Smith, M. and Zeichner, K.M. (2005) *Studying Teacher Education: The Report of the AERA Panel on Research and Teacher Education*. Mahwah, NJ: Lawrence Erlbaum Associates.
Darling-Hammond, L., Hammerness, K., Grossmann, P., Rust, F. and Shulman, L.S. (2005) The design of teacher education programmes. In L. Darling-Hammond and J. Bransford (eds) *Preparing Teachers for a Changing World* (pp. 390–441). San Francisco: Jossey-Bass.
Dewey, J. (1910) *How We Think*. Boston, DC: Heath and Co.
Eraut, M. (1994) *Developing Professional Knowledge and Competence*. London and New York: The Falmer Press.
Farrell, T.S.C. (2007) *Reflective Language Teaching: From Research to Practice*. London: Continuum.
Freeman, D. and Johnson, K.E. (1998) Reconceptualizing the knowledge-base of language teacher education. *TESOL Quarterly* 32, 397–417.
Freeman, D. (2002) The hidden side of the work: Teacher knowledge and learning to teach. A perspective from North American educational research on teacher education in English language teaching. *Language Teaching* 35, 1–13.
Grossman, P. (2008) Responding to our critics: From crisis to opportunity in research on teacher education. *Journal of Teacher Education* 59 (1), 10–23.
Jay, J.K. and Johnson, K.L. (2002) Capturing complexity: A typology of reflective practice for teacher education. *Teaching and Teacher Education* 18, 73–85.

Johnson, K.E. (2009) Trends in second language teacher education. In A. Burns and J.C. Richards (eds) *The Cambridge Guide to Second Language Teacher Education* (pp. 20–29). Cambridge: Cambridge University Press.

Kelly, M. and Grenfell, M. (2004) The European Profile for Language Teacher Education: A Frame of Reference. Online at http://www.lang.soton.ac.uk/profile/index.html

Kemmis, S. (1985) Action research and the politics of reflection. In D. Boud, R. Keogh and D. Walker (eds) *Reflection: Turning Experience into Learning* (pp. 139–163). London/New York: Routledge.

Korthagen, F.A.J. (2010) Situated learning theory and the pedagogy of teacher education: Towards an integrative view of teacher behaviour and teacher learning. *Teaching and Teacher Education* 26, 98–106.

Mehlmauer-Larcher, B. (2010) Die Unterstützung von Reflexionsprozessen in der Lehrer-Innenbildung mit Hilfe des EPOSTLs (European Portfolio for Student Teachers of Languages). In C. Altmayer, G. Mehlhorn, C. Neveling, N. Schlüter and K. Schramm (eds) *Grenzen überschreiten: sprachlich – fachlich – kulturell* (pp. 51–61). Baltmannsweiler: Schneider-Verlag Hohengehren.

Mehlmauer-Larcher, B. (2011) Die Implementierung des EPOSA am Fachdidaktischen Zentrum Englisch der Universität Wien. In D. Newby and A. Horak (eds) *Die Implementierung des Europäischen Portfolios für Sprachlehrende in Ausbildung (EPOSA) in der Lehrer/innenbildung in Österreich: Beispiele der guten Praxis*. Graz: ÖSZ.

Moon, J.A. (1999) *Reflection in Learning and Professional Development: Theory and Practice*. London: Kogan Page.

Newby, D. (2007) The European portfolio for student teachers of languages. *Babylonia* 3, 23–26.

Newby, D., Allan, R., Fenner, A-B., Jones, B., Komorowska, H. and Soghikyan, K. (2007) *European Portfolio for Student Teachers of Languages: A Reflection Tool for Language Teacher Education*. Graz: Council of Europe Publishing. Online at http://epostl2.ecml.at

Noffke, S.E. and Brennan, M. (2005) The dimensions of reflection: A conceptual and contextual analysis. *International Journal of Progressive Education* 1 (3), 58–81.

Richards, J.C. (2008) Second language teacher education today. *RELC Journal* 39 (2), 158–177.

Roberts, J. (1998) *Language Teacher Education*. London: Arnold.

Schön, D.A. (1987) *Educating the Reflective Practitioner: Towards a New Design for Teaching and Learning in the Profession*. San Francisco: Jossey-Bass.

Shulman, L.S. (1987) Knowledge and teaching: Foundations of the new reform. *Harvard Educational Review* 57 (1), 1–22.

Wallace, M.J. (1991) *Training Foreign Language Teachers: A Reflective Approach*. Cambridge: Cambridge University Press.

Widdowson, H.G. (1990) *Aspects of Language Teaching*. Oxford: Oxford University Press.

Wideen, M., Mayer-Smith, J. and Moon, B. (1998) A critical analysis of the research on learning to teach: Making the case for an ecological perspective on inquiry. *Review of Education Research* 68 (2), 130–178.

Zeichner, K.M. and Liston, D.P. (1996) *Reflective Teaching: An Introduction*. Mahwah, NJ: Lawrence Erlbaum Associates.

Part 4
Addressing Established Paradigms

11 NESTs Versus Non-NESTs: Rethinking English-Language Teacher Identities

Irena Vodopija-Krstanovic

1 Introduction

In English-language teaching (ELT), the native speaker (NS) has been held up as a benchmark for knowledge about language (Davies, 2003) and represents an ideal in ELT methodology (Holliday, 1994; 2005). The NS/non-native speaker (NNS) dichotomy is said to divide the TESOL world, in which native English speaker teachers (NESTs) are often privileged over non-native English speaker teachers (non-NESTs), who are regarded as inferior in knowledge and performance, a notion that has influenced employment policy, teaching methods and language use (Braine, 1999, 2010). The NS/NNS divide is rooted in a 'linguistic caste system' of which one is either a permanent member and insider or is excluded from the group (Kachru & Nelson, 2001: 20).

However, the overarching spread of English as an international language fostered discussions about the status and the changing 'ownership of English' (Widdowson, 1994: 377), bringing into question the appropriateness of the NS linguistic ideal (Jenkins, 2007; Seidlhofer, 2000). Indeed, the static conceptualisation of the ideal NS seems far removed from the sociocultural contexts where English is taught and learned and, in reality, it is not always clear who is a NS anyway (Sharifian, 2009).

Besides, today, the majority of English teachers are non-NESTs who work in different educational cultures and local realities across the world (Canagarajah, 2005) and it is questionable whether the NS can be considered the ideal teacher (Moussu & Llurda, 2008; Phillipson, 1992).

Despite the discussions, the NS construct still has far-reaching implications on teaching, teacher knowledge and teacher struggle to construct a viable professional identity. 'Native speakerism' has contributed to teachers' feelings of insecurity and has had profound effects on teacher identity and the teacher's sense of self-worth (McKay & Bokhorst-Heng, 2008).

In line with these views, the aim of this chapter is, in the first place, to examine two elements of teachers' cognition as essential to their work as

EFL teachers: native speaker ideology and language teacher identity. In the second place, by exploring teacher/student teacher conceptualisations of NESTs/NNESTs within a language teacher education programme in Croatia, the study explores teacher positioning and questions essentialist categorisations of ELT professionals. And third, it is intended as a critical contribution from the Croatian context to the literature on socially situated meanings of education (Clarke, 2008; Hawkins, 2004; Johnson, 2009a; Richards, 2008).

2 NEST/NNEST Identities

For a long time, SLA narrowly viewed identity through the NS/NNS lens (Firth & Wagner, 1997) and by implication, in ELT, English-language teacher identities were also conceptualised with reference to a one-to-one relationship with nativeness to English. The assumption that the native language is central to individual identity is potentially reductive as it relies on essentialised notions of fixed traits and suppositions that identity is relatively stable and unproblematic (Holliday, 2005). The underlying essentialist premise is that there exists a fixed identity based on the stable native/non-native core of the self as 'the imprint of a monolithic culture embodied in the individual' (Clarke, 2008: 26).

Indeed, the native-language-and-identity ideology is problematic for at least two reasons: first, the mother tongue is seen as a true part of one's identity, and second, it forms a hierarchical division whereby that which is 'more authentic' is valued more highly; thus, the 'native language is designated as determinative of authenticity' (Myhill, 2003: 81). Furthermore, language is 'not only [...] a linguistic system but also [...] a social practice in which experiences are organized and identities negotiated' (Norton, 2010: 351), hence, viewing the English language as the defining trait of a teacher's identity, the natural state of being, fosters reductive generalisations about teacher abilities and behaviour.

With the contemporary understanding of identity as constructed and not intrinsic (Block, 2007; Duff & Uchida, 1997; Norton, 2000), ELT professionals have the power to be flexible. Hence, teachers can create their professional identities, to follow their own inclinations, in order to build their teacher identities in a way that works for the individual and the context.

However, in order to have more flexibility and autonomy in the negotiation of teacher identity, it is necessary to understand how mainstream native speaker discourse constructs teachers and teacher knowledge. Accordingly, it is increasingly important for education programmes:

to engage teachers in an exploration of the political status of English in today's world, the role it can play in maintaining positions of privilege and inequality, and the role the notion of 'native speaker' has played in TESOL. (Richards, 2008: 18)

3 NEST/NNEST Knowledge

In the light of the current discussions, it would appear that language teacher identities are more complex than the binary NEST/NNEST distinction and its appertaining qualities. Indeed, the NEST/NNEST dichotomy is associated with cultural expectations that deny cultural and personal variations, identifications and individual differences that exist among ELT professionals, ranging from ethnicity, education, age and personality to professional expertise (Holliday, 2005). Yet, in TESOL, the hierarchical distinction NEST/NNEST has perpetuated discourse on the abilities of NNESTs and their professional expertise.

If we look at NS/NNS teacher expertise, it seems to be conceptualised through knowledge of English, which places the NEST in an advantageous position of the ideal teacher (Llurda, 2005; Phillipson, 1992) and seriously undermines teacher learning and education (Johnson, 2009a). Clearly, if the native language is a benchmark of teacher knowledge and teaching practice, what role, if any, does teacher education play? Can teacher knowledge be measured only on linguistic grounds? Teachers are not linguistic virtuosos, but are, above all, individuals with prior experiences, personal values and beliefs that inform their knowledge about teaching (Freeman & Johnson, 1998), which is located in contexts where teachers learn and teach (Johnson, 2006).

Following these discussions, it might be useful to further explore language teacher knowledge in the light of Shulman's (1986) teacher knowledge framework and Tsui's (2003) conceptualisation of teacher expertise.

According to Shulman (1986), teacher knowledge can be analysed as (a) subject matter content knowledge (e.g. English), (b) pedagogical content knowledge and (c) curricular knowledge.[1] It is evident that knowledge of English does not necessarily subsume knowledge of pedagogical content or the curriculum. Hence, a justifiable argument would then be that NESTs are highly proficient, but do not, by default, have a superior linguistic knowledge for teaching (Reeves, 2009). Besides, NNESTs are better able to predict the learner's challenges, or as Seidlhofer (1999: 238) argues, 'native speakers know the destination, but not the terrain that has to be crossed to get there; they themselves have not travelled the same route'.

Let us now take a look at Tsui's (2003) distinction between the state of expert performance and the process of attaining expert knowledge. While claims have been made about NEST expert performance with reference to English, it is unlikely that similar claims could be made relative to the process of attaining expert performance. Indeed, expertise in teaching is a complex issue and includes continual renewing of knowledge, exploring and contextualising pedagogical possibilities, problematising, tackling challenges and expanding skills in new domains (Tsui, 2009), none of which are directly relevant to native speakerism. From this it would follow that a professional teacher identity grounded in expertise is not necessarily rooted in native speakerism.

4 Conceptual Frameworks

This study draws on conceptual frameworks of sociocultural teacher education and language teaching and identity to explore culturally and socially situated NEST/NNEST identities in the light of NS discourse and thus to develop understandings of the complex question of language teachers' identities.

4.1 Sociocultural Teacher Education

The sociocultural teacher education framework is used as a theoretical lens for analysing the knowledge, experience, practice and positioning of a group of teachers, i.e. university lecturers and student teachers (prospective EFL teachers) in a language teacher education programme in Croatia.

A view of teacher learning rooted in sociocultural theory considers how the participants, the context and social processes shape learning, which emerges through social interaction (Richards, 2008) and explores the political, social and ideological dimension of teacher education (Hawkins & Norton, 2009; Johnson, 2009a).

This being so, a teacher knowledge base can no longer draw only on the linguistic features of the English language and how it can be taught and learned (Richards, 2008), but should take into account teacher identity, diversity and the native/non-native divide (Miller, 2009) as well as the social and cultural position of English in the world and the way it influences teachers, learners and ELT (Franson & Holliday, 2009). In other words, the sociocultural framework constitutes premises for understanding teachers and teaching in the light of (a) the overarching question of ideology and power relative to language teaching (Hawkins & Norton, 2009; Norton, 2000), (b) the centrality of teacher identity in language teaching (Miller,

2009; Varghese et al., 2005), (c) teacher knowledge as situated within a specific sociocultural context (Johnson, 2009a, 2009b) and (d) the different social-cultural roles teachers and learners enact through interaction (Norton, 1997, 2000). It is evident that in today's complex educational realities, awareness of the sociocultural implications of teaching is a part of the teacher's knowledge base.

In summary, the sociocultural framework is not 'a methodology or an approach how to do L2 teacher education' but is instead 'a theoretical lens, a mindset, or way of conceptualising teacher learning that informs how teacher educators understand and support the professional development of L2 teachers' (Johnson, 2009a: 16).

4.2 Language Teaching and Identity

The sociocultural turn in TESOL has led to increased research on the role the broader context plays in the process of teacher learning and the shaping of language teacher identities (Clarke, 2008; Duff & Uchida, 1997; Johnson, 2009a; Petric, 2009; Tsui, 2007; Varghese et al., 2005), which was explored in a variety of contexts and framed in different ways.

In this chapter, I take a post-structuralist view of identity as a dynamic, hybrid and changeable category contextually situated and constantly in the process of becoming, as individuals position themselves through interactions and negotiate different subject positions (Block, 2007; Norton, 2000; 2010). From language teacher identity research, I draw on five themes. First, identity is not a static, deterministic construct that EFL teachers and student teachers bring to the classroom and take away unchanged (Kramsch, 1993). Second, in educational practices, identities and beliefs are negotiated and constructed through language (Duff & Uchida, 1997; Norton, 2010). Third, identity is negotiated in specific sociocultural and political contexts (Duff & Uchida, 1997). Fourth, the ideological and political implications of ELT influence the identity formation of teachers and student teachers (Pennycook, 2001). And fifth, learning to teach is a process of identity formation (Clarke, 2008).

In brief, a post-structuralist approach questions binary oppositions, stable truths and 'monolingual and monocultural biases' (Pavlenko, 2002: 295).

5 The Study

5.1 Research Aims

The research is guided by the question: how is the legacy of the native speaker and the distinction NEST/non-NEST conceptualised by lecturers and learners and reflected in classroom practice? Through the voices of the participants, all lecturers and student teachers in a language teacher education programme in Croatia, the study researches different lecturer/student teacher positioning in NS ideologies as a move toward a more complex conceptualisation of teaching, teacher knowledge and teacher identities than the presence/absence of the NS feature.

5.2 Method

The research presented here is part of a larger qualitative study situated within the interpretative framework. The prime source of data in this study is derived from two rounds of individual interviews with six lecturers (three NESTs and three non-NESTs) and 25 NNS student teachers. I used an unstructured or informal conversational interview characterised by spontaneous generation of questions in a natural flow of interaction (Patton, 2002) and constrained by the research goals (Weiss, 1994). Although the interviews in this study were not guided by any predefined questions, I did keep in mind the underlying research theme of teaching, teacher knowledge and teachers' lived experiences in light of the native speaker discourse. Hence, the interviews were loosely guided by the interviewer's topic and were conceptually grounded in the understanding that interview responses are the products of interpretive practice whereby knowledge is cooperatively constructed in context by interaction partners in interview conversations (Kvale & Brinkmann, 2009).

All the interviews were recorded except for two student teacher interviews and one lecturer interview during which notes were taken. The interviews lasted anywhere from 60 to 120 minutes and were transcribed verbatim. To ensure confidentiality for the participants, the names of the interviewees were withheld by mutual agreement and the female gender is used throughout the article, as only three of the interviewees were male.

During the analysis, the interview data were coded to link responses to the emerging concepts and categories. The categories were generated by repeated reading, comparing and grouping interview texts into similar topics until a cluster was apparent. Each cluster constituted a theme that was named and labelled, such as the four themes presented in Section 6 of this chapter, namely: (a) the power of the NS ideal, (b) the status of NESTs and NNESTs in a Croatian teacher education context, (c) teacher identities and NS ideology and (d) teachers and teaching practices in light of the NS discourse.

5.3 Participants and the Context

The research site is an English department in a Croatian university and the participants in the study were all university lecturers or student teachers in the language teacher education programme. The lecturers taught EFL and content courses in different disciplines and the student teachers were in their final year of studies and had completed their pre-service practicum.

At the time of the study, the knowledge base of the teacher education programme was traditionally positioned in a language-based foundation that drew from (a) linguistics, (b) language-learning theory and (c) ELT methodology as the practical component (Richards, 2008). Teacher education is understood as the development of a theoretical background from different disciplines, which aids abstract conceptualisations and in-depth understandings of the complexities of teaching, whereas teacher training addresses the development of specific skills and competencies to meet particular goals (see Widdowson, 1990). In this programme, the NS ideal was firmly entwined in the very fabric of teacher education. This is not surprising as teacher education maintains the existing educational power structures and dominant discourses (Phelan, 2001).

6 Data Analysis

The four themes that emerged in this study will be examined in the light of the discussions so far: (a) the power of the NS ideal, (b) the status of NESTs/non-NESTs, (c) teacher identities and ideology and (d) teachers and teaching practices.

6.1 The Power of the NS Ideal

Mention has been made that, in the past, native speakership was a birthright and not a controversial issue (Kramsch, 1998). In contrast, today, questions are raised as to who the NS is and what the NS knows by virtue of being one (Davies, 2003; Sharifian, 2009; Widdowson, 1994). With English being increasingly used in multilingual contexts, the language is adapted and altered, by uses and users, as a creative means for constructing and expressing diverse identities (Jenkins, 2007; Kachru, 1992; Seidlhofer, 2000).

However, in this context, the recent discussions surrounding English and the NS ideal have had little influence on the dominant professional discourse, which uses the NS as the yardstick. Hence, in the teacher education programme, the NS is the unquestionable methodological and linguistic ideal. In other words, the NESTs represent a culture 'from which spring the ideals of both the English language and of English language teaching methodology' (Holliday, 2005: 6). This is not surprising as ELT pedagogy is centrally produced and, as such, promotes (and is promoted by) the global ELT materials industry (Kumaravadivelu, 2006). This position has undoubtedly influenced the student teachers' personal knowledge, their value system and understanding of teacher knowledge. In the following extract, a student teacher states 'we are raised' and 'we were taught' according to the NS ideal, the foundation of the teacher education programme:

> S: We are raised like this we have (...) we were taught to speak correctly and (...) excellently.
> T: So, what do you have in mind when you say correctly and excellent?
> S: Native speakers.
> T: And by native speakers you mean?
> S: I don't know (...) native speakers (...) generally people who (...) native speakers (...) native language connected with language on television CNN (...) BBC.
> T: UK or U.S.?
> S: Not necessarily I also perceive you as a native speaker.
> T: But I don't see myself as a native (...) no.
> S: But I compare your language and the language of some other professors and you are much closer to the ideal.
> T: The ideal that you have in mind?
> S: Yes, the ideal is not necessarily reached only by people born in the U.S. or UK.(NNS student teacher)

To the student teacher, the NS is a real construct and a part of a teacher's identity; however, it is negotiable and not necessarily obtained only by birthright, but is attainable through language proficiency. More specifically, the NS does not seem to be predetermined on ethnolinguistic grounds but is generated in context.

From the above extract, it would appear that identity construction is a negotiation between how one is seen by others and how one sees oneself (Blackledge & Pavlenko, 2001). The differences in understandings of the NS between the student teacher and lecturer lead to a disparity between self- and perceived teacher identity. In the eyes of the student teacher, NS group membership is obtained through linguistic proficiency, which suggests that one can become an NS. In fact, research conducted into self and perceived NS/NNS identities of English teachers has shown a gap between chosen and perceived identity, suggesting that conceptualisations of NS/NNS may be fluid (Inbar-Lourie, 2005) and NS status may be a matter of self-ascription and identification by others (Davies, 2003).

The position that an NS can be constructed through language and on the basis of convincing personal evidence of identity was corroborated by another interviewee. In fact, she claims that an NS is someone who is regarded credible enough to 'pass' as an NS:

> S: I would like to go to English speaking countries (...) you can't learn the language really well here. For example (...) when I was in the UK I saw these windows and I kept on saying what nice windows (...) what nice windows and then I learned they were called bay windows. English teachers should know the language well, much better than the students (...) like native (...) yes like native speakers (...) like professor X.
> T: Is this the ideal?
> S: No the native speaker is not really my ideal it could also be a non-native speaker who has learned the language really well.
> T: Really well?
> S: Yeah, like my aunt who works as a speech therapist in Cambridge. You can't tell she is not from the UK. (NNS student teacher)

If we examine this extract in the light of the student teacher's beliefs, personal values and positioning surrounding English, it would appear the teacher's professional image is closely linked with expertise in English, which can only be developed in anglophone countries. Lantolf and Johnson (2007: 884) state that:

> L2 teachers typically enter the profession with largely unarticulated, yet deeply ingrained, everyday concepts about language, language learning, and language teaching that are based on their own L2 instructional histories and lived experiences.

The student teacher's perspective is an example of deep-rooted values concerning teacher knowledge. Clearly, the native speaker is the point of reference.

Native speakerism plays a pivotal role in teacher identity with pronunciation as its most salient marker (Jenkins, 2007). Hence, there seems to be widespread prejudice against foreign-sounding speech (Dalton-Puffer *et al.*, 1997; Mahboob, 2005). Likewise, in this context, NNS accents are stigmatised and lecturers are expected to imitate NS models, a position reiterated by the linguistics courses in the teacher education programme, in particular the phonology course.

This being so, it is not surprising that student teachers not only criticise lecturers whose pronunciation is distinctly non-native, but also raise questions about their professional identity, expertise and qualifications:

> It's the pronunciation. It's the British accent that's some kind of prestige (...) Some of our teachers here have an awful pronunciation. The idea that those professors have a doctoral degree in English (...) and they talk like that. I know they didn't have TV back then (...) We will be professors [i.e. school language teachers] one day, so if you are going to teach others then you have to know how to speak English, and pronunciation is part of that. (NNS student teacher)

In this context, teacher knowledge seems to be embedded in the widely criticised assumption 'if you can speak the language you can teach it' (Johnson, 2009a: 41). It is evident that the credibility of a lecturer's professional identity is defined by knowledge of English and a 'proper accent' as conceptualisations about teacher knowledge and expertise are grounded in the centrality of the NS. In fact, even the validity of a PhD degree is questioned on grounds of English-language proficiency.

In contrast to the above opinion, recent discussions on the sociopolitical implications of English posit that it would be more realistic not to treat the NS model as the pronunciation norm and goal (Jenkins, 2007; McKay, 2002). A direct objection to the modeling of NS accents was raised by a NEST:

> Some of the professors here speak a sort of very snobbish English, like X. I mean, terribly posh (...) And a lot of other people I met. So, obviously, they'd internalized some sort of model in their stays in England which carries a slightly old fashioned sense of prestige. (NEST lecturer)

What is perceived by student teachers as the ideal NS pronunciation for English lecturers sounds quaint or stilted to the NEST, and a marker of excellence by one measure becomes a faux imitation by another. In a similar vein, Seidlhofer (1999: 237) criticises the modelling of NS accents whereby students are expected to 'ape' NSs as closely as possible. Mahboob (2005) also explains that the NS model for pronunciation should be reconsidered as SLA evidence has shown that the majority of adult learners will never be able to attain it.

In brief, knowledge formation is not value free (Canagarajah, 2002) and teachers' ways of thinking and conceptualisations of what constitutes English teacher knowledge are embedded in their language learning experiences and teacher education programmes (Johnson, 2009a). From the data, it appears that the educational system produces and reproduces NS ideology and attaches value to NS identity as a marker of teacher expertise.

6.2 The Status of NESTs/Non-NESTs in a Croatian Teacher Education Context

In all ELT institutions in this context, the NS is a key selling point. In the English department brochure, the NS is advertised as an asset, and private language schools market the NS as the real deal. This is not surprising since the public discourse on ELT reflects widespread assumptions about native speakerism and teaching and there is a tendency for the English teacher job market to favour NSs (Braine, 1999). A case in point was made by an informant who strongly objected to discrimination in hiring practice when an NS with no qualifications in ELT was employed in the English department, whose aim is to educate and train prospective language teachers. It is evident that this action is a self-defeating position that undermines the very mission of the department.

The implication of this orientation towards English is that it perpetuates the NS ideal and raises the following questions: (a) is ELT a birthright, (b) how is teacher knowledge conceptualised in this context and (c) what is the role of teacher education?

> Now look at X (...) we hired just because she is a (...) native speaker (...) no training in ELT (...) she is not an English teacher (...) I don't even know what her qualifications are. I couldn't teach Croatian and nobody would hire me. And just because she is a native (...) what about teaching methods? (NNEST lecturer)

Clearly, the interviewee's personal philosophy on teaching places value on teacher education over native speakerism. She states that the NEST is not a qualified lecturer; hence, teacher knowledge is not obtained by birthright. The NNEST foregrounds teacher education in an attempt to highlight positive aspects of her own professional identity as she struggles for power and positioning within the educational context dominated by a discourse that highlights language over language pedagogy.

The NS issue is further elaborated by a NEST who sees herself as a selling point for 'authentic language' and a guarantee that the student will not be taught 'school English' or a 'twice-removed English', i.e. from non-NESTs who learned it from their NNS teachers in an EFL context:

> We fill in the gap (...) we get the students to talk. It's not that we talk to the student (...) the students talk and that fills that oral skills gap, and if your faculty doesn't have any then you cannot boast. You have to boast that you have native speakers otherwise (...) how do you know everything is not happening in Croatian. You can teach everything in English, but still when you have the native speaker (...) (NEST lecturer)

It appears that the 'myth of the superiority of the NS is used as a bait' (Petric, 2009: 141) to attract students and differentiate between the 'value' of NESTs/NNESTs for the department. This distinction leads to the stratification of ELT professionals and denigration of local (teacher) knowledge (Canagarajah, 2002). It would seem that, in spite of NNESTs' education and training, doubts are raised about their ability to realise the communicative language teaching (CLT) ideal. As a result, NNEST professional identity is marginalised as language and authenticity become central to teaching in a site of contestation of ELT professionals. Widdowson (1994: 386) cautions about the undisputed influence of the native speaker as '[w]hat they say is invested with both authenticity and authority'.

In short, the data in this section raises the question: what does it mean to be an EFL lecturer in this context and what does he/she need to know? In the light of the discussions, there seems to be a need to re-examine the ideology underlying the teacher education programme in the Croatian EFL teacher-education department under investigation and question assumptions surrounding notions of nativeness and authenticity in academia. In our particular context, it would seem necessary to deemphasise the role of native-like language proficiency in the teacher education programme (Freeman & Johnson, 1998).

6.3 Teacher Identities and Native-Speaker Ideology

Mention has been made that it is doubtful whether teacher identities can be conceptualised as fixed entities based on nativeness in English (or lack thereof). Research suggests that, although the majority of teachers consider themselves to be either NSs or NNSs (Medgyes, 1994), some do not see themselves as belonging exclusively to one category (Brutt-Griffler &

Samimy, 2001). Directly relevant to this position is the following extract, in which a lecturer positions herself within the NS discourse:

> I do not see that the characteristics of the immutable categories are adequate or appropriate to define me as a teacher or as an individual. First (...) I disapprove of being labelled as linguistically deficient, in comparison to the linguistic ideal. Second (...) I disagree that my teaching expertise be defined in terms of a mediocre pedagogical paradigm. If I attempt to look at my identity in terms of the NEST/non-NEST categories, it is not fixed but socially constructed and depends greatly on context and circumstances. At times (...) I see myself closer to the NEST category (...) in terms of ELT methodology (...) When I look at myself in the context of my work environment, then I am closer to a non-NEST. Perceptions by others as to where I belong may also vary depending on circumstances. Occasionally I am perceived as a NEST [...]. Some Croatian EFL teachers perceive me as a near-NEST, [...] My colleagues at the department, however, do not perceive me as a NEST (...) [...] the NESTs are exclusively members of Inner Circle countries, and I am one of them, the Croatian staff. (NNEST lecturer)

The extract highlights how the negotiation of NS/NNS and professional identities is contextualised and implicated in social relationships. One of the key aspects of being a native speaker is 'about groups and identity' (Davies, 2003: vii). Hence, the NNEST lecturer sees her identity in relational terms as she identifies with and takes up different subject positions at different times. According to Barker (2008: 243), identity can be understood as 'an emotionally charged description of ourselves'. Directly relevant to this interpretation are descriptions of the multifarious perceptions of the informant: an NS by NESTs, a near NEST by non-NESTs, NNS by non-NESTs and, based on nationality, a self-ascribed non-NEST. The initial perception of NEST identity gradually changes to non-NEST through contextualisation and the negotiation of different subject positions.

The NNEST resists the NS linguistic ideal and objects that her teaching expertise is labelled second best in comparison to the NS pedagogical ideal. The implication is that, in the lecturer's mind frame, there exists a concrete NS pedagogical ideal. Johnson (2009a: 7) states that in the past, approaches to teacher education focused on identifying good patterns of teaching and 'what effective teachers do'. In this context, good patterns of teaching, i.e. the NS language-teaching ideal (Holliday, 2005) are integrated in the theoretical content of the teacher education programme and put into practice in the methodology course. The NNEST overtly rejects the labelling, but nevertheless builds a professional identity by positioning herself within the professional world as a progressive local teacher who is closer to the language-teaching ideal (Holliday, 2005). In other words, the teacher resists native-speakerism as a benchmark for comparison of the self, but draws on the ideal to affirm her professional identity.

Let us now look at the distinction NEST/non-NEST identity from a NEST's perspective. In the following extract, a NEST describes the transition from being identified as an NS to being perceived as a professional:

> I would describe students' perception of me as both an individual and a professor as proceeding through three general phases. [...] the first phase lasts for the first two or three classes wherein I am perceived as an object of curiosity in the sense that I am a real foreigner from the legendary Wild West of the US and that there is much that is unknown and mysterious about me [...]. Following about the second or third class students can get a sense that I am not all that much unlike them [...]. By the fourth class [...] students seem resolved, above all else, to determine what it is exactly that I expect of them in class and what elements are to be the most important in determining their grades. Finally, [...] students make a final judgment surrounding my ethos as they see it, the fairness of my grading methods, and the overall impression that I have left upon them. (NEST lecturer)

In contrast to the other NESTs, this lecturer does not see herself as the teaching or linguistic ideal, but as an authentic 'artefact of culture'. While native speakerism is a significant factor in initial contact with student teachers, later, the lecturer's professional identity emerges in the forefront in the transition from the NS collectivity to the individual teacher, i.e. from American to professional. In the changeover, the NEST is not defined by native speakerism but by teacher knowledge and an approach to teaching embedded in personal values, understandings of the context and the rational and ethical decisions she makes.

In short, the teachers come to the profession from different educational backgrounds and have different understandings about the context and different teaching experiences. Each is unique.

6.4 Teachers and Teaching Practices in Light of the NS Discourse

Research on NEST/non-NESTs has frequently focused on comparing competencies and highlighting their strengths and weaknesses in order to make claims about teacher knowledge in two areas: language and pedagogical skills. For example, strengths attributed to non-NESTs are: knowledge about language, good learner models and guides and the capacity to understand student teachers' difficulties and needs (Arva & Medgyes, 2000; Medgyes, 1994). In contrast, NESTs are appreciated for their language proficiency, fluency and cultural knowledge (Cheung & Braine, 2007; Mahboob, 2004). From this it would follow that teacher knowledge is binary; the NESTs know the language and culture and NNESTs know about the language.

In the light of the discussions above, it seems that the respective strengths and weaknesses of NESTs/NNESTs are reflected in their pedagogical styles. In fact, Brown (2007: 242) states that some aspects of CLT might pose a challenge for less proficient non-NESTs, while 'dialogues, drills, rehearsed exercises and discussions (in the first language) of grammatical rules are much simpler for some nonnative speakers to contend with'. From this perspective, it is the NNESTs who might find CLT challenging. However, it is likely that teachers may struggle with CLT for reasons other than language proficiency (e.g. weak education, lack of training, expectations of the local educational context, personal values and beliefs, to name a few).

A case in point was made by a NEST interviewee who criticised NESTs at a North American university for using traditional teaching methods. A fair assumption regarding these NESTs' competences would be that they are proficient enough to use CLT, nevertheless, they resort to lectures and conduct traditional teacher-fronted classes:

> I can say now being back in the States (...) that I watch some of my colleagues and they do very teacher-fronted learning, and they don't do small groups and I look at them (...) well (...) it's hard (...) because I don't think they really try (...) And they don't know how to. (NEST lecturer)

Clearly, NEST/NNEST generalisations in relation to CLT and dominant teaching practices should be contextualised and taken with caution as teaching expertise is a personal endeavour and some teachers just 'don't know how'. Derwing and Munro (2005) criticise blanket statements about NESTs/NNESTs and make their case for a contextualised approach that focuses on specific teaching/learning requirements and appropriate teacher training. In fact, they state that teachers need a similar knowledge base regardless of their L1.

With respect to NEST/non-NEST teaching practices in the Croatian context, the interview data yielded contradictory information about lecturers' teaching. While some student teachers claimed that classes taught by NESTs were different, others did not differentiate between the groups, as can be seen in the two extracts:

> She wasn't really different than Croatian professors (...) not really. I expected something revolutionary (...) but it wasn't that different. We had some midterms, some tests but the teaching techniques and tools were not different (...) It was just a lecture. (NNS student teacher)

> The teaching methods of the NESTs differ and they like to talk (...) interact with us. They are not so theory focused while the locals are theory focused. They are just different (...) more friendlier (...). (NNS student teacher)

The second extract suggests that local lecturers focus on the theoretical aspects of language while NESTs focus on communication. Johnson (2009a) explains that the knowledge base of teacher education has traditionally assumed that teachers need to acquire a theoretical understanding about language that they can transmit to their students to help them acquire the theory or use it in meaningful communication. Although research has shown that teachers fail to transfer the knowledge to classroom language teaching (Johnson, 2006), in this context, the knowledge base of language teacher education is indeed envisioned as a 'repository knowledge of inert facts' (Johnston & Goettsch, 2000: 466) about linguistic theory, which teachers attempt to transmit to their students.

From the data it can be observed that teaching is complex and contingent on personal characteristics, context, teaching conditions, values, beliefs, education and training and personal development, and is not necessarily defined by nationality. Deterministic conceptualisations of 'who is a better teacher', as defined by group membership, deny individual agency, creativity and teacher responsibility and undermine the role of teacher education and teacher development.

7 Conclusion

In ELT, the NS seems to be a taken-for-granted theoretical construct with far-reaching implications on teachers, learners, teacher knowledge base and teaching in local realities. It is evident that to understand teaching, learning and teacher learning, it is necessary to understand teachers' positioning relative to TESOL and their local contexts, 'and in order to understand teachers, we need to have a clearer sense of who they are: the professional, cultural, political, and individual identities which they claim or which are assigned to them' (Varghese et al., 2005: 22).

This study highlights the language teacher education context as an interaction site where teacher identities shift according to situation and subject positions. The findings suggest that identities are complex, dynamic, dialogic and contingent on the interaction of sociocultural and educational factors. At a more theoretical level, the discussions in the study invite a rethinking of how the NS ideal is intertwined in teaching, teacher development and teacher identity. The distinction NEST/non-NEST, albeit reductive, is ubiquitous and reflected in teacher and student conceptualisations of identities, teachers' work and the language teacher education programme. As a result, the pervasive influence of the NS construct has far-reaching implications on teacher development as the NS/NNS division sustains a static essentialist conceptualisation of teacher (professional) identities rather than encouraging personal development and teacher growth.

Departing from the sociocultural framework, it seems necessary to reflect on the current teacher education paradigm in this context and to question a teacher knowledge base anchored in the NS ideal and a 'value neutral' knowledge about the English language, linguistics and ELT methodology to be transferred into language classrooms. In our particular context, this would mean re-examining teacher education in light of the emerging trends: (a) the power and ideology of NS discourse, (b) the post-structuralist conceptualisation of identity, (c) the global spread of English as an international language (d) the sociocultural and critical approaches to teacher education.

More specifically, in our department, we would need to first re-examine the limitations of the traditional language teacher education programme and define a knowledge base that expands on the contentious (NS) linguistic ideal and 'value-free' language pedagogy to develop teachers' critical knowledge into a sustainable professional knowledge base. Second, awareness should be raised of the dominant discourse in applied linguistics, TESOL and teacher education, i.e. the power relations and NS ideology within ELT. Third, the teacher education programme should address the local context while at the same time not losing sight of the global ELT environment and EIL. Fourth, it should be emphasised that expertise is attainable through continuous professional development, regardless of the L1 background. And finally, given the growing literature on language teacher identities and the multiple identity positions from which teachers engage in teaching, the programme should place new importance on understanding the way teachers conceptualise themselves relative to the

NS discourse and TESOL, as well as the identities they construct for themselves in their local realities.

In closing, with the sociopolitical turn in TESOL, there is a growing need to critically analyze the current teacher education paradigm and the epistemological underpinnings that have guided our profession. By acknowledging the implicit and explicit role that NS ideology plays in ELT and the effect it has on teacher identities, values and knowledge in a given context, we will be able to better attune the teacher education programme with the emerging sociocultural trends, and thus shape the development of teachers' professional identities.

Note

(1) For further discussion, see also Hüttner and Smit, Mehlmauer, Reichl, and Tsui in this volume.

References

Arva, V. and Medgyes, P. (2000) Native and non-native teachers in the classroom. *System* 28 (3), 355–372.
Barker, C. (2008) *Cultural Studies: Theory and Practice*. Thousand Oaks, CA: Sage Publications.
Blackledge, A. and Pavlenko, A. (2001) Negotiation of identities in multilingual contexts. *The International Journal of Bilingualism* 5 (3), 243–257.
Block, D. (2007) The rise of identity in SLA research, post Firth and Wagner. *The Modern Language Journal* 91 (5), 863–876.
Braine, G. (ed.) (1999) *Non-Native Educators in English Language Teaching*. Mahwah, NJ: Lawrence Erlbaum Associates.
Braine, G. (2010) *Non-Native Speaker English Teachers: Research Pedagogy and Professional Growth*. New York: Routledge.
Brown, H.D. (2007) *Principles of Language Teaching and Learning*. New York: Pearson Education.
Brutt-Griffler, J. and Samimy, K. (2001) Transcending the nativeness paradigm. *World Englishes* 20 (1), 99–106.
Canagarajah, S. (2002) Reconstructing local knowledge. *Journal of Language Identity and Education* 1 (4), 243–239.
Canagarajah, S. (ed.) (2005) *Reclaiming the Local in Language Policy and Practice*. Mahwah, NJ: Lawrence Erlbaum Associates.
Cheung, Y.L. and Braine, G. (2007) The attitudes of university student-teachers towards non-native speakers English teachers in Hong Kong. *RELC Journal* 38 (3), 257–277.
Clarke, M. (2008) *Language Teacher Identities: Co-constructing Discourse and Community*. Clevedon: Multilingual Matters.
Dalton-Puffer, C., Kaltenboeck, G. and Smit, U. (1997) Learner attitudes and L2 pronunciation in Austria. *World Englishes* 16 (1), 115–128.
Davies, A. (2003) *The Native Speaker: Myth and Reality*. Clevedon: Multilingual Matters.
Derwing, T.M. and Munro, M.J. (2005) Pragmatic perspectives on the preparation of teachers of English as a second language: Putting the NS/NNS debate in context. In

E. Llurda (ed.) *Non-Native Language Teachers: Perceptions, Challenges and Contributions to the Profession* (pp. 179–191). New York: Springer.

Duff, P. and Uchida, Y. (1997) The negotiation of teachers' sociocultural identities and practices in postsecondary EFL classrooms. *TESOL Quarterly* 31 (3), 451–486.

Firth, A. and Wagner, J. (1997) On discourse, communication and (some) fundamental concepts in SLA research. *Modern Language Journal* 81 (3), 286–300.

Franson, C. and Holliday, A. (2009) Social and cultural perspectives. In A. Burns and J.C. Richards (eds) *Second Language Teacher Education* (pp. 40–48). Cambridge: Cambridge University Press.

Freeman, D. and Johnson, K.E. (1998) Reconceptualizing the knowledge-base of language teacher education. *TESOL Quarterly* 32 (3), 397–417.

Hawkins, M.R. (ed.) (2004) *Language Learning and Teacher Education: A Sociocultural Approach*. Clevedon: Multilingual Matters.

Hawkins, M. and Norton, B. (2009) Critical language teacher education. In A. Burns and J.C. Richards (eds) *Second Language Teacher Education* (pp. 30–39). Cambridge: Cambridge University Press.

Holliday, A. (1994) *Appropriate Methodology in Social Context*. Cambridge: Cambridge University Press.

Holliday, A. (2005) *The Struggle to Teach English as an International Language*. Oxford: Oxford University Press.

Inbar-Lourie, O. (2005) Mind the gap: Self and perceived native speaker identities of EFL teachers. In E. Llurda (ed.) *Non-Native Language Teachers: Perceptions, Challenges and Contributions to the Profession* (pp. 265–281). New York: Springer.

Jenkins, J. (2007) *English as a Lingua Franca: Attitude and Identity*. Oxford: Oxford University Press.

Johnson, K.E. (2006) The sociocultural turn and its challenges for second language teacher education. *TESOL Quarterly* 40 (1), 235–257.

Johnson, K.E. (2009a) *Second Language Teacher Education: A Sociocultural Perspective*. New York: Routledge.

Johnson, K.E. (2009b) Trends in second language teacher education. In A. Burns and J.C. Richards (eds) *Second Language Teacher Education* (pp. 20–29). Cambridge: Cambridge University Press.

Johnston, B. and Goettsch, K. (2000) In search of the knowledge base of language teaching: Explanations by experienced teachers. *Canadian Modern Language Review* 56 (3), 437–468.

Kachru, B.B. (ed.) (1992) *The Other Tongue: English Across Cultures* (2nd edn). Urbana: University of Illinois Press.

Kachru, B.B. and Nelson, C.L. (2001) World Englishes. In A. Burns and C. Coffin (eds) *Analysing English in a Global Context* (pp. 9–25). London: Routledge.

Kramsch, C. (1993) *Context and Culture in Language Teaching*. Oxford: Oxford University Press.

Kramsch, C. (1998) The privilege of the intercultural speaker. In M. Byram and M. Fleming (eds) *Language Learning in Intercultural Perspective* (pp. 16–31). Cambridge: Cambridge University Press.

Kumaravadivelu, B. (2006) *Understanding Language Teaching*. New York: Routledge.

Kvale, S. and Brinkmann, S. (2009) *Interviews: Learning the Craft of Qualitative Research Interviewing*. Thousand Oaks, CA: Sage Publications.

Lantolf, J.P. and Johnson, K.E. (2007) Extending Firth and Wagner's (1997) ontological perspective to L2 classroom praxis and teacher education. *The Modern Language Journal* 91 (5), 875–890.

Llurda, E. (ed.) (2005) *Non-Native Language Teachers: Perceptions, Challenges and Contributions to the Profession*. New York: Springer.

Mahboob, A. (2004) Native or nonnative: What do student-teachers enrolled in an intensive English program think? In L. Kamhi-Stein (ed.) *Learning and Teaching from Experience: Perspectives on Nonnative English Speaking Professionals* (pp. 121–147). Ann Arbor: University of Michigan Press.

Mahboob, A. (2005) Beyond the native speaker in TESOL. In S. Zafar (ed.) *Culture, Context, and Communication* (pp. 60–93). Abu Dhabi: Center of Excellence for Applied Research and Training and the Military Language Institute.

McKay, S.L. (2002) *Teaching English as an International Language: Rethinking Goals and Approaches*. Oxford: Oxford University Press.

McKay, S.L. and Bokhorst-Heng, W. (2008) *International English in Its Sociolinguistic Contexts*. New York: Routledge.

Medgyes, P. (1994) *The Non-Native Teacher*. London: Macmillan.

Miller, J. (2009) Teacher identity. In A. Burns and J.C. Richards (eds) *Second Language Teacher Education* (pp. 172–181). Cambridge: Cambridge University Press.

Moussu, L. and Llurda, E. (2008) Non-native English-speaking English language teachers: History and research. *Language Teaching* 41 (3), 315–348.

Myhill, J. (2003) The native speaker identity and the authenticity hierarchy. *Language Sciences* 25 (1), 77–97.

Norton, B. (1997) Language, identity and the ownership of English. *TESOL Quarterly* 31 (3), 409–429.

Norton, B. (2000) *Identity and Language Learning*. London: Longman.

Norton, B. (2010) Language and identity. In N.H. Hornberger and S.L. McKay (eds) *Sociolinguistics and Language Education*. Bristol: Multilingual Matters.

Patton, M.Q. (2002) *Qualitative Research and Evaluation Methods* (3rd edn). Thousand Oaks, CA: Sage Publications.

Pavlenko, A. (2002) Poststructuralist approaches to the study of social factors in second language learning and use. In V. Cook (ed.) *Portraits of the L2 User* (pp. 277–302). Clevedon: Multilingual Matters.

Pennycook, A. (2001) *Critical Applied Linguistics: A Critical Introduction*. Mahwah, NJ: Lawrence Erlbaum Associates.

Petric, B. (2009) I thought I was a Westerner; it turns out I am an Easterner: EIL migrant teacher identities. In F. Sharifian (ed.) *English as an International Language: Perspectives and Pedagogical Issues* (pp. 135–150). Bristol: Multilingual Matters.

Phelan, A.M. (2001) Power and place in teaching and education. *Teaching and Teacher Education* 17 (5), 583–597.

Phillipson, R. (1992) *Linguistic Imperialism*. Oxford: Oxford University Press.

Reeves, J. (2009) A sociocultural perspective on ESOL teachers' linguistic knowledge for teaching. *Linguistics and Education* 20 (2), 109–125.

Richards, J.C. (2008) Second language teacher education today. *RELC Journal* 39 (2), 158–177.

Seidlhofer, B. (1999) Double standards: Teacher education in the expanding circle. *World Englishes* 18 (2), 233–245.

Seidlhofer, B. (2000) English as a mother tongue vs. English as a lingua franca. *VIEWS* 9 (1), 51–68. Online at http://www.univie.ac.at/Anglistik/ang_new/online_papers/views/VIEW00_1.pdf

Sharifian, F. (ed.) (2009) *English as an International Language: Perspectives and Pedagogical Issues*. Bristol: Multilingual Matters.

Shulman, L.S. (1986) Those who understand: Knowledge growth in teaching. *Educational Researcher* 15 (2), 4–14.

Tsui, A.B.M. (2003) *Understanding Expertise in Teaching*. Cambridge: Cambridge University Press.

Tsui, A.B.M. (2007) Complexities of identity formation: A narrative inquiry of an EFL teacher. *TESOL Quarterly* 41 (4), 657–680.

Tsui, A.B.M. (2009) Teaching expertise: Approaches, perspectives and characterisation. In A. Burns and J.C. Richards (eds) *Second Language Teacher Education* (pp. 190–197). Cambridge: Cambridge University Press.

Varghese, M., Morgan, B., Johnston, B. and Johnson, K. (2005) Theorizing language teacher identity: Three perspectives and beyond. *Journal of Language, Identity and Education* 4 (1), 21–44.

Weiss, R.S. (1994) *Learning from Strangers: The Art of Qualitative Interview Studies*. New York: The Free Press.

Widdowson, H.G. (1990) *Aspects of Language Teaching*. Oxford: Oxford University Press.

Widdowson, H.G. (1994) The ownership of English. *TESOL Quarterly* 28 (2), 377–389.

12 Multilingualism Pedagogy: Building Bridges between Languages
Eva Vetter

1 Introduction

The present contribution investigates in how far the multilingualism perspective is likely to bring about changes for teaching languages and hence for language teachers and teacher education in Europe. It starts out from the assumption that within the scope of multilingualism, the linguistic resources in the language users' minds are to be seen as – more or less – integrated components of a linguistic repertoire and that language learning means developing the linguistic repertoire further. Hence, teaching languages is to be interpreted as supporting and encouraging learners during this multi-layered process. Since the single language taught or learned is part of a complex whole that comprises all linguistic capacities of language users, taking into account the whole repertoire instead of teaching single languages in isolation is assumed to be highly advantageous for the learning and acquisition processes. These dynamics across languages can be considered a major characteristic of multilingualism pedagogy.

The present chapter will ask in how far the pedagogic perspective on multilingualism impacts upon teaching languages and particularly upon educating (student) teachers. Its main aim is to contribute to the investigation with respect to the following questions: What are the main issues at stake when talking about languages in education? In how far does multilingualism – as an area of research and as a European policy endeavour – prepare new grounds for teacher education? How should teachers be educated in order to situate their pedagogic actions within a framework of multilingualism?

In order to answer these questions, this chapter will proceed in four major steps: firstly, it will be shown in how far the multilingualism perspective impacts upon approaching language(s) in educational settings: The growing awareness of linguistic diversity and its educational consequences has blurred well-established categorisations of languages and thus calls for new perspectives on languages in education (Section 2). In a second step, I will ask in how far recent multilingualism research (Section 3.1) and the European language policy debate (Section 3.3) may contribute to developing new perspectives of this kind, while at the same time new questions will be raised. Furthermore, this section is also concerned with terminological and conceptual issues arising from the multilingualism debate (Section 3.2). Thirdly, the major characteristics of multilingualism pedagogy will be outlined and some concrete approaches will be presented (Section 4). The last section concentrates on the consequences of the multilingualism debate for language teacher education. It will be asked in how far European language policy provides for concrete incentives with regard to language teacher education (Section 5.1) and finally three major guidelines will be presented along which teacher education should be developed when multilingualism is the aim of teaching (Section 5.2).

2 Blurred Boundaries: Language(s) in Education

Languages in education may differ considerably in various ways, i.e. with regard to their visibility, their institutional role, the competence pupils are supposed to achieve or the abilities pupils (and sometimes also teachers and staff) already have, as well as with regard to the prestige of these languages at school and in society at large. It is generally assumed that linguistic diversity in education goes well beyond pedagogic scenarios and asks about the multilingual repertoire of the actors (pupils, teachers, staff), which can be quite heterogeneous. Hence, the languages heard in the corridors or seen on the walls of schools are to be taken into consideration just like the foreign languages taught there.

A perspective on linguistic diversity demonstrates that categorisations of languages in education are generally rather problematic if simplistic groupings (e.g. mother tongue versus foreign language teaching, etc.) are to be avoided and if the complexity of linguistic practice is to be taken into due account. Even well-established pragmatic categories such as the differentiation between languages of instruction, which are usually also taught as a subject, and languages belonging to the foreign-language category, as well as regional or minority languages, are not as clear-cut as they might appear at a first glance: first, data referring to these categories are not always comparable across countries (Key Data on Teaching Languages at School in Europe 2005 and 2008 are a good example) and second, the pupils' linguistic background at home and in their peer group may overlap with the languages at school to very different degrees. To give an example, the languages of instruction may or may not be the pupils' first or second languages and they may even not be part of the pupils' extracurricular life world. The difficulty of putting languages into separate boxes is further illustrated by the example of Content and Language Integrated Learning (CLIL). Here, a 'foreign' language – very often English – may be at stake, although for a purpose that differs from that of traditional foreign-language teaching.

Multilingual education can be considered as a possible – and positive – reaction to linguistic diversity in schools, although it may also evolve from rather 'monolingual' educational contexts. Definitions of multilingual education oscillate between a pragmatic focus when, e.g. stressing the importance of using more than two languages as languages of instruction (García et al., 2006) and a focus on multilingualism as an educational aim (for an overview, see Cenoz, 2009: 31). Nevertheless, there seems to be a growing understanding that multilingual education is more than an organisational task and that the adoption of multilingualism as a pedagogic aim requires specific effort. Hence, multilingual education itself has come to be considered as an achievement rather than a state that can be taken for granted. Multilingualism pedagogy would then refer to approaches through which the specific pedagogical aim of multilingualism is to be achieved.

Looking at languages from the perspective of linguistic diversity, multilingual education and multilingualism pedagogy require an intensive debate on the meaning of multilingualism and on languages in education. It goes without saying that continuing to look at languages in terms of discrete isolable boxes such as 'foreign languages' might appear to be a simpler task, but it rarely accounts for the highly complex and cross-cutting nature of language practice.

3 The Impact of Multilingualism Research and Language Policy

3.1 Research in Multilingualism and Language Acquisition

Multilingualism research and research in language acquisition constitute two closely interrelated areas of scientific interest. On the one hand, multilingualism research has been increasingly developing into an independent research area in the last decades, with language acquisition and learning traditionally constituting important research topics within this research area. On the other hand, research into language acquisition and learning itself is more and more concerned with multilingualism, and there seems to be a growing awareness of the intricate relationship between these two strands. The recent interest in multilingualism research must, however, not obscure that multilingualism has been investigated for a long time (see, e.g. Jessner, 2008: 16–17 for an overview). There are nevertheless some significant differences between the more recent and growing scientific interest in multilingualism and early multilingualism research, which have been brought about by the main social, linguistic and political driving forces behind present-day research.

As to the social dimension, one can observe an 'increased sensitivity towards socio-cultural diversity' and a 'great variety of (socio-)linguistically based issues and problems at the societal level which have arisen from increased migratory movements' (Franceschini, 2009: 29). Both the increased sensitivity as well as social issues relating to multilingualism have slowly but surely contributed to a reinterpretation of linguistic diversity and multilingualism. Hence, beside the awareness that multilingualism might be a problem, there is also a more positive view of it, as it were, a 'change in perspective towards the value contained in multilingualism at the individual and societal level' (Franceschini, 2009: 30). Following Franceschini, this perspective encourages a certain tendency in language teaching and learning research, namely a trend towards considering languages in interpersonal interaction instead of narrowly focusing upon the individual and his/her competencies, and towards the complex and variable constellations in which the languages are embedded instead of studying languages as isolated and isolable entities. This tendency matches with observations from sociolinguistic research, which has been highlighting that languages do not coexist peacefully side by side, but are linked to each other through asymmetric relations of power originating from quite diverse features such as status and prestige of the languages, number of speakers, cultural background, identity and attitudes, etc. (e.g. Rindler, 2007). It is particularly from the anthropological perspective on language learning and acquisition (Schwerdtfeger, 2000a, 2000b) or in biographical approaches (Krumm, 2001) that the sociolinguistic components of the languages to be learned or acquired have been taken up. These approaches have stressed that many aspects of language learning, such as language choice, targeted competencies, etc., cannot be separated from sociolinguistic issues of this kind (e.g. Hu, 2003; Pavlenko & Blackledge, 2006).

As to the linguistic aspects of present-day research, it can be outlined that recent psycho- and neurolinguistic research provides evidence that multilingualism constitutes an apt starting point for language learning and teaching research since it underlines that, at the individual level, language learning is linked to all linguistic resources the learners already have at their disposal (e.g. Cenoz et al., 2008; Cook, 2003; De Angelis, 2007; Hall et al., 2006; Kecskes, 2010). It can thus be concluded that even if the acquisition of one specific language is at the focus of interest, the other linguistic resources of the individual mind have to be taken into account as well. Or, as the International Association of Multilingualism puts it in its statutes: 'the study of multilingualism provides the basis for understanding all types of language acquisition and learning, maintenance and attrition' (www.iamultilingualism.org).

As to the last point, i.e. the political dimension of the scientific interest in multilingualism, it cannot be overlooked that multilingualism has developed into a powerful and comprehensive framework that stimulates research into language acquisition while, at the same time, it appears to be inspired itself by this research (see Section 3.2). Since at least in Europe, language competence primarily derives from educational contexts, language education policy represents an area of political interest of particular importance.

The social, linguistic and political driving forces behind current multilingualism research have led multilingualism research and research in language acquisition to grow even closer together. Hence, there is also a growing awareness that language teaching and learning research can fruitfully be seen (and carried out) through a multilingual lens. The elaboration of what we can name 'multilingualism pedagogy' is but one implication of this multilingual scope.

3.2 Terminological and Conceptual Issues

The outlined shift towards languages (plural!) and multilingualism, which has sometimes been considered paradigmatic (e.g. De Cillia, 2008), goes along with an intense terminological and conceptual debate. Without going into the details of this debate (see Jessner, 2008; Kemp, 2009), I would like to direct attention to the plurilingual approach, which is described in section 1.3 of the CEFR (Common European Frame of Reference, Council of Europe, 2001) and is generally associated with the Council of Europe's language policy (see also Section 3.3). The CEFR is very clear about the integrative and intercultural nature of plurilingualism in conceiving of plurilingual competence as a complex competence that is fed by all linguistic knowledge as well as by the linguistic and cultural experiences of the individual. In contrast to additive conceptions of multilingualism, the Council's approach suggests a holistic, multi-faceted, dynamic and individual vision that is open to partial competence and circulations, mediations and passages between languages and cultures, to name but the most evident changes (Coste & Moore, 2009: v). The plurilingual approach is particularly well in line with current models of multiple language acquisition as presented in Jessner (2008). These models are all based upon the assumption that the use and acquisition of two or more languages can only be assessed adequately when the individual's linguistic resources are taken into consideration as a whole, i.e. when languages and varieties are not focused upon in isolation. To put it another way, these models suggest a strong link between retrospective multilingualism, i.e. the diversity of language competence that pupils bring to their education, and prospective multilingualism, i.e. the target of achieving competence in other languages through education. It has to be said, however, that only some of these models – such as the multilingual processing model (Meißner, 2004) – have come to be integrated into multilingualism pedagogy until now. There is, however, no doubt that the conceptualisation of language acquisition and learning as multilingual or plurilingual processes may be highly significant for language pedagogy: pupils most likely have two or more languages and/or varieties in their linguistic repertoire and the classroom is characterised by highly diversified linguistic practices. Since research provides evidence that all these languages impact on language learning in one way or in another, it is thus quite reasonable to assume that language teaching may benefit from the pluri- or multilingual scope.

3.3 Some Open Questions Related to Language Policy

In general, European language policy efforts are directed towards further developing linguistic competences among Europeans. In short, more Europeans are to gain competences in more languages. Multilingualism understood in this way has constituted the overarching pedagogic objective of European language education policies for more than two decades. Various recent documents issued by the European Union and the Council of Europe, the two major players in the field of European language policy, are full of suggestions as to how this objective can be achieved (e.g. Béacco, 2007; COM [2005] 596 final; COM [2008] 566 final; Commission of the European Communities, 2007; Council of Europe 2001; Fleming 2009).

The policy efforts are, however, not as straightforward as they might appear at first sight, since a common understanding of the concept of multilingualism or plurilingualism and the political aim behind the policy endeavour has, as yet, not been successfully negotiated. As to conceptual issues, the plurilingual approach has become a prominent strategic concept. Attempts to operationalise plurilingualism are, however, rare and not very well known. The study conducted by Coste et al. (2009), contains concrete incentives for implementing plurilingualism in school settings and is also very clear about the objective of a language policy directed towards plurilingualism, which should encourage every learner to achieve an integrating communication competency spanning a large number of languages and cultures and encompassing not only general competences at different levels, but also balanced partial competences fostering receptive skills. (Trim, 2009: vi)

This study could at the same time have initiated an intense debate on the conceptual nature of multilingualism/plurilingualism as well as an investigation into the social construction of multilingualism in Europe. The evident lack of this kind of debate gives rise to a range of contradictions with regard to European language education policy. To give an example, the European Union's 'mother tongue + two' strategy and the Indicator for Language Competence (COM [2007] 184; COM [2005] 596) suggest an additive conception of multilingualism in stressing the importance of competences in distinct languages. Similarly, the introduction of educational standards currently rather suggests a view of languages as isolated entities in which a specific competence should be reached – without, however, starting out from one integrating competence in the way the plurilingual approach suggests. Moreover, in choosing Europe's most widely taught languages for assessment, the Indicator for Language Competence suggests that some languages are more relevant than others. The European Language Portfolio, in contrast, is open to all linguistic and cultural experiences and hence succeeds in mapping the linguistic repertoire and the individual and intercultural shaping of this repertoire. It is evident that the additive conception of multilingualism is difficult to combine with the integrative conception of plurilingual and pluricultural competence.

As to the contradictions arising from the lacking consensus with respect to the political aim behind the policy endeavour, it must be stressed that multilingualism in Europe has come to be seen as a venue for demands and scenarios that go well beyond language. Following influential documents issued by the European Union (e.g. Opinion of the European Economic and Social Committee on 'Multilingualism', 2009; Languages Mean Business 2008; COM [2008] 566 final; Commission of the European Communities 2007; COM [2005] 596 final) and the Council of Europe (e.g. Béacco, 2007; Fleming, 2009), the language issue has become embedded in quite different fields of action: in the economic discourse connected with individual and societal advantage, and also in the discourse on democratic citizenship and social cohesion. The diverse demands and scenarios profoundly impact upon how the pedagogic goal, i.e. multilingualism/plurilingualism, is interpreted and implemented. Beyond that, there is also a lack of a consensus with regard to the question if language policy should adopt a top-down (Opinion of the European Economic and Social Committee on 'Multilingualism', 2009) or a bottom-up approach (Maalouf, 2008).

It goes without saying that discrepancies and open questions of this kind do not provide for a secure political frame for pedagogic approaches. It must, however, be stressed that there is strong scientific evidence for looking at language acquisition and learning in terms of plurilingualism and that beyond the insecurities mentioned in this section, multilingualism continues to figure as the outstanding goal of European language policy. These are the grounds on which multilingualism or plurilingualism pedagogy has been developing.

4 Multilingualism Pedagogy: A Brief Overview

Multilingualism pedagogy is to date far from representing one single and coherent approach and the different realisations currently available can vary considerably with regard to their specific focus. Looking backwards and forwards when thinking about the pupils' linguistic repertoire, i.e. taking the dynamics between the retrospective and the prospective view into account, is probably its most pertinent feature.

Against the background of what has been said about languages in education, it goes without saying that integrating the languages pupils bring with them and the languages that are learned and used in the educational contexts is a highly complex task. Hence, although the assumption that all components of the multilingual mind interact in one way or another is commonly shared, pedagogic approaches towards multilingualism do make choices and decide which languages should be integrated into teaching and learning and which should not. The number of languages to be explicitly taken into account constitutes one, rather simple, criterion of differentiation and highlights two extremes: on the one hand, there are approaches that integrate the widest possible range of languages, such as *Jaling*, or *Eveil aux langues* (Candelier, 2003, 2004), and on the other hand, there are approaches for developing competencies in a specific language on the basis of one (or more) language(s) already acquired, such as English as a bridge language for Romance intercomprehension (Klein & Reissner, 2006). Another criterion would be the typological relationship between languages. Here, one could differentiate between approaches that confine themselves to typologically related languages, and others that go beyond the language family. Starting out from the target competence, one could, for example, differentiate between approaches that aim at developing a wide range of skills (reception, production, interaction, etc.) and others that are restricted to specific skills.

A valuable contribution to multilingualism pedagogy, which has been developed at the European Centre for Modern Languages (ECML) of the Council of Europe by a research group coordinated by Michel Candelier, is the framework of reference for pluralistic approaches to languages and cultures. By pluralistic approaches, which the group understands as the opposite of 'singular approaches', they mean 'didactic approaches which use teaching/learning activities involving several (i.e. more than one) varieties of languages or cultures' (Candelier, 2007: 7). Candelier and his colleagues distinguish between four major groups: the intercultural approaches, 'awakening to languages', the inter-comprehension of related languages and integrated didactic approaches to different languages studied (in and beyond the school curriculum). Among these, the last three are linguistically focused and specifically relevant in the present context.

'Awakening to languages' is the translation that the authors propose for *l'éveil aux langues* in projects such as *Evlang* and *Jaling* (Candelier, 2003). This stresses the plurilingual and pedagogic character of this group of approaches, and differentiates it from the language awareness movement, from which it has developed. Approaches within the 'awakening to languages' group refer to the language of education and any other linguistic varieties, even those not learnt at school. Hence, the focus is on retrospective multilingualism: all languages children are equipped with are valued, and children should become more sensitive both to their own language and to other languages. The knowledge about languages and cultures should help them to develop a positive attitude towards multilingualism and multiculturalism and to develop metalinguistic competence as well as learning strategies, which are likely to support future language learning.

In contrast to 'awakening to languages', integrated didactic approaches set a clear prospective focus upon languages learnt at school. The first language (Castellotti, 2001) or the first foreign language (Hufeisen & Neuner, 2004) is used in order to facilitate the learning of further foreign languages.

The third category, inter-comprehension, also focuses upon prospective multilingualism. Unlike the first two groups however, this category comprises approaches that have a clear tendency towards developing partial, particularly receptive skills within a language group (e.g. EuroCom for Romance, Germanic and Slavic languages, http://www.eurocomresearch.net/). Beyond this, inter-comprehensive approaches may also develop traditional skills (e.g. ICE, Galanet) or go beyond a language group (Klein & Reissner, 2006).

Many of the approaches mentioned within these three groups were supported at the European level. Thus, they are outcomes of concrete language policy activities and are linked to the diversified demands associated with European multilingualism. They differ, however, with respect to various aspects, such as the pedagogic dimension (e.g. lower or higher degrees of learner-centredness, etc.) or their foundation in models of language acquisition. All options developed within multilingualism pedagogy are, in a broader sense, based upon bridging the gap between languages. The relationships between languages may differ substantially with regard to their nature: Some approaches rather focus upon the emotional and attitudinal component of the relationship between the languages, e.g. by valuing all languages learners bring with them equally. Others stress the linguistic component, which is the case, for example, when languages are to be compared with regard to their structural properties. Despite these differences multilingualism pedagogy sees languages in relation to other languages and strives towards taking benefit from these relationships for the teaching and learning of languages.

5 What Teachers Should Know about All This

5.1 Teacher Competences from the Language Policy Perspective

Against the background of the wide range of approaches within multilingualism pedagogy, the ambitious character of the European policy endeavour, and the many questions that still remain open, one might be tempted to ask what teachers should know about all this. From what has been said above, it should have become clear that it is difficult to ignore the issue of multilingualism when talking about languages in educational contexts: multilingualism is a social fact, research in teaching and learning languages is substantially inspired by multilingualism research and lastly, within Europe, multilingualism has turned into a political goal. So, if multilingualism can no longer be ignored, what are teachers supposed to know and do about it? Should they become accustomed to all the different approaches in order to be able to apply them according to the specific context of teaching? Or should they rather be familiar with the concept of plurilingualism itself, its political contextualisation and contradictory interpretations? In how far would they have to be acquainted with research results and the role of language in the educational context in general?

These are questions that are likely to arise when teacher education and training is at stake. Here, two points will be made: first, the Council of Europe provides for an important cornerstone with respect to teacher education (Béacco, 2007). Second, multilingualism is not just a knowledge set to add to existing curricula for language teachers, but calls for a paradigmatic change since it relates to the teachers' competences in a very broad sense: Taking up the competences which the CEFR defines for language learners, a multilingual turn in teacher education would affect the teachers' declarative knowledge (savoir), their skills and know-how (savoir-faire) and existential competence (savoir-être), as well as their ability to learn (savoir-apprendre).

Returning to the first point, there seems to be a general awareness of the importance of language teacher education, since issues relevant for teacher education are raised in several language policy-related reports (e.g. Commission of the European Communities, 2007; Strubell et al., 2007). The Guide for the Development of Language Education (Béacco & Byram, pilot version 2001, revised version 2003), one of the first documents raising the question of plurilingualism with regard to teacher education, is a descriptive and programmatic document that demonstrates the complexity of the questions involved in language teaching. Its main version (Béacco, 2007) refers to four elements to be taken into consideration in initial and continuing teacher education: the European objective of plurilingual education and its educational and political goals, the notion of plurilingual competence, more didactic content 'such as teaching approaches based on competences with proficiency levels defined according to reference levels', and the development of the teachers' own linguistic repertoire (Béacco, 2007: 77 f.). Moreover, the guide recommends taking into account the different types of language teacher that should be educated, distinguishing between four groups of teachers, i.e. pre-school teachers familiar with early language-learning methods, primary school teachers, secondary school teachers and subject teachers who are able to teach their subject in a variety other than the national variety.

Language teacher education is a good example for the collaboration between the Council of Europe and the European Union. 'Improving language teaching' represents one of the three broad areas defined in the European Commission's Action Plan for language learning and linguistic diversity (COM [2003] 449 final). Arguing for a holistic approach to the teaching of language and for connections between the different languages at stake in the educational setting, as well as for multilingual comprehension approaches, the European Union's Action Plan is well in line with the Council's plurilingual approach and gave rise to the European Profile for Language Teacher Education: A Frame of Reference (Kelly et al., 2004). The European Profile aims to serve as a checklist and guideline for teacher education programmes. Part II comprises the Frame of Reference, which represents 40 key elements for language teacher education in four sections (Structure; Knowledge and Understanding; Strategies and Skills and Values).

Issues relating to multilingualism are raised several times, although in a rather abstract and vague manner, e.g. in item 5, 'Experience of an intercultural and multicultural environment' and in item 13, 'Close links between trainees who are being educated to teach different languages'. Under item 13, suggested activities include joint seminars or workshops for future teachers of different languages, which could focus on the European dimension and concepts such as plurilingualism and pluriculturalism. The Values section comprises key elements like 'Training in the diversity of languages and cultures' (item 36), which recommends, e.g. that future teachers are familiar with the central notion of plurilingual and pluricultural competence set out in the CEFR. In this context, teachers 'could be encouraged to choose their materials to reflect linguistic and cultural diversity as much as possible' (Kelly et al., 2004: 83).

However, the Profile for Language Teacher Education lacks more concrete suggestions for plurilingual teacher education, which also holds true for the *European Portfolio for Student Teachers of Languages* (Newby et al., 2007),[1] a reflection tool for language teacher education that is based upon the Profile. The Portfolio remains rather vague with regard to plurilingualism. To give an example, the descriptor 'I can take into account the knowledge of other languages learners may already possess and help them to build on this knowledge when learning additional languages' (Newby et al., 2007: 17) is one of the most explicit descriptors relating to plurilingual issues. The descriptor lacks a more precise differentiation of retrospective and prospective language knowledge, as well as of the different kinds of relationships that may be constructed between the languages. Hence, the knowledge of a home language that is not part of the language family of the language(s) to be learnt is likely to play a profoundly different role from that of a foreign language of the same linguistic family. There are completely different strategies at stake if this kind of retrospective multilingualism is to be taken into account for future language learning. In encouraging future teachers to reflect upon their own language learning experiences, the European Portfolio for Student Teachers of Languages succeeds, however, in raising awareness of the linguistic repertoire as a whole.

A further step in order to come closer to the specific competences that teachers require if they are to adopt multilingualism or plurilingualism as the goal of teaching could be to look at CARAP (Framework of reference for pluralistic approaches to languages and cultures). As a reference framework 'of the knowledge, skills and attitudes which could be developed by [...]

pluralistic approaches' (Candelier, 2007: 11), CARAP provides for sets of descriptors which precisely focus upon the European Council's concept of plurilingualism. It goes without saying that CARAP cannot simply be transferred to teacher education since it does not address (student) teachers, but anyone responsible for curriculum development and teaching materials as well as teacher educators. Moreover, CARAP is restricted to three of the four competences: it describes knowledge sets (savoir), skills (savoir-faire) and attitudes (savoir-être) and lacks the component of ability to learn (savoir-apprendre). Despite these limits and the necessary modifications, CARAP may be a good starting point for coming closer to the competences plurilingual teachers should possess. To give an example, the descriptor 'Can use the knowledge and skills available in one language for understanding another one and expressing oneself in it' is further specified by the following descriptors 'Can use the similarities between languages as strategies for understanding and producing language' and 'Can identify first language (L1) reading strategies and apply them in learning other languages (L2[...])'. The first group is further refined by various descriptors such as, e.g. by 'Can construct a grammar of hypotheses (a set of hypotheses about the ways in which languages correspond or do not correspond)' (Candelier, 2007: 87). It goes without saying that there is still a certain amount of work to be done, but European language policy provides for valuable grounds on which to build a model of teacher education for plurilingualism or multilingualism.

5.2 Three Major Guidelines for Teacher Education

The guidelines presented here link up with the author's previous work on teacher education (Vetter, 2008, 2009), which started out from empirically identified obstacles to multilingualism in educational contexts which were interpreted as parts of a cycle of monolingualism. In brief, student teachers appear to have a utilitarian conception of multilingualism that sharply contrasts with their emotional sympathy for the language(s) they actually teach. During teacher education (at least in Austria), they are not systematically confronted with multilingualism and only rarely experience multilingual teaching in multilingual teaching projects. Moreover, schools seem to perpetuate the monolingual habitus since teachers tend to cooperate within groups of languages, but not across languages. Student teachers are in fact very open towards learner-centred pedagogic approaches that they relate to teaching and learning a specific language, but not in connection with multilingualism. The following suggestions are meant to break this cycle of monolingualism in order to allow teachers to best cope with multilingual realities, to benefit from existing language knowledge and to help their learners prepare for lifelong learning. They can be formulated as recommendations for language teacher education programmes and as a frame for describing competences as mentioned in the previous section. The three guidelines relate to

(1) debating multilingualism / plurilingualism and its impact;
(2) adopting learner-centred pedagogic approaches for multilingualism and
(3) facilitating positive linguistic and intercultural experiences.

The first guideline refers to the multilingualism/plurilingualism debate and should address its highly complex nature. In this context, it seems appropriate to start out from the notion of language and the functions of language, the difficulty of drawing lines between languages from a (psycho-, neuro-, pragma- and socio-) linguistic point of view, before investigating linguistic diversity and the various demands it is associated with. The language policy perspective will, of course, have to be complemented by scientific insights. As multilingualism research is a young and very active field of research, it is not so much a question of acquiring certain clearly defined knowledge sets (savoir), but of learning what questions can be raised in the context of multilingualism in educational settings and how to position one's own future teaching activity within the diverse and complex relationships at stake.

The second major guideline starts out from the assumption that if the linguistic repertoire is to be conceived of as an integrated whole, learner-centred and differentiated approaches are of the utmost importance. The pupils' linguistic repertoire is individually shaped and likely to comprise linguistic varieties unknown to their teachers and many of their classmates. Taking the whole repertoire as a reference point for future language learning cannot do without phases of learner autonomy and other learner-centred approaches which involve a re-definition of the teacher's role in language teaching. If teachers learn how to re-adapt innovative pedagogies within a multilingual scope, they will surely benefit from moving an important step further towards a more concrete operationalisation of the plurilingual approach.

It is the student teachers as learners who are addressed by the third major guideline. Intercultural and plurilingual experiences should be an integral part of their education and will, thus, primarily impact upon their 'savoir-faire' and 'savoir-être'. The opportunity to make first-hand experiences related to multilingualism opens up a wide range of options, from teaching practice in highly multilingual and multicultural classes to language learning experiences. The further development of the future teachers' own linguistic repertoire in a multifaceted and plurilingual way, for instance, will not only make them more flexible with regard to future teaching settings, but will first and foremost give them insights into the highly complex character of being and/or of becoming multilingual and acting as a multilingual individual.

These guidelines open up a variety of concrete realisations, such as the option of becoming a teacher for a language group instead of for one single language. These teachers may teach Russian or French, for example, with the prospective aim in mind to teach other Slavic or Romance languages (for partial skills) at a later stage. Another option would involve training CLIL teachers in international or minority languages (migrant and regional) against the background of multilingualism. Changes like the ones outlined here require a firm conceptual and transversal basis and they would benefit from a secure political frame. The insecurities with regard to conceptual and political grounds have been discussed in the previous sections. Nevertheless, the concept of plurilingualism, the respective elaborations with regard to teacher education and the guidelines mentioned above represent a promising starting point for a new teacher education.

6 Concluding Remarks

The multilingualism scope profoundly impacts upon the status of languages in education. It highlights existing linguistic diversity, the heterogeneity of language practices in educational settings and hence the necessity to critically reflect upon well-established categorisations of languages and language use. There is common agreement that the adoption of multilingualism as an educational aim requires a specific commitment and effort. Multilingualism pedagogy represents an effort of this kind. The salient characteristics of multilingualism pedagogy, i.e. the dynamics between the retrospective and the prospective view of teaching and learning languages, calls for crossing the bridge between languages.

Multilingualism pedagogy has developed in close relationship with multilingualism research, a young and currently very active field of research, which in Europe is moreover intrinsically related to language policy issues. Here, the Council of Europe's plurilingualism concept represents an interesting approach that is in line with the scientific modelling of multilingual processes. However, the lack of an intensive debate about the concept of plurilingualism and multilingualism as well as about the aim of multilingualism policy actually gives rise to a number of controversial issues. Despite the many questions which are still open, there is no doubt that a multilingual or better: a plurilingual scope has a strong impact on teaching languages and hence upon educating teachers. The three guidelines that have been proposed in the present contribution are intended as a first step towards a more profound debate in this area.

Note

(1) See also the contribution by Barbara Mehlmauer-Larcher on the use of EPOSTL in teacher education in this volume.

References

Béacco, J-C. (2007) *From Linguistic Diversity to Plurilingual Education: Guide for the Development of Language Education Policies in Europe*. Strasbourg: Council of Europe. http://www.coe.int/T/DG4/Linguistic/Source/Guide_Main_Beacco2007_EN.doc

Béacco, J-C. and Byram, M. (2003) *Guide for the Development of Language Education Policies in Europe: From Linguistic Diversity to Plurilingual Education*. Strasbourg: Language Policy Division, Council of Europe. http://www.coe.int/t/dg4/Linguistic/Source/FullGuide_En.pdf

Candelier, M. (2003) *L'éveil aux langues à l'école primaire: Evlang: bilan d'une innovation européenne*. Bruxelles: De Boeck & Larcier.

Candelier, M. (coord.) (2004) *Janua Linguarum: The gateway to languages. The introduction of language awareness into the curriculum: Awakening to languages*. Graz: European Center of Modern Languages.

Candelier, M. (coord.) (2007) *CARAP: Framework of reference for pluralistic approaches to languages and cultures*. Graz: European Center of Modern Languages. http://carap.ecml.at/Portals/11/documents/C4pub2007E_20080302_FINAL.pdf

Castellotti, V. (2001) *La langue maternelle en classe de langue étrangère*. Paris: CLE international.

Cenoz, J. (2009) *Towards Multilingual Education: Basque Educational Research from an International Perspective*. Bristol: Multilingual Matters.

Cenoz, J., Hufeisen, B. and Jessner, U. (eds) (2008 [2001]) *Looking Beyond Second Language Acquisition: Studies in Tri- and Multilingualism*. Tübingen: Stauffenburg Verlag.

COM (2003) 449 final, Communication from the Commission to the Council, the European Parliament, the European Economic and Social Committee and the Committee of the Regions: Promoting Language Learning and Linguistic Diversity. An Action Plan 2004 – 2006. http://eur-lex.europa.eu/LexUriServ/LexUriServ.do?uri=COM:2003:0449:FIN:EN:PDF

COM (2005) 596 final, Communication from the Commission to the Council, the European Parliament, the European Economic and Social Committee and the Committee of the Regions: A New Framework Strategy for Multilingualism. http://ec.europa.eu/education/languages/archive/doc/com596_en.pdf

COM (2007) 184 final, Communication from the Commission to the Council: Framework for the European survey on language competences. http://ec.europa.eu/education/policies/2010/doc/com184_en.pdf

COM (2008) 566 final, Communication from the Commission to the Council, the European Parliament, the European Economic and Social Committee and the Committee of the Regions: Multilingualism. An asset for Europe and a shared commitment. http://ec.europa.eu/education/languages/pdf/com/2008_0566_en.pdf

Commission of the European Communities (2007) Final Report: High-level group on multilingualism. http://ec.europa.eu/education/policies/lang/doc/multireport_en.pdf

Cook, V.J. (2003) The changing L1 in the L2 User's Mind. In V.J. Cook (ed.) *Effects of the Second Language on the First* (pp. 1–18). Clevedon: Multilingual Matters.

Coste, D. and Moore, D. (2009) Foreword. In D. Coste, D. Moore and G. Zarate (eds): *Plurilingual and Pluricultural Competence* (pp. V–VI). Strasbourg: Council of Europe. http://www.coe.int/t/dg4/linguistic/Source/SourcePublications/CompetencePlurilingue09web_en.pdf

Coste, D., Moore, D. and Zarate, G. (2009) *Plurilingual and Pluricultural Competence: With a Foreword and Complementary Bibliography. Studies towards a Common European Framework of Reference for Language Learning and Teaching* (French version originally published in 1997). Strasbourg: Council of Europe. http://www.coe.int/t/dg4/linguistic/Source/SourcePublications/CompetencePlurilingue09web_en.pdf

Council of Europe (2001) *Common European Framework of Reference for Languages: Learning, Teaching, Assessment*. Cambridge: Cambridge University Press.

De Angelis, G. (2007) *Third or Additional Language Acquisition*. Clevedon: Mulitilingual Matters.

De Cillia, R. (2008) Plädoyer für einen Paradigmenwechsel im Umgang mit Mehrsprachigkeit in der Schule. In M. Frings and E. Vetter (eds) *Mehrsprachigkeit als Schlüsselkompetenz: Theorie und Praxis in Lehr- und Lernkontexten* (pp. 69–84). Stuttgart: Ibidem.

Fleming, M. (2009) *Languages of Schooling and the Right to Plurilingual and Intercultural Education*. Intergovernmental Conference Report. Council of Europe: Language Policy Division.

Franceschini, R. (2009) The genesis and development of research in multilingualism: Perspectives for future research. In L. Aronin and B. Hufeisen (eds) *The Exploration of Multilingualism: Development of Research on L3, Multilingualism and Multiple Language Acquisition* (pp. 27–61). Amsterdam: John Benjamins.

Galanet, Plateforme de formation à l'intercompréhension en langues romanes. http://www.galanet.eu/

García, O., Skutnabb-Kangas, T. and Torres Guzmán, M. (2006) Weaving spaces and (de)constructing ways for multilingual schools: The actual and the imagined. In O. García, T. Skutnabb-Kangas and M. Torres Guzmán (eds) *Imagining Multilingual Schools: Languages in Education and Glocalization* (pp. 3–47). Clevedon: Multilingual Matters.

Hall, J.K., Cheng, A. and Carlson, M.T. (2006) Reconceptualizing multicompetence as a theory of language knowledge. *Applied Linguistics* 27 (2), 220–240.

Hu, A. (2003) *Schulischer Fremdsprachenunterricht und migrationsbedingte Mehrsprachigkeit*. Tübingen: Narr.

Hufeisen, B. and Neuner, G. (2004) *The Plurilingualism Project: Tertiary Language Learning – German after English*. Graz: European Centre for Modern Languages.

ICE, Programme InterCompréhension Européenne. http://logatome.eu/ice.htm

International Association of Multilingualism. http://www.iamultilingualism.org

Jessner, U. (2008) Teaching third languages: Findings, trends and challenges. State-of-the-art article. *Language Teaching* 41(1), 15–56.

Kecskes, I. (2010) Dual and multilanguage systems. *International Journal of Multilingualism* 7 (2), 91–109.

Kelly, M., Grenfell, M., Allan, R., Kriza, C. and McEvoy, W. (2004) European profile for language teacher education: A frame of reference. University of Southampton. http://www.lang.soton.ac.uk/profile/report/MainReport.rtf

Kemp, C. (2009) Defining multilingualism. In L. Aronin and B. Hufeisen (eds) *The Exploration of Multilingualism: Development of Research on L3, Multilingualism and Multiple Language Acquisition* (pp. 11–26). Amsterdam: John Benjamins.

Key Data on Teaching Languages at School in Europe, Eurydice: Brussels; 2005 edn. http://eacea.ec.europa.eu/eurydice/ressources/eurydice/pdf/0_integral/049EN.pdf; 2008 edn. http://eacea.ec.europa.eu/about/eurydice/documents/KDL2008_EN.pdf

Klein, H.G. and Reissner, C. (2006) *Basismodul Englisch: Englisch als Brückensprache in der romanischen Interkomprehension*. Aachen: Shaker (Editiones EuroCom 26).

Krumm, H.-J. (2001) *Kinder und ihre Sprachen: Lebendige Mehrsprachigkeit*. Wien: Eviva.

Languages mean Business (2008) Languages mean Business: Companies work better with languages. Recommendations from the Business Forum for Multilingualism established by the European Commission (2008)-Online Document: http://ec.europa.eu/dgs/education_culture/publ/pdf/language/davignon_en.pdf

Maalouf, A. (2008) A rewarding challenge: How the multiplicity of languages could strengthen Europe. Proposals from the Group of Intellectuals for Intercultural Dialogue set up at the initiative of the European Commission. http://ec.europa.eu/education/languages/archive/doc/maalouf/report_en.pdf

Meißner, F.-J. (2004) Transfer und Transferieren: Anleitungen zum Interkomprehensionsunterricht. In H. G. Klein and D. Rudtke (eds) *Neuere Forschungen zur Europäischen Interkomprehension* (pp. 39–66.). Aachen: Shaker.

Newby, D., Allan, R., Fenner, A-B., Jones, B., Komorowska, H. and Soghikyan, K. (2007) *European Portfolio for Student Teachers of Languages: A Reflection Tool for Language Teacher Education*. Graz: Council of Europe Publishing. Online at http://www.ecml.at/mtp2/publications/C3_Epostl_E_internet.pdf

Opinion of the European Economic and Social Committee on 'Multilingualism' (2009/C 77/25). Official Journal of the European Union. http://eur-lex.europa.eu/LexUriServ/LexUriServ.do?uri = OJ:C:2009:077:0109:0114:EN:PDF

Pavlenko, A. and Blackledge, A. (eds) (2006) *Negotiation of Identities in Multilingual Contexts*. Clevedon: Multilingual Matters.

Rindler Schjerve, R. (2007) Language conflict revisited. In J. Darquennes (ed.) *Contact Linguistics and Language Minorities* (= Plurilingua XXX) (pp. 37–50). St. Augustin: Asgard.

Schwerdtfeger, I. C. (2000a): Leiblichkeit und Grammatik. In H. Düwell, C. Gnutzmann and F. G. Königs (eds) *Dimensionen der Didaktischen Grammatik: Festschrift für Günther Zimmermann zum 65. Geburtstag* (pp. 281–303). Bochum: AKS-Verlag.

Schwerdtfeger, I.C. (2000b) Anthropologisch-narrative Didaktik des fremdsprachlichen Lernens. *FLuL* 29, 106–123.

Strubell, M., Vilaró, S., Williams, G. and Williams, G.O. (2007) The diversity of language teaching in the European Union: Final Report. A Report to the European Commission. Directorate General for Education & Culture. http://ec.europa.eu/education/languages/eu-language-policy/docs/diversity_en.pdf

Trim, J.L.M. (2009) Introduction. In D. Coste, D. Moore and G. Zarate (eds) *Plurilingual and Pluricultural Competence* (pp. vi–vii). Strasbourg: Council of Europe. http://www.coe.int/t/dg4/linguistic/Source/SourcePublications/CompetencePlurilingue09web_en.pdf

Vetter, E. (2008) Italienisch-, Spanisch- und FranzösischlehrerInnen: Grenzen und Möglichkeiten ihrer Ausbildung zur Mehrsprachigkeit. In J. Laakso (ed.) *Ungarischunterricht in Österreich: Perspektiven und Vergleichspunkte/Teaching Hungarian in Austria: Perspectives and Points of Comparison* (pp. 85–114). Wien: LIT-Verlag.

Vetter, E. (2009) Mehrsprachigkeit: Neue Herausforderungen für die Aus- und Weiterbildung von Fremdsprachenlehrer(innen). In A. Polleti (eds) *Sprachen als akademische Schlüsselkompetenz?* (pp. 147–153). Bochum: AKS-Verlag.

Subject Index

A

Assessment (see: testing and assessment)

B

Biographical learning XVIII, 149, 155

C

Change management 155
Classroom interaction 38–39, 42, 67, 85
Coaching XIV, 72, 149, 150, 156
Cognition XV, 20, 38, 39, 44, 52, 101–120, 128, 133–135, 138–139, 167, 207
Collaborative assessment (see: testing and assessment)
Common European Framework of Reference for Languages (CEFR) 59, 104, 107–108, 114–115, 117, 119, 146, 179, 192, 232, 238–239
Communicative approach to language teaching (CLT) 5, 8–9, 62, 83, 87, 94–96, 97, 105, 108, 115, 218, 221
Communicative competence 5, 8–9, 107, 115, 191
Communicative event 42, 106–115, 107, 108, 118, 119, 171
Communicative practice 47
Communicative task XVII, 87, 89, 92, 94
Competence and performance 106–107, 114
Constraints on teachers' work 39, 45, 46–52, 71, 91, 97, 124
Construction of practice 129, 135
Content knowledge (see: teacher knowledge)
Conversation analysis 38, 42, 51
Cooperative network learning (see: network learning)
Corpus linguistics 171, 172

D

Development of practice 46–51

E

E-learning 158
English as a lingua franca (ELF) 84
English for specific purposes (ESP) XVIII, 164–184
European language policies 229, 230–235, 237–240, 241, 242
European Language Portfolio (ELP) 146, 149, 153, 158–159, 160, 161, 194, 201, 234
Experiential knowledge (see: teacher knowledge)

F

Focus on form / focus on forms XVII, 11, 42, 44, 87–88, 89, 90, 92, 93–94, 99
Formulaic language 86, 173
Frames, schemata, scripts 108, 116–119, 132, 171

G

Genre analysis 169–175, 181
Grammar XVII, 6, 8, 14, 43, 61, 83–97, 101–120, 123, 167, 170, 172–175, 240
  – grammar teaching: implicit / explicit XV, XVII, 83–97, 101, 115
  – grammatical competence 104, 107–108, 116
  – grammatical notions 110–114, 116–118
  – pedagogical grammar XVII, 38, 101, 103, 108, 109, 111, 115–119
Group work 21, 26–29

I

In-service teacher education XV, XVIII, 60, 80, 134, 145–161, 167
Inter-comprehension 235, 236

K

Knowing-in-action 23–25

L

Language assessment (see: testing and assessment)
Language teaching methodology 50, 147, 155, 214
Language testing (see: testing and assessment)
Linguistic diversity 228, 229–230, 238, 241, 242
Literature in the EFL classroom 124, 127, 129–133, 136, 138

M

Materials development 167, 168–175, 182
Meaning-making competences XVIII, 125, 131–132, 133, 137, 138
Models for teacher education XVII, 34, 57–80, 125, 126, 166, 183, 188, 240
Moments of practice XVII, 38–52
Motivation 20, 32, 45, 91, 131
Multilingual education 230
Multimodality 167, 169–171, 173–175, 178

N

Native speakerism / native speaker ideal 207, 210, 215, 217, 220
Native speaker English teachers (NEST) / non-native speaker English teachers (NNEST) XIX, 207– 224
Network learning 145, 148, 151, 156, 158–160

O

Organisational learning 152–153, 159, 160

P

Pattern practice 7–8
Pedagogical content knowledge (PCK) (see: teacher knowledge)
Pedagogical grammar (see: grammar)
Pluriculturalism 139, 234
Plurilingualism 232, 233–235, 237–242

Portfolio XVIII–XIX, 62, 71, 146, 158, 160, 186–202, 234, 239
Presentation – Practice – Production (PPP) model 84–85, 88–90, 94
Practical knowledge (see: teacher knowledge)
Pre-service teacher education XV, XVI, XVIII, 75, 78, 127–129, 134–135, 138, 145, 164 167, 168, 170, 186–202
Process writing 30, 32
Professional development / professionalism XIII, XIV, 26, 45, 58, 60, 66, 69, 70, 74, 78, 80, 189–190, 197, 200, 211, 123
Project management 150, 151, 153, 156, 161

R

'Real' English 9–10, 11–12
Reflection XIV, XV, XVI, XVIII, 19, 25–26, 34, 70, 101, 110, 124, 125, 133–139, 153, 157, 186–202, 239
 – reflective autobiographical writing 136
 – reflective practice XV, XIX, 25, 133, 165

S

Schemata (see: frames, schemata, scripts)
Scripts (see: frames, schemata, scripts)
Self-assessment (see: testing and assessment)
Situated knowledge (see: teacher knowledge)
Skill-based language teaching 88–89
Sociocultural framework 210–211, 223
Standardization / standardized tests (see: testing and assessment)
Subject matter knowledge (see: teacher knowledge)

T

Tacit knowledge (see: teacher knowledge)
Task-based language learning (TBL) / task-based language teaching (TBLT), task-based instruction 9, 85, 154
Teachability hypothesis 85, 89
Teacher cognition XV, 128, 133, 139, 167
Teacher development XVI, 67, 68, 70, 148, 149, 150, 151–152, 222, 223

Subject Index

Teacher identity 207–208, 210, 211, 214–215, 223
Teacher knowledge XIV, XVI, XVII, 16–34, 38–52, 125, 166, 207, 208, 209, 210–211, 212, 214, 215, 216, 217, 218, 220, 221, 222, 223
- content knowledge XVIII, 19–21, 34, 126–127, 133, 136, 138, 165–168, 170, 180, 182, 183, 209
- experiential knowledge XVIII, 38, 52, 78, 168
- pedagogical content knowledge (PCK) XIV, XVIII, 20–21, 34, 38, 124, 126–127, 133, 135, 138, 164–184, 188, 191, 202, 209
- practical knowledge 17–18, 19, 23, 52
- situated knowledge 22–23
- subject matter knowledge XIV, 19–21, 34, 166–167, 169, 181, 183, 188
- tacit knowledge XVII, 23
Teachers' beliefs XV, 129, 137, 215
Teaching materials XVIII, 91, 102, 108, 120, 146–147, 148, 167, 169, 179, 180, 181, 183, 240

Teaching practice XVII, XVIII, XIX, 3, 39, 51, 124, 125–126, 127–128, 133, 148, 149, 157, 165, 167, 170, 183, 187, 190, 193, 194, 198, 209, 212, 213, 220–202, 241
Teaching situation, characteristics / contexts 23, 39, 43, 44, 46–52, 75, 92, 96, 97, 124, 154, 157–158, 167, 169, 171, 183, 189, 199
Testing and assessment XV, 31, 48, 49, 57–80, 190, 193–194, 234
- assessment culture 63–64, 66–67
- assessment for learning / assessment as learning 63–64, 66–67, 70, 77
- assessment literacy XVII, 57–80
- assessment qualifications 68–70
- collaborative assessment 65, 70–72, 77, 80
- self-assessment XVIII, 62, 75, 135, 186–187, 192–195, 197– 202
- standardization / standardized tests XVII, 49, 57, 59, 74, 191
- test instrument 61–62, 65, 67, 74
Translation 4, 14, 72–74, 83, 236

Name Index

A

Abell, S.K. 166
Achard, M. 102
Achermann, B. 146
Adolphs, S. 171
Akbari, R. 190, 198
Allaei, S.K. 31
Allwright, D. 38
Anderson, J.R. 120
Appel, J. XVII, 38, 39, 42, 50, 52
Arva, V. 221
Auer, P. 42

B

Bachman, L.F. 62, 70, 71
Bailey, K.M. 38, 66, 74
Ball, D.L. 20, 126, 127
Bamford, J. 131
Banks, F. 133
Barker, C. 219
Barnwell, D. 61
Bartlett, L. 190
Bass, H. 20
Baughman, K. 45
Béacco, J.-C. 233, 234, 238
Beck, C. 134
Bennett, N. 21
Bereiter, C. 32
Berliner, D.C. 44
Berry, A. 140
Bezemer, J. 174
Bhatia, V.K. 170, 171, 172
Birdsong, D. 102
Black, P. 66
Blackledge, A. 214, 231
Block, D. 208, 211
Bokhorst-Heng, W. 207
Borg, S. 52, 128–129, 133–134, 136, 139
Borko, H. 25
Bosshard, H.U. 146
Bowden, H.W. 90
Boyles, P. 57, 60
Braine, G. 207, 217, 221

Breen, M. 39, 46, 49, 50
Brennan, M. 189
Brindley, G. 77, 78
Brown, G. 116
Brown, J.D. 66, 74
Brown H.D. 221
Bruner, J. 17
Brutt-Griffler, J. 218
Bullough, R.V. 45
Burns, A. 134
Burton, J. 134, 135, 136, 189

C

Calderhead, J. 21, 38
Canagarajah, S. 207, 217, 218
Canale, M. 115
Candelier, M. 235, 236, 240
Canniveng, C. 167
Carless, D. 95
Carlsen, W. S. 20
Carroll, J.B. 65
Carter, R. A. 10, 130, 131
Castellotti, V. 236
Cenoz, J. 230, 231
Chalker, S. 103,111
Chamot, A. 120
Chapelle, C. 57
Cheung, Y.L. 221
Christmann, U. 132
Chu, H. 24
Clandinin, D.J. 19, 38
Clark, C.M. 38, 48–49
Clarke, M. 208, 211
Cochran, K.F. 20
Cochran-Smith, M. 187
Connell, R. 46
Connelly, F.M. 19
Cook, G. 14, 86
Cook, V. J. 231
Coste, D. 232, 233
Coulthard, M. 38
Croft, W. 105, 106
Crookes, G. 85
Cruse, D.A. 105
Crystal, D. 173

D

Dalton-Puffer, C. 215
Darling-Hammond, L. XIII, 193
Davidson, F. 66, 71
Davies, A. 68–69, 207, 213, 215, 219
Day, R.R. 131
De Angelis, G. 231
De Cillia, R. 232
De Florio-Hansen, I. 130
De Kop, S. 102
De Rycker, T. 102
Dekeyser, R. M. 86, 89, 102
Delanoy, W. 131,
Denscombe, M. 49
Derwing, T.M. 221
Dewey, J. 134, 189 – 190, 199
Ding, Y. 86
Dirven, R. 103
Doff, A., 105
Donaldson, J. 132
Doppler, K. 149, 155, 156
Duff, P. 208, 211
Duranti, A. 42
Dweck, C. 155

E

Earl, L. 63
Edmondson, W. 130, 131
Elbaz, F. 17–19
Ellis, N.C. 86, 102
Ellis, R. 85, 86, 87, 88, 90
Ellis, V. 133
Eraut, M. 34, 190

F

Farrell, T.S.C. 135, 190
Feiman-Nemser, S. 39, 46
Fenner, A.B. 102
Fenstermacher, G.D. 34
Fernandez-Balboa, J.-M. 166
Fillmore, C. J. 116
Firth, A. 208
Fleming, M. 233, 234
Floden, R.E. 39, 46, 48–49
Fotos, S. 102
Franceschini, R. 231
Franson, C. 210
Freeman, D. 38, 70, 78, 127, 188, 190, 209, 218
Fries, C.C. 7–8
Fröhlich, E. 155
Fulcher, G. 66
Fullan, M. 155, 156
Furlong, J. XIII

G

Gao, S.L. 25
García, O. 230
Gardner, S. 87–88
Gaskell, E. 113
Gautschi, P. 155
Gess-Newsome, J. 166
Gipps, C. 62, 63
Goettsch, K. 222
Goffman, E. 42
Golombek, P.R. 45
Graden, E.C. 45
Graham, C. 86
Grenfell, M. 186, 191–192
Grossman, P. 20, 166, 187

H

Haas, W. 146
Halász, L. 130
Hall, J.K. 231
Halliday, M.A.K. 104, 115, 116
Hashweh, M. 20
Hatch, A. 46
Hawkins, M. 208, 210
Heindler, D. 115
Hesse, M. 130
Heywood, D. 20
Hinkel, E. 102
Holland, N.N. 130
Holliday, A. 207, 208, 209, 210, 214, 219– 220
Holme, R. 102
Howatt, A.P.H. 4
Hu, A. 231
Hu, G. 95
Hufeisen, B. 236

Name Index

Hutchins, E. 39, 41, 46, 51
Hutterli, S. XVIII, 147
Hüttner, J. XVIII, 34, 52, 140, 168, 169, 170, 171–172, 175, 178, 202, 224
Hymes, D.H. 5, 6, 8, 9, 104, 106

I

Inbar-Lourie, O. 62–63, 67, 215

J

Jackendoff, R. 104–105, 109, 112
Jackson, P.W. 16
Jakobovits, L.A. 62
Jay, J.K. 190–191
Jenkins, J. 207, 213, 215, 216
Jessner, U. 231, 232
Jewitt, C. 174
Johnson, D.W. 71
Johnson, K. 5, 47, 88, 89, 102
Johnson, K.E. XIV, 127, 133, 188, 200, 208, 209, 210, 211, 215, 216, 217, 218, 219, 222
Johnson, K.L. 190–191
Johnson, R.T. 71
Johnston, B. 222
Jones, L.L. 20
Jones, R.L. 62

K

Kachru, B.B. 207, 213
Kaltenböck, G. 172
Kattmann, U. 126
Kecskes, I. 231
Keller, R. 147
Kelly, M. 186, 191–192, 238–239
Kemmis, S. 191
Kemp, C. 232
Kennedy, C. 151
Kind, V. 166, 167, 181
Klein, H.G. 235, 236
Kleinsasser, R.C. 76
Koballa, T.R. 166
Korthagen, F.A.J. XVI, 124, 128, 187
Kosnik, C. 134
Kramsch, C. 130, 131, 211, 213
Kramsch, O. 130

Krashen, S. 85, 89, 90, 102
Kraus, N. 176, 178–179
Kress, G. 174
Krumm, H.-J. 231
Kumaravadivelu, B. 214
Küppers, A. 130

L

Lado, R. 7–8
Lampert, M. 39, 127
Langacker, R.W. 104, 105
Lantolf, J.P. 215
Latchem, C. 147
Laufer, B. 95
Lauterburg, C. 149, 156
Lave, J. XVI, 21, 22, 24, 32
Lee, D. 104
Legutke, M. 50
Leinhardt, G. 23
Leki, I. 31
Lenz, P. 146
Leung, C. 67
Lightbown, P.M. 89
Liston, D.P. 190
Littlemore, J. 102
Llurda, E. 207, 209
Long, M.H. 85, 87, 90, 102
Lortie, D.C. 46, 128
Loughran, J. 140
Lunenberg, M. 140
Lynch, B.K. 71
Lyster, R. 90

M

Ma, L. 20
Maalouf, A. 235
Maciel, R.F. 152
Magnusson, S. 166
Mahboob, A. 215, 216, 221
Maley, A. 84
Malone, M. 57, 61, 62
Mann, S. 78
Marks, R. 166
Martinez, M. 167
Matthiessen, C.M.I.M. 104
May Yin, T. 161

Mayer, K. 179–182
McCarthy, M. 9–10
McKay, S.L. 207, 216
McNamara, T. 64, 77
Measor, L. 45
Medgyes, P. 218, 221
Mehlmauer-Larcher, B. XVIII, 34, 140, 172, 183, 189, 196, 224, 243
Meißner, F-J. 233
Miller, E. 21, 47
Miller, J. 210
Minsky, M.
Mitchell, R. 50
Moon, J.A. 189
Moore, D. 232
Morgan-Short, K. 90
Moussu, L. 207
Müller-Reim, A. 179–182
Munby, H. 17, 21
Munro, M.J. 221
Myhill, J. 208
Myles, F. 50

N

Neale, D.C. 20
Nelson, C.L. 207
Neuner, G. 236
Newby, D. XVII, 101, 102, 103, 107, 108, 111–112, 115, 123, 145, 151, 186, 191, 192, 193–194, 198, 239
Ng, M. 31
Niemeier, S. 102
Noffke, S.E. 189
Nonaka, I. 152–153, 160
Norris, J.M. 86
Norton, B. 208, 210, 211
Numrich, C. 45
Nunan, D. XIII, 38
Nünning, A. 132

O

Oatley, K. 130
O'Loughlin, K 75
O'Malley, J.M. 120
Ortega, L. 86

P

Palmer, A.S. 70, 71
Paran, A. 130
Patton, M.Q. 212
Pavlenko, A. 211, 214, 231
Pennycook, A. 211
Peterson, P.L.M. 38
Petric, B. 211, 218
Phelan, A.M. 213
Phillipson, R. 207, 209
Pienemann, M. 48, 85
Polanyi, M. 23–24
Postholm, M.B. 135
Putnam, R.T. 25

R

Reeves, J. 209
Reichl, S. XVIII, 34, 52, 137, 183, 202, 224
Reissner, C. 235, 236
Richards, J. 106
Richards, J.C. 48, 72, 85, 105, 126, 134, 187, 200, 208, 209, 210, 213
Richardson, V. 125
Rindler Schjerve, R. 231
Roberts, J. 128, 135, 136, 139, 189
Robinson, B. 147
Robinson, P. 87, 90, 102
Rodgers, T.S. 48, 105
Roever, C. 64, 77
Rollnick, M. 20
Roulet, E. 38
Russell, T. 21
Ryle, G. 17, 23–24

S

Salaberry, M.R. 90
Samimy, K. 219
Scardamalia, M. 32
Scheffler, A. 132
Schendl, H. 139
Schmid, H.-J. 116
Schmid, S. 176, 78–79
Schmidt, R. 86

Name Index

Schmitt, N. 173
Schneider, R. 131
Schön, D.A. 16, 17, 24, 25–26, 34, 134, 135, 188
Schreier, M. 132
Schwab, G. 52
Schwerdtfeger, I.C. 231
Scribner, S. 22
Seedhouse, P. 38, 42, 44, 50, 85
Seidlhofer, B. 95, 207, 209, 213, 216
Seilman, U. 131
Semmelrock, N. 175–177
Sendak, M. 132
Senge, P.M. 156
Shak, J. 87–88
Sharifian, F. 207, 213
Shavelson, R.J. 38
Shepard, L.A. 63
Shohamy, E. 61
Shulman, L.S. XIV, 17, 19–20, 32, 34, 38, 126, 134, 165–166, 183, 188, 209
Silvia, P.J. 131
Sinclair, J.M. 38, 171
Singh, G. 126
Skandera, P. 173
Skehan, P. 83, 85, 102
Smit, U. XVIII, 34, 52, 140, 168, 169, 202, 224
Smith, D.C. 20
Smith, R.G. 21
Spada, N. 89
Spolsky, B. 59, 61, 62
Sprague, K. 146
Stanley, J. 31
Steiner, B. 175–177
Stern, H.-H. 38
Stern, P. 38
Stevick, E.S. 50, 51
Sterman, J.D. 156
Stiehl, J. 166
Stiggins, R.J. 57, 60, 63, 67
Stotz, D. 146
Stoynoff, S. 57
Strubell, M. 238
Studer, T. 146
Surkamp, C. 132
Suter, C. 146

Swain, M. 85, 115
Swales, J.M. 170, 171, 172
Swan, M. 85, 96, 103, 112–114

T

Takeuchi, H. 152–153, 160
Taylor, L. 63–64, 77
Teasdale, A. 67
Thomas, H. 50
Tribble, C. 171, 172
Trim, J.L.M. 110, 234
Truscott, J. 90
Turnbull, M. 85
Tsui, A.B.M. XVII, 17, 25, 26, 30, 31, 33, 38, 45, 52, 183, 202, 209, 210, 211, 224

U

Uchida, Y. 208, 211
Ungerer, F. 116
Ur, P. 96, 130, 131

V

Van Dijk, E.M. 126
Van Ek, J.A. 110
Van Leeuwen, T. 174
Varghese, M. 211, 223
Vetter, E. XIX, 240
Viëtor, W. 4
Vilches, M.L.C. 148, 152–153, 155

W

Wagner, J. 38, 208
Wallace, M.J. 70, 125, 165, 188–189
Walter, C. 113
Waters, A. 148, 152–153, 155
Wedell, M. 149, 152, 155, 159, 161
Weiss, R.S. 212
Weskamp, R. 130
Wharton, S. 75
White, R.V. 148
Widdowson, H.G. XVI–XVII, 3, 6, 7, 12, 70, 101, 104, 109, 120, 145, 165, 168, 170, 188, 207, 213, 218
Wideen, M. 187

Wiliam, D. 66
Wilkins, D. 104, 105, 110
Wilson, S.M. 19, 20
Wineburg, S. 20
Wolf, D. 62
Wong, J.L.N. 25
Woods, D. 38, 45, 46
Wray, A. 86, 173

Y

Young, R. 47
Yule, G. 116

Z

Zeichner, K.M. 187, 190

For Product Safety Concerns and Information please contact our EU Authorised Representative:

Easy Access System Europe

Mustamäe tee 50

10621 Tallinn

Estonia

gpsr.requests@easproject.com

www.ingramcontent.com/pod-product-compliance
Ingram Content Group UK Ltd.
Pitfield, Milton Keynes, MK11 3LW, UK
UKHW021941200326
4879IPUK00004B/37